Afghanistan in the Cinema

Afghanistan in the Cinema

MARK GRAHAM

University of Illinois Press
URBANA, CHICAGO, AND SPRINGFIELD

Library of Congress Cataloging-in-Publication Data
Library of Congress Cataloging-in-Publication Data
Graham, Mark, (Mark A.), 1970-
Afghanistan in the cinema / Mark Graham.
p.   cm.
Includes bibliographical references and index.
ISBN 978-0-252-03527-2 (cloth : alk. paper)
ISBN 978-0-252-07712-8 (pbk. : alk. paper)
1. Afghanistan—In motion pictures.
I. Title.
PN1995.9.A35G73   2010
791.43'658581—dc22   2009038149

For Fauzia, Dean, and Zayn
Light follows every darkness

Contents

Acknowledgments

This book could not have been written without the kindness and generosity of many people from all over the world. From Afghanistan there was Roya Sadat in Herat and Ibrahim Faizi in Kabul, who shared with me Sadat's remarkable film. From the United Kingdom, Corinne Fowler and Jude Davies made their scholarship available to me, as did Fadwa El Guindi and Richard A. Voeltz in the United States. Farhad Azad, publisher of the online Afghan literary journal *Lemar-Aftaab,* demonstrated the generosity for which Afghans all over the world are renowned.

Elizabeth Fifer, my graduate school mentor at Lehigh University, provided both constructive criticism and encouragement, as did Dawn Keetley at Lehigh and Louis Schwartz at Kutztown University. My thanks also go to the dedicated team at the University of Illinois Press, especially to my editor Joan Catapano, assistant editor Rebecca McNulty, and copy editor Carol Burwash.

Most of all I would like to thank my family—my parents, Kenneth and Michele Graham, and especially my wife, Fauzia Nouristani, who inspired me not only to begin this book but also to finish it.

Introduction

Haunted Eyes

Her name, as if that matters, is Sharbat Gula. For nearly twenty years, no one outside of Afghanistan knew who she was. But they knew her face. I don't think I've ever been in an Afghan restaurant where I didn't see her staring at me, either from a photograph or a clumsily painted facsimile. Originally seen on the June 1985 cover of *National Geographic,* Steve McCurry's photograph of Sharbat Gula has become, especially now with the destruction of the Buddhas of Bamiyan, the new Afghan icon, the very embodiment for Westerners and Afghans alike of her long-suffering nation.

It is not hard to understand why her image has fascinated so many viewers and made it perhaps the most famous photograph ever to come out of the magazine. You see it immediately: those *eyes.* The cover captions it this way: "Haunted eyes tell of an Afghan refugee's fears."

Certainly, Sharbat would have known fear. When she was six years old, Russian bombs killed her mother and father. She and the remnants of her family had fled the Soviet assault on her country—a savage, decade-long invasion and occupation that left the nation devastated.

But if there is fear in those "sea-green eyes," there is also much more. A later *National Geographic* writer, looking at Afghanistan from a different perspective, noticed something else: "Her eyes challenge ours. Most of all, they disturb. We cannot turn away."[1]

Contrary to the magazine's original caption, this writer reveals the hidden truth of the image: Sharbat's eyes may be haunted, but they also have the power to haunt *us.* It is not simply that they elicit pity. True, her *chador* is tattered (a fact that embarrassed her when she first viewed the portrait), and her unwashed face grimaces in a hunger both physical and emotional.

But the little girl's face is not broken or humiliated. It violates what we expect and what we want to know. The photograph is, after all, of a little Afghan girl living in a tent. What does she have to be defiant about? She does not (as one might expect) cry out for us in helpless desperation. Rather, she stares at us with what looks like defiance, even anger. It is a gaze that meets ours, head-on. Her eyes overpower the camera itself, surmounting its ways of seeing in such a way that even the photographer was surprised when he first developed the image: "How still and quiet it appeared," he later wrote.[2]

In that quiet stillness lies great power, a somewhat unsettling quality that involves Sharbat Gula's ability to return our gaze. She, and the Afghanistan she embodies, stares back at us like a private abyss suddenly made public. Those beautiful sea-green eyes are like the sea itself, gorgeous but implacable, protean yet primeval, sublime and resolutely self-sustaining. Despite war, death, and displacement, she can, and does, exist on her own terms. For this reason, she challenges and disturbs.

From the perspective of empire, especially the current key player of the Great Game, the United States, the truth of Sharbat Gula's gaze is embarrassing and, worse, threatening. Steve McCurry's other photograph of Sharbat on the April 2002 cover of *National Geographic* frames the inner conflict over her image in an indelible way by presenting her now as a woman, holding the photograph taken all those years ago. There's just one problem: *we can't see her.*

Clad in the *chadari* (in Arabic, burqa), the traditional veil that covers a woman from head to toe, Sharbat's eyes are dim shadows behind the delicate mesh. The veil obscures her body completely, dematerializes it into an amorphous and abstract field of violet color. Geometric patterns and pleats flow over the surface in shadowy rivulets. The pyramidal composition of the photograph recalls a Leonardo da Vinci Madonna, except that here the Virgin's veil has grown all-encompassing, and the child she cradles to her bosom is her lost self, staring back at us even from beneath the *chadari*.

Sharbat holds this mirror of resistance to us, reflecting our innermost fears. Unlike the complacent mother and child of Renaissance art, grounded in sentimentality and naturalism, this Muslim Madonna refuses to be dominated by Western ways of seeing. Her invisibility behind the *chadari* now corresponds with the photograph she holds, the icon of her defiance. It allows her to look at us without being seen.

This is perhaps the most frustrating realization of all, a phenomenon Malek Alloula analyzes in *The Colonial Harem:* "The [veiled] woman does not conceal herself, does not play at concealing herself. But the eye cannot catch hold of her."[3] For a culture that prides itself on its ability to see, penetratingly, into the very nature of things, this poses the direst of challenges. Western assumptions of intellectual and cultural superiority are fixated on dreams of panoptic visuality. For Michel Foucault, the panopticon (Jeremy Bentham's design for a perfect prison where the inmates could always be observed but not observe themselves) provides a fitting metaphor of how Western modernity surveils its metaphysical opponents.

Surveillance implies an ability to see into every part of a thing, for such total vision equals total knowledge, predicated on the absolute materiality of the real. Look at an archetype of early modern visuality, Rembrandt van Rijn's *The Anatomy Lesson of Dr. Nicolaes Tulp* (1632), to see the mechanism already in working order. In the painting, a small group of authoritative men cluster in a dark room, presided over by the doctor himself, lecturing above the dissected remnants of a cadaver. For modernity, merely gazing at the flesh is not enough. One must probe beneath it, inside it, strip it away in a desperate attempt to clutch the innermost adytum where absolute power waits like a prize.

Science is not the only Western discourse that yearns for omnipotence through visuality. Imperialism also depends on total surveillance to effect its hegemony over subject peoples. In this imperial way of seeing, the bodies of its subjects become colonized by the Western gaze, reduced to a quintessence quite divorced from social forces like history, politics, or culture. Such a state, according to David Spurr, "enable[s] both visual possession of the body and an interposition of technique which safely conceals the body of the observer."[4] With the observer in a privileged position of objectivity, values can be metamorphosed into truth with the shape-shifting effectively hidden and mystified.

The knowledge validation process is a highly fragile mechanism. All it takes is for someone to look back. Or to draw the curtain. Sharbat Gula does both. In the later image, this Afghan peasant woman has the audacity to photograph us. The *chadari* here curiously resembles the drape beneath which nineteenth-century photographers hid themselves while performing their craft. The portrait itself stands in for the camera, her face the image on the lens imprinted on the eyes of a dying dream of total power.

This is a sacred image in the purest sense of the term: set apart, exclusively appropriated, both holy and wholly itself. In this sense, the veiled woman, who embodies something both external and internal to her, reflects the Qur'an, often veiled itself by a cloth in Muslim households to preserve its sacred nature and testify to its immanent yet transcendent power. What emerges from the shadowy folds of the *chadari* to stare back at us then is not simply Afghanistan but Afghanistan *as* Islam, as an independent and resistant force. The two are combined. Afghanistan, never dominated, despite three misbegotten attempts by the British and one by the Russians, fuses here with Islam, itself the single most powerful opponent of Western intellectual, scientific, and spiritual hegemony. The subaltern does not have to speak here. She merely needs to be. Indeed, the Afghan woman as Muslim archetype was never a subaltern at all.

As soon as this fact comes out into the open, as it did after September 11, 2001, the rhetoricians of empire scurry for cover, dodging behind age-old smoke screens and stereotypes. A cursory glance at the accompanying article in the 2002 issue of *National Geographic* reveals this process at work. The story's very existence reflects the need to somehow palliate Sharbat Gula's gaze. The mere idea of going back into Afghanistan to seek her indicates the new-found American power asserted over the region, testifying to the benefits of the imperial project there. Now we can look at her again—look at someone who has eluded our gaze for so long.

The journey, cast in the romantic language of the travelogue, becomes a quest, a "search for the girl with green eyes." Ironically, they find her near Tora Bora, formerly a hideout for Osama bin Laden. "Names have power," and so, the writer implies, do people with the power to name. Now they can put a label to those previously anonymous eyes: a rustic name meaning "Nectar Flower." Having flaunted this power to label, the author proceeds to the next step: classification. She notes that Sharbat Gula is "Pashtun, that most warlike of Afghan tribes." Her eyes seem to "burn with ferocity." No one knows her exact age in a place where "stories shift like sand." She is a simple woman whose day revolves around her children, household chores, and prayer.

When interviewed, Sharbat Gula seems to confound the expectations of the journalist. Rather than bemoan the *chadari,* she calls it "a beautiful thing to wear, not a curse." Instead of jeering the ousted regime, she says, "Life under the Taliban was better. At least there was peace." This coming from a woman belonging to a "tribe" that the writer earlier claims "[is] only at peace when they are at war." Shouldn't she be more depressed, the article ponders, after all she went through? "Such knife-thin odds . . . that she could be found. . . . How, she was asked, had she survived?" Her tacit answer: "It was the will of God."[5]

A second encounter and again the same response: dignity, confidence, and now something else—faith in God, in Islam. On every count she has parried the ideological assault, remained resolutely herself. Eyes or words, it makes no difference. The end result is the same: There is another who *sees.* And now, *speaks.*

In answer to her, a sidebar above the article displays two men, one an FBI forensic examiner and the other a computer science professor at the University of Cambridge. One would have to look hard to find two men more representative of the Establishment than these. On the desks before them lie photographs of Sharbat's face and blowups of her eyes. The officials' purpose is to positively verify that the woman interviewed in Afghanistan was *the* girl. Thankfully, we have these men who can "authenticate" Sharbat's eyes as really hers—an astounding accomplishment. Even better, the Cambridge prof has invented "automatic iris recognition," irises being like fingerprints. Now Sharbat can be efficiently processed, booked, and printed.

This dissection of eyes from face once again evokes Rembrandt's Dr. Tulp and the scientific authority conveyed by a more penetrating vision. The photographer carries the analogy even further, illuminating the men in a Baroque tenebroso. Here, despite Sharbat Gula's existence, despite her eyes and words, Western men can still loom over her with the self-satisfied complacency of the expert. Only they, it seems, can truly "dis-cover" her. By looking at images of Afghanistan, especially ones prepared for consumption in the West, the viewer can easily deconstruct such hegemonic discourses at work. A shopworn set of clichés, they lie at the surface like a brittle patina. But looking for the real Afghanistan requires more work. Indeed is it even possible to see the "real" Afghanistan—and if so, then what?

Afghanistan may at some point recede from the world's headlines. The press will move on to other disasters, all in the vain hope of redemptive closure and a boost to sagging approval ratings. But Afghanistan has a funny way of creeping into the news again sooner or later, reasserting itself with the annoying insistency of the truth and of problems that refuse to go away, even after dropping a billion dollars' worth of bombs.

If Afghanistan has become an archetype of the abyss not only staring but also talking back at us, then perhaps we should listen to it. Perhaps, like Sharbat Gula, it wants peace rather than war. Perhaps it wants secular education as well as faith. Perhaps it wants what we call "modernity"—only without having to surrender the very things that make Afghanistan itself. But before we can listen to Afghanistan and the plethora of Afghan voices, we have to find them somewhere. One such place to look is in the cinema.

In recent years, films like *Kandahar* and *Osama* have attracted extraordinary international attention and garnered a healthy dose of jury prizes, Palmes d'Ors, and Golden Globes. For many Westerners, the Afghanistan of these movies *is* Afghanistan. Most college libraries, if they have any movies at all on Afghanistan in their collection, own *Kandahar* and *Osama*. These films have been primary vehicles for shaping Western discourse about the rights of Muslim women, the *chadari,* and the nature of Islam as a "clashing civilization" opposed to Western, supposedly secularist modernity. These knowledge-making monologues, as responses to Afghanistan's ideological challenge, need themselves to be examined and evaluated in the contexts of the rhetorical and discursive worldviews that create them as well as the films that mirror and shape them—if for no other reason than they fuel policies that can either heal or bring increased suffering to a nation that has already suffered far too much.

For most Western audiences, *Kandahar* was the first time they had journeyed inside "authentic" Afghanistan with real Afghans. Films from the 1980s like *High Road to China, The Living Daylights,* and *Rambo III,* while all being set in the country during various time periods, were filmed in other locations like Israel and Yugoslavia. Of course, no Afghan actors were used in these films. Neither was there any attempt (except perhaps with *Rambo,* surprisingly enough) to be accurate in any way in the portrayal of Afghans' culture and languages. *High Road to China* (1982), for example, features Brian Blessed, an English actor, playing a "Waziri" (Pashtun) warlord who uses an invented language, dresses like a Russian Cossack, and rolls his eyes and laughs maniacally. In *The Living Daylights* (1987), James Bond (ever that expert on world cultures) calls his lover "*khaista*" while lounging with her in a supposedly Afghan room that looks as if it were outfitted in a Moroccan casbah. When she asks him what *khaista* means, he says, "It means 'beautiful' . . . in Afghan." Alas, anyone mildly literate on the subject knows of course that there is no such language as "Afghan"; people speak many languages there, including Pashto, Dari, and numerous others. *Khaista,* as it turns out, is indeed a word spoken by Dari-speaking Afghans, except that it means "slow"—actually a more appropriate adjective for the typical piece of Bond cheesecake.

Naturally, the student of cultural anthropology does not rely too heavily on Tarzan films of the 1930s and '40s for accurate information on Africa. Nor does the American historian trust John Ford Westerns to provide sensitive or even mildly objective representations of Native Americans. Rather, scholars tend to examine these films for what they tell us about the people who made and viewed them, not the people they're supposedly about. This sort of critical perspective, while common coin in academia, remains far from the intellectual norm in general society. While peoples of different races or religions continue to be stereotyped in the media, some marginalized groups have successfully struggled to represent themselves through a decades-long tradition of revisionist films that attempt to counter racist and imperialist points of view.

Because no such long-standing revisionist project has occurred regarding the representation of the Muslim world, it is much more difficult for the casually informed viewer to assess the validity of Mohsen Makhmalbaf's Afghanistan in *Kandahar* or Siddiq Barmak's *Osama*. Especially in the case of Afghanistan, there have been so few films about the country that when one comes along that appears authentic, even usually well-reasoned viewers embrace it precisely because there are no critical faculties in place by which its image might be falsified. This presents a serious problem for viewers seeking to learn about the empirical realities in Afghanistan.

Sooner or later, when examining Western discourse on Afghanistan (and the Islamic world as a whole), Orientalism makes an appearance. Originally Orientalism was the name given to the academic study of the Middle East (and the rest of Asia), but Edward Said redefined the term in a series of critical attacks on Orientalists that would culminate in *Orientalism* (1978) and *Covering Islam* (1981). In these two volumes, Said tried to do to Western knowledge what he felt it had done to the Muslim world. By classifying its principles, deconstructing its ethnocentric biases, and subverting its alleged expertise, Said turned the tables on a discipline that insisted, as Francesco Gabrieli did, that "the East is theoretically a desert,"[6] open to the predations of Marxists, fundamentalists, and other unsavories if not for the tender attentions of Western superpowers.

Said noted several themes that pervaded Orientalist discourse, despite its varied and contentious proponents. These included the belief that (1) the East and West were irreconcilably different, the former irrational and static, while the latter was characterized by reason and a spirit of intellectual and cultural innovation; (2) abstractions and dehistoricizing were preferable to contextualization and concrete evidence; and (3) the Western subject, being rational, provided the most objective and desirable witness and judge of what exactly the Islamic world was all about. Orientalism was, therefore, according to Said, a discursive force with authoritative power to analyze and penetrate the East, a "Western style for dominating, restructuring, and having authority over the Orient."[7]

Two epistemological issues emerge from Said's work. First, do Orientalism and its predatory visuality entail a specifically *Western* way of seeing the East that is as monolithic and self-conscious as Said at times suggests? And second, if Orientalism essentially warps reality to bolster imperial power, will one ever find a "real" Orient beneath the facade that one can, with some degree of certainty, truly *know*? The last question is especially pertinent for a discussion of Afghanistan and the cinema, precisely because the way Afghans are represented directly affects American popular opinion on the continued wars there.

Luckily, a number of films have recently appeared that in some ways engage the Western gaze with the intensity of Sharbat Gula. What these films say about Afghanistan, Islam, and the West involves an often surprising and always disturbing blend of propaganda and poetry, jeremiad and jihad. Most of these films, because of their exposure in the West and their subsequent power to (in part) form the discourse on Afghanistan, are necessary tools with which to analyze the "rhetoric of empire" here and abroad, as well as hearing aids tuned to a people like us and yet different, with whom we desperately need to talk and, most important, listen.

PART 1

Imperialist Nostalgia

1 Getting in Touch with Our Inner Savage

The Horsemen

Before the 1970s, Afghanistan did not exist in the cinematic dreamworld of the West. Afghans featured briefly in lowbrow "Rule Britannia" films like *King of the Khyber Rifles* (1953) and *Carry On . . . Up the Khyber* (1968), but Afghanistan itself did not become the subject of a Western feature film until John Frankenheimer's *The Horsemen* (1971). Scripted by Academy Award winner Dalton Trumbo, *The Horsemen* was the first (and only) twentieth-century American feature film ever to be shot in Afghanistan itself, with the cooperation of Afghan Films, the national production company. At the time that Frankenheimer was making his picture, President Richard Nixon was abandoning Afghanistan to increased Soviet patronage, paving the way for an

The Vanishing Afghan: Uraz (Omar Sharif) prepares to ride into the sunset.

eventual coup that led to the Russian invasion of 1979. The film thus stands as a poignant relic of an Afghanistan at the twilight of its innocence—before the seizure of power by Daoud Khan, before Nur Muhammad Taraki, before the Soviets, before the horror.

Based on a novel by French author Joseph Kessel, *The Horsemen* tells the story of the proud and ambitious Uraz, who seeks to eclipse his father Tursen's legendary prowess in *buzkashi,* the Afghan national pastime. In this game that one commentator has called a "cross between dirty polo and open rioting," riders struggle to transport the *buz,* a headless goat or calf carcass stuffed with sand (and weighing close to a hundred pounds), around a post a mile away and return to the game's starting point and goal, the "circle of justice."[1] When Uraz the young *chapandaz* (master player of *buzkashi*) fails to win the championship game in Kabul, he embarks on a perilous journey back to his home. Along the way, his servant Mukhi and Zereh, a beautiful and independent Kuchi nomad woman, scheme to kill him and steal his prize horse, Jahil. The redoubtable Uraz holds them off, even after a village doctor amputates his fractured and infected leg. Devastated with the thought that he might never ride again, the *chapandaz* hides the secret even from his own father until the climax, when he and Jahil are reunited in a masterful display of horsemanship.

In evoking this rough and rugged story, *The Horsemen* clearly aspires to a documentary way of seeing. The issue of authenticity was a crucial one for the director: "Was this an accurate picture of what life is like in Afghanistan? Yes! Life is like this in Afghanistan, exactly the way I depicted it. I spent a lot of time there, I saw a lot there, but this was a story that I loved reading. I identified completely with that character."[2] On location in Kabul, Frankenheimer made a point to highlight the ethnographic, filming an array of barbers, dyers, bakers of naan, blacksmiths, and snake charmers. Evocative juxtapositions abound: automobile traffic interspersed with donkeys, Mercedes sedans with women in purple *chadaris.*[3] There are mosques and minarets and a muezzin calling to the heights where the camera floats, observing both the pristine Kabul River and the traffic coursing beside it. Frankenheimer sees Afghanistan with an almost childlike wonder and depth of feeling, conscious of having gone where no one had gone before, at least in the American cinema.

Despite his claim of having "been there" sufficiently long to portray the "real" Afghanistan with exactitude, Frankenheimer, like every other traveler, has packed some ideological baggage to take with him on his excursion into the unknown. Thus he transitions easily from talking about Afghanistan as a place to enjoying it as "a story." As Steven H. Clark has written, "[T]he appeal to the testimony of the eyewitness itself may be deconstructed into an illusion of an experiential present embedded in a commentary that necessarily exceeds and transgresses those criteria of authenticity. Seeing presupposes believing."[4] But what exactly is it that Frankenheimer sees (and believes)? Nothing less than a cinematic vision of an almost prehistoric, uncorrupted world—what the director himself called "the most beautiful country I've ever seen."[5]

That almost preternatural beauty is the focus of a series of majestic establishing shots at the beginning of the film. Vast desert wastes of ice appear, so terrifyingly raw and jagged that they look as if they have stood unchanged since the world began. They soon give way, in a startling juxtaposition, to dusty steppes and deserts, cerulean lakes, and irrigated fields that glitter like tesserae in a gentle plain of unremitting green. In such a place, men can be men again and cling to ancient codes both "bold and barbaric" as the film's trailer puts it. One such man appears astride his horse, a rifle slung across his shoulder, a living icon perched atop the Khyber Pass of our dreams. For a brief moment, the viewer could be forgiven for believing that the frontier has not disappeared, that a lost world lingers on the edge of ours, a savage haven for the self to rediscover what it has surrendered to modernity.

The film's sublime landscape effortlessly evokes Albert Bierstadt's nineteenth-century paintings of Yosemite. Both portray an untouched reserve of primitive Eden, a fountain of spiritual youth that Manifest Destiny had placed in our hot and eager hands. Encountering the massive scale of the American continent had all the trappings of a religious experience. This idea of the romantic sublime inspired Thomas Gray to say of the Chartreuse Mountains in 1739: "Not a precipice, not a torrent, not a cliff but is pregnant with religion and poetry."[6] The vast power and presence of nature lies at the very heart of romantic mythology, a stand-in for medieval faith eclipsed by Enlightenment rationality. Into the natural world the romantics projected their need for a primeval place of origins, a sacred space that could act as foil to the deceitful and alienating labyrinths of self and city that characterized the modern metropolis. While the tropes stayed more or less the same from one continent to the next, there were a few local variations. Europeans had their Alps and Roman ruins, Americans had the frontier.

The fantasy of the Wild West so well known today was already being massproduced by late-nineteenth-century pop culture. Thanks to the likes of Ned Buntline, Buffalo Bill Cody, and Owen Wister, Americans came to imagine a pristine and uninhabited wilderness lying on the rim of their democratic experiment. Like Jean-Jacques Rousseau, who described the Alps as "abysses beside me to make me afraid,"[7] the West for Americans was a boundary that was both terrifying as well as self-affirming. But where European travelers would face down their existential dread by taking a hike in the mountains, most Americans encountered the sublime with the sole intent of slaughtering and dominating it.

Crossing the Atlantic, the romantic quest transformed into what Richard Slotkin has called a "regeneration through violence," by which the American national consciousness could define itself by a struggle against the forces of wilderness and savagery. The outcome was Manifest Destiny but required a dangerous yet necessary association with the very forces against which American civilization arrayed itself. Only by merging into the regenerative chaos of Western wilderness could America as a nation be born.[8]

While such sentiments circulated for many centuries in captivity tales and dime novels before the advent of cinema, the Western genre provided the most visceral and epic expressions of this myth of conquest, transmuting genocide into nation building by producing "an Other whose destruction is not only assured but justified."[9] This narrative became increasingly persistent with the rise of American preeminence following World War II. Not coincidentally, Westerns as a genre in film reached their apex in the 1950s, their popularity paralleling America's self-consciousness as civilizing agent and superpower. *The Horsemen* came at the tail end of this trend, with its native hero struggling to live his traditional way of life. That these traditions are doomed to fall before the onslaught of civilization is a given, as it is in most other Westerns that long for a return to the primitive. Thus when the film shows jets streaming overhead, interrupting Tursen's speech to his *chapandaz,* it recalls an identical scene in *Lonely Are the Brave* (1962), also scripted by Dalton Trumbo.[10] In this earlier film, a lone cowboy rides across an iconic Western landscape only to have the vision shattered by some fighter planes streaking across the sky. The only difference between the two stories is that in Afghanistan the Indians, rather than the cowboys, are the heroes.

Like the imagined Wild West, *The Horsemen* represents nature as a kind of social Darwinist paradise: a vicious interspecies battle for power and survival with the strong always coming out on top. The film features many scenes of animals viciously attacking each other, from partridge and camel fights to furious head-butting rams. But more than anything, it is the violence of *buzkashi* (literally "goat pulling") that transforms the film's ideology into visual spectacle. Under Frankenheimer's direction and Claude Renoir's masterful cinematography, the sport becomes positively iconic. At the time of the film's release, film critic Roger Ebert glowingly wrote, "There hasn't been a sustained action sequence on this scale since the chariot race in *Ben-Hur.*"[11] The costumes of the *chapandaz* are authentic in every detail, and in the remarkable eleven-minute *buzkashi* sequence, it is mostly real *chapandaz* who play the game, no holds barred. Frankenheimer even went so far as to hire Habib, one of Afghanistan's most famous *buzkashi* players, to serve as technical advisor as well as appear in the sequence itself.[12]

Only just two years before filming, Frankenheimer later recalled, the Afghan government had outlawed the use of knives during play.[13] Whips, however, were still used to devastating effect on competing riders (and still are), resulting in routine bruises, lacerations, and broken bones. For some, the final outcome can be death. Toward the end of the match, a brief shot catches a dead horse being dragged from the field by a very modern tow truck and crane. Animals were very visibly harmed in this production because that's what happens in Afghanistan on the mythic frontier, where violence inextricably binds both men and beasts.

Strong-willed humans like Uraz inhabit that bestial space with animal combatants, defying the forces of nature and time. "They ride today as if it were still yesterday," the film's trailer boldly proclaims, "as though there were no tomorrow. They ride with a savage frenzy that defies our civilization. They live by a code as bold and barbaric as the ancient game they play." Frankenheimer likewise asserted in an interview that, "Afghanistan itself has not changed in over a thousand years."[14]

The trailer's ballyhoo falls squarely within a long-established mode of representing the developing world. Despite the seemingly authoritative medium of the camera, many critics have uncovered the ways in which documentary films and photographic journalism can construct a vision of the globe that reinforces a naturalized hierarchy between civilized and savage, modern and traditional, the West and everywhere else. In step with many other mainstream sources of ethnography (such as *National Geographic*), *The Horsemen* revels in exotic dress and ritual, noble and virile savages, the identification of America with the modern future, and the rest of the world with the prehistoric past.

These noble savages are the sole inhabitants of *The Horsemen*'s dreamscape. Happily they little resemble those Afghan buffoons and treacherous zealots of earlier "Rule Britannia" films. Instead they serve heroically to uphold an admirable and ancient patriarchal social code. They have no need for anything other than their horses, their honor, and their *buzkashi*.

This representation of the native other also differs from those one could see in contemporary revisionist Westerns like *Little Big Man* or *A Man Called Horse* (both 1970). In these films, despite their sympathetic depiction of the Lakota people, the white man remains the locus of agency as well as of the drama itself. Through his eyes, the culture of the Native Americans continues to be interpreted and evaluated. In *The Horsemen*, on the other hand, Afghans act autonomously in an indigenous social and cultural space that the film represents as meaningful and attractive. By doing so, Frankenheimer takes the logic of revisionist Westerns one step further, dispensing with the white mediator in order to more perfectly immerse the civilized audience into savage spectacle.

Astride his beloved Jahil, the white stallion so reminiscent of the Lone Ranger's Silver, Uraz evokes all too clearly the lone rider of the western frontier, displaced now in the Afghan landscape. The noble savage par excellence, this premodern Übermensch spends much of the narrative asserting his God-given right to be the alpha male. He and his fellow Afghans synthesize the two archetypal Western characters: cowboy and Indian. They even look like a strange fusion of the two with their knee-high leather boots, long cloaks, and distinctively Asian features. As a result, Uraz unites in one person the American self and its Asian other—not the Asia against which Americans were fighting at the time, but the comfortable and colorful barbarism of travelogue and frontier mythology.

The first time Uraz appears on-screen, he is watching a gruesome and all-too-real camel fight on which he has bet a respectable number of afghanis. The horseman's isolated presence fills most of the frame, thrown in relief by the background with all its distant little men who hustle and bustle meaninglessly. Not caring if he wins or loses, Uraz represents the quintessential aristocrat, a man who was born to ride, born to win, and born to lead, elevated from the masses by an innate master morality that would make Friedrich Nietzsche envious.[15]

As the savage par excellence, Uraz displays not only heroism but also a propensity for ignorance and cruelty. After tumbling off his horse in Kabul, he clings to the superstitious belief that pages from the Qur'an can disinfect and heal his gashed leg. He deliberately baits his faithful servant Mukhi, inciting him to steal the horse and slay him in the mountain passes of the ancient road. Similarly he toys with Zereh's attraction to him, at first spurning her advances because she is "untouchable" (a concept well known in Hinduism but foreign to Islam), and then trying rape her.[16] This cruelty, paradoxically, appears to be a by-product of his rebellion against tribalism and against the father whose fame and power he covets. If Uraz embodies certain admirable savage principles, he lives by others that are pathologically antisocial, even sociopathic. This ambiguity lies at the heart of his character as well as the ways in which Westerners have traditionally viewed the Islamic world: as a place where men can be real men but at the same time can thus indulge in excesses that horrify even as they titillate.

For the Western viewer of *The Horsemen*, Uraz thus facilitates communication between a civilized consciousness and the inner primitive in a dream of unrestrained power. Such a process had become all the more pertinent at the time of the film's release in light of the Vietnam War, in what would eventually become a U.S. defeat by developing-world insurgents. As it turned out, things had not been going so well for America in the "Indian country" of the 1960s, both in Vietnam and at home. Myths had been seriously tarnished if not demolished, including the iconic self-image of America as civilizing agent and champion of the underdog. Most damaging (at least for Cold Warriors) was the onslaught of the so-called Vietnam syndrome, what neoconservative guru Norman Podhoretz called "the sickly inhibitions against the use of military force."[17]

For the United States in 1970, unquestionable triumph in war seemed elusive, if not impossibly out of reach. In this light, Frankenheimer's film emerges as an attempt to solve the plight of Uraz, essentially the problem of military defeat and disrepute, so that the warrior within can be rehabilitated and unleashed again. These themes were not exactly invisible to contemporary critics. Vincent Canby, in his 1971 review, claimed that *The Horsemen* was "designed to glorify machismo of the most ignorant, savage sort, the cult of manliness that has, I suspect, its closest civilized equivalent in the totalitarian political movements of the 1930's."[18]

Fascism and Kennedy liberalism (Frankenheimer was a devoted follower of Robert Kennedy) initially seem to make strange bedfellows. But *The Horsemen* reveals such tension to be largely illusory. Indeed it evokes a "new frontier" (after John F. Kennedy's speech of July 16, 1960) in order to reconcile the decade's initial hopeful promise with its later miserable failures. In the face of bewildering social change, many Vietnam-era artists and intellectuals had found solace in a vision of the heroic past where conservative or nationalistic norms could still be valorized and rendered as ineluctable as biological laws. For Frankenheimer, as with others of his generation, the return to the native became not simply a form of flight but a desperate search for meaning, for myth, and for a firm ground in the anomie of the post-1960s era. In this sense, the film acts as a kind of prophecy of the decades to come, in which the United States would continue to use Afghanistan to stage its own fantasies of revenge and total victory.

Not so long ago, things had made sense. The rhetoric of American nationalism, with its obsession with unconditional surrender and unparalleled power infused with moral righteousness, had imprinted itself within the consciousness of a generation. The greatest generation, as it would come to be known, had fought the forces of tyranny and won the big one that made America a superpower.

But now, in Vietnam, there didn't seem to be a clear-cut victory. And absolute power, at least on the ground in villages like My Lai, had little to do with righteousness, or even sanity. For those who staked so much of themselves on the image of American imperial power as redemptive, the Vietnam era was not so much a political as it was a spiritual crisis. People reacted to this crisis with varying amounts of emotional courage or intellectual cowardice. For some, the ones who took to the streets and burned their draft cards, imperial power never recovered its hold on them. But for others, most notably the neoconservatives who would eventually orchestrate a twenty-first-century war on terror in Afghanistan, it was not American might that posed the biggest challenge but American weakness.[19]

Enter the horse.

In *The Horsemen,* Jahil is not simply an animal but a character—perhaps the major one. Most of the plot revolves around a desperate and vicious struggle to gain possession of this magnificent steed, whose name just happens to mean, in Dari, "savage."

For Uraz, this savagery is a birthright. It belonged at first to his father, a venerable and powerful leader now gone to seed. Resentful and impetuous, Uraz bristles to take the old man's place. But at the moment of truth in the *buzkashi* arena, he fails the test, falling from Jahil and breaking his leg. His momentary weakness leads to a castration both painful and ridden with shame—because at the crucial point, Uraz failed to measure up to his father, to muster enough savagery to make himself one with Jahil and achieve absolute victory. That is the secret of his missing leg. Any Freudian worth his or her salt would notice the link with Oedipus, whose name means "with the inflated leg." Uraz's leg is indeed inflated, his boot stuffed first with a cast, then with the Qur'an, then finally (when it is has been cut off) with cloths to make it bulge.

At the same time that he must deal with his own personal loss, Uraz also fends off attacks on what's left of his authority from Mukhi and Zereh, the former a member of the lower classes and the latter a nomad woman. In the wake of his defeat, traditional hierarchies break down and those on the bottom begin to assert themselves, indeed to even dare to assume the reins of power.

Of course, these underlings can never understand the symbiotic bond Uraz shares with the animal, none except Tursen, who owns the horse and who alone has proved his ability to master it. Nevertheless, the younger man chafes against his alpha-male father and the tribal mentality he represents. Throughout the film, there are hints that Tursen, as noblest of savages, is also a "vanishing Indian," a model moving fitfully into obsolescence. His son must fill the power vacuum, but he knows that the world Tursen inhabited no longer exists. Time has changed and so have the rules. The "ancient road" he pursues, and on which he becomes symbolically castrated, does not lead Uraz to redemption. Rather, his father's old age and infirmity goad the young *chapandaz* to reveal his own wounds—and thus make him realize, as all sons must, that he should not expect to be his father.

In this new world and new time, Uraz must forge a different kind of relationship with his father's horse, with Jahil, with savagery. And so, in the film's climactic scene, he rides before the assembled *chapandaz* and other dignitaries in a dazzling display of horsemanship. As they stare at him, agape, the one-legged Uraz weaves around the horse like a trick rider, man and animal fused in what can only be called a dance. After performing and thus enacting his remodeled union with the "savage," a relationship in which he and Jahil become one, Uraz rides his horse into the sunset, moving on to different lands where he can train others in the art of *buzkashi*.

The political agenda is startlingly transparent, just as it was in Frankenheimer's early work *The Manchurian Candidate*. Far from an ethnographic documentary, *The Horsemen* plays like a neoconservative dream—or a prophecy. The dreamscape of Western filmography and the genocidal frontier myth provide the stage on which Vietnam-era angst segues to a war without end. If Tursen represents the ideals and moral authority of the greatest generation and its just war, then Uraz embodies all too clearly the Vietnam vet lost in "Indian country," where it was not only politically necessary but even biologically imperative to harness savagery in order to safeguard civilization. The consequent blueprint for the future would thus be no "sickly inhibitions against the use of force" but, rather, a reinvention of the political arena as neo-social Darwinist battlefield, where nations, like the *chapandaz,* play the next great game for the big prize.

The *chapandaz* are so attractive to Frankenheimer because they suggest that unrestrained patriarchal power can easily renaturalize the hierarchy between master and slave, whether it be in the home or between nations. Modernity, with all of its repressions and its moral equivalence, dissolves before the ineluctable energy of these masculine and militarist paragons. "We are men of a different breed," Tursen intones, "conceived in the loneliness of desolation. Born with the smell of paradise in our nostrils, bred to pursue death as lesser men pursue women. Infatuated all our lives with dreams of the tomb. The rage . . . craving to make death our whore." This Nietzschean credo makes it clear that because Afghans exist in intimate contact with death and do not fear personal pain, neither should they flinch from the possibility of inflicting it on others.

Years later, after the war in Vietnam was lost, Frankenheimer would return to this theme in *Black Sunday*. Released in 1977 and written by Thomas Harris of Hannibal Lecter fame, *Black Sunday* follows a Palestinian terrorist plot to attack the 80,000-member audience of the Super Bowl with a Goodyear blimp crammed full of explosives.

The later film's counterpart to Uraz is Lander, the pilot of the blimp and lover of the terrorist leader. Like Uraz, who failed in the moment of truth, Lander collapsed under torture as a POW in Vietnam. As it did with the *chapandaz,* this lack of resolve leads to castration. His inability to stand up under enemy attack leads to sexual impotence after the war. "They took it away from me," Lander says of other Americans, against whom he now plots revenge.

To foil this nefarious scheme, the film introduces David Kabakov, a Mossad agent who, in the course of the narrative, overcomes his own temporary "sickly inhibitions against the use of force" to return to shooting people without remorse. Like *buzkashi,* the Super Bowl provides a spectacular arena against which these forces of national resilience and antiwar "terrorism" can duke it out in a final battle royal.

Melani McAlister has written that *Black Sunday* is the "first film to take the Vietnam Syndrome as its theme," expressing both horror over a "battered masculinity" and the need to solve this problem through unapologetic and brutal violence.[20] The loss in Vietnam (according to the film's logic) had nothing to do with the insurgents themselves and everything to do with the emasculated leaders who did not have the guts, viciousness, and will to *win.* The Israeli Kabakov teaches a valuable lesson in dealing with terrorists: Violence should be employed without restriction and without mercy. When one comes "to see both sides," his partner intones, "that is never good."[21] This ability to win without conscience or remorse, this Machiavellian drive to absolute victory at any cost, transcends any other consideration. It is the prize above all others to attain. In Frankenheimer's eyes, the Americans had a lot to learn from Afghanistan. After the Afghans' victory over the Soviets, the director expressed his envy: "[Y]ou could see why the Russians never beat them. Nobody could ever beat them."[22]

Frankenheimer's and Trumbo's view of Afghan society and of the primeval past it represents is, like *Black Sunday,* a cautionary tale on what it takes to win the unconditional surrenders that provide our national regenerations through violence. If American military defeats were viewed as emasculation, then the prescription seems to be misogyny, homosocial bonding, and relentless aggression.[23]

Afghanistan in 1970 had so far managed to preserve itself from the messiest entanglements of the Cold War. Like Pahlavi-era Iran, it was not yet characterized as a bastion of religious fundamentalism but rather an exotic and alluring backwater, frequented by a generation of adventure tourists and hippies who came there for the local color and cheap dope. Emptied of its complexity and its history, Afghanistan could become for a while the sublime frontier, a cinematic training ground for the next generation of not-so-noble American savages. In such a way did we begin to sow the wind.

2 Butch and Sundance in Afghanistan

The Man Who Would Be King

As the United States escalated its war in Afghanistan in the first years of the twenty-first century, Western commentators struggled to frame the conflict. To bring up the immediate cause of the devastation naturally drew attention to the Russian invasion. But to do that would require admitting the embarrassing fact that the same terrorists who were now our targets had previously been our allies, equipped and trained by our own intelligence agencies. In order to avoid any taint of association with the new enemy, the institutional memory of the press had to reach further back in time to make sense of Afghanistan.

Almost inevitably, they arrived at the works of Rudyard Kipling, following a long-standing practice of transposing nineteenth-century views of Afghani-

The Empire Besieged: Afghans surround Danny Dravot (Sean Connery).

stan onto the present. Kipling continues to be revered as an authority on a country that he saw only once in his life, briefly crossing the border while on assignment for a newspaper. His own negative experience there (he was either shot at or threatened at knifepoint by a Pashtun tribesman) colored all of his future writings on the country. Consequently, as Corinne Fowler has pointed out, Kipling popularized the notion of an essentialized Afghan ferocity and bloodthirstiness, which in turn "creates a primary focus on Afghans as perpetuators (rather than victims) of violence."[1]

In the wake of 9/11, a host of pundits began to invoke Kipling's Afghanistan. Richard Reeves urged his audience to "read Kipling to understand Afghanistan and Iraq."[2] Ben Macintyre, in the prologue to his biography of the first American adventurer in Afghanistan, wrote that Kipling's story "The Man Who Would Be King" made a "profound and lasting impression" on him. As a foreign correspondent, he had first encountered the tale in Peshawar, while covering the Afghan defeat of the Soviets. Reading Kipling, he remembers, was a favored pastime of reporters in the region, men who "were all living out [their] romantic fantasies in a land that invited and nourished them."[3] Another writer in the fall of 2001 called Kipling the "literary immortal of the hour," whose 1888 novella had gained sudden relevance now that Afghanistan was once again being invaded by a Western power.[4]

The 1975 film *The Man Who Would Be King*, directed by American auteur John Huston, also gained relevance. Like its literary source, Huston's film follows the romantic and ill-fated quest of two British soldiers of fortune, Danny Dravot and Peachey Carnehan, who conspire to loot the treasures of the fabled Kafiristan (modern-day Nuristan). After a short but adventurous walk through the Hindu Kush, they effortlessly usurp power from the hapless King Ootah and use their military training to build an army that soon unifies the country. With the savage yet rich land pacified, they enter the fabled city of Sikandergul, where superstitious natives worship Danny both as the divine son of Alexander the Great and as absolute monarch. Of course when you're at the top, there's nowhere else to go but down. Despite Peachey's objections, the man who would be king refuses to leave with the riches they've acquired, deciding to stay on permanently as benevolent dictator. But all his best-laid plans come undone when his Kafir bride bites his face at the wedding, drawing blood. Realizing that no god can bleed, the fanatical priesthood casts Danny to his death from a rope bridge and crucifies Peachey, who returns to India to recount their tragic tale.

In the eighty-seven years between the writing of the story and the production of the movie, the situation had gotten even more out of hand for the British Empire and its partners in crime. The British had to part ways with the Raj, the Belgians gave up the Congo, and the French begrudgingly departed from Algeria and Indochina—as did America, much to its own dismay. Despite suffering casualties more than twenty times those of the U.S. forces, the Vietnamese had managed to withstand one of the most vicious onslaughts in the twentieth century. But while Franz Fanon could write exultantly of "A Dying Colonialism," many in the West emerged from the era of decolonization unnerved and upset, especially in an America increasingly under siege from forces without and within.

As the 1970s began, Arab nations finally asserted themselves by turning off America's energy tap. Women were burning bras, men were burning draft cards, and inner-city African Americans were burning their homes in rage and frustration at dreams still deferred. The military had come under fire for war crimes in My Lai, while the president had been forced to resign or face impeachment hearings. Heroes were tarnished, and the patriotic fervor of the Cold War now seemed at best corny, at worst grotesque.

At this precise moment of American imperial vulnerability, Huston delivered his retro epic, appropriately starring Sean Connery. The aging former James Bond was a perfect choice for the role of Danny Dravot. In this tale of imperialism gone awry, who better to play the lead than 007 himself, a little aged and worse for wear now, like the political system he once served. At his side was Michael Caine as Peachey Carnehan. Caine was no stranger to the genre, having starred in *Zulu* (1964), one of many historical epics like *Lawrence of Arabia* (1962) and *Khartoum* (1966) that harkened back to the glory days of the British Empire as decolonization began. With such a track record, these two compelling and charismatic actors could admirably embody the empire besmirched, dragged through the mud, and kicked in the rear.

Of course this perception of self-degradation was also largely a product of self-pity, or what Tom Engelhardt has called the "dominant whine." Despite the tens of thousands of American dead in the Indochina war, the Vietnamese, Cambodians, and Laotians suffered in the millions. Such a focus on the losses of the invader masked those of the invaded and turned the aggressor into the victim. As the 1970s progressed, this image of the United States as victim became only more entrenched, allowing conservatives to reconstruct support for unrestrained military violence in the developing world.[5]

Empire Follows Art

The Man Who Would Be King provides ample illustrations of the dominant whine. Huston likes his imperialists—and wants the audience to identify with them. These "real" men display a machismo that would have made Huston's friend Ernest Hemingway proud. The effect is so hyperbolic that it seems almost obvious to label the overall tone "ironic"—a tongue-in-cheek critique of exploitation. As Richard A. Voeltz has written, *The Man Who Would Be King* is a "conflicted film," an "anti-imperialist, orientalist epic" that is "both imperialistic and critical of that imperialism."[6] But its anti-imperialism is not so much ambivalence about the nature of such aggression as it is a nostalgic longing for a past that is both quaint in its unvarnished honesty as well as dismally unattainable in the current political climate of decolonization. Despite Huston's affection for Danny and Peachey and their style of leadership, his film engages, by necessity, with world events that had made such a leadership style increasingly untenable. The failure of the United States in Vietnam had not just been a military one. It had also created a cognitive dissonance—the Vietnam syndrome—that got in the way of unflinching support for war. To resort to the cornball anticommunist rhetoric of the 1950s was now no longer possible. The recent war had all too clearly exposed the sharp contrast between the self-righteousness of American nationalism and the atrocities committed in its name.

Militarists thus employed a number of strategies to render any further interventions palatable to a public that had grown sick of war. Some resorted to Machiavellian realism, asserting that foreign policy must continue to be aggressive, if only because that is how the "real" world operates. Howard Zinn has noted, however, that such realism is "seductive because once you have accepted the reasonable notion that you should base your actions on reality, you are too often led to accept, without much questioning, someone else's version of what that reality is."[7]

Elsewhere, a jaded and often self-parodying cynicism became the order of the day—because it leads all too often to inaction. No one will feel the need to protest another war if they imagine that war to be inevitable. Similarly, why bother preventing or protesting wartime atrocities if these are unavoidable, almost automatic effects of war itself? Such a viewpoint easily dovetailed with the mass media's fascination with the irony and bad taste of camp. Thus *The Man Who Would Be King* and many other reactionary films of its era (notably *The Wild Bunch*) extol the momentarily discredited "leadership principle" of American militarism by giving it an ironic face. One way to make authoritarianism attractive again was to make it fun.[8]

To once again enable future imperial action, these ideologues would have to induce cultural amnesia. That is, they would have to help us forget a crucial imperial lesson of Vietnam: It's more fun to invade a country than it is to occupy it. Peachey and Danny know this all too well. They cannot stomach the sickly tedium of actually running the empire once they conquer it. Nor can they abide the rapid reassertion of the British class system that Huston makes apparent as soon as Kipling and Peachey meet. They are the everymen of the empire, the heroes who have been callously cast on the rubbish heap of history. As such, their position is akin both to the stigmatized Vietnam vets of the film's era as well as to the mythic cowboys of contemporary Westerns who tamed the Wild West but must now give way to more civilized inhabitants.

Once you face the heart of darkness and get in touch with the inner savage, it's hard to come home. When Kipling suggests they return to England, Danny scornfully says, "Not after watching Afghans come howling down out of the hills and taking battlefield command when all the officers had copped it!" Only in that moment while fighting the Afghans can they be more than the class they were born into. With India tamed (it's not "big enough"), there is nowhere else for them to go but into the next frontier. In the mountainous regions of the Hindu Kush, they hope to find a place where a man "isn't crowded and can come into his own." Such a savage wilderness promises them the chance to finally "be themselves." And a place of warring tribes, Danny says with a grin, is also a land of opportunity. They will be worshipped as deities and in the process "loot the country four ways from Sunday." Speaking of his film's heroes, Huston noted (without irony), "They think and act large. Not many leaders are this way today."[9]

Westerns often voice similar sentiments. The lone heroes of these films always journey to the supposedly empty space of the desert to escape something: the constraints of a mechanistic industrial age, a prudish social code, or perhaps simply themselves. In the wilderness, they can be reborn. There they can establish contact with the sublime forces of nature and "be themselves" according to the way nature intended, not the caste system of urban America or, in this case, Anglo-India. Only by converting open space to private property can they be fully actuated human beings. Only by being alone can they feel truly secure.

This insecurity ultimately stems from a deep-seated awareness of their tentative position in the colony. Wherever they initially go, the men seem to be swallowed up by crowds (as in the film's establishing shots), whose sheer numbers are vast, their languages bewildering. Peachey and Danny want to escape these multitudes because crowds imply others, or simply the Other. By fleeing from them, the two adventurers engage in a romantic regression to nature in order to isolate themselves from the anxiety of change as well as from the apprehension of the subjugated majority. The psychological dynamic has asserted itself in American history most obsessively in the South, where whites exercised a brutal yet tenuous power over an oppressed African American population they knew could easily overwhelm them.

By 1975, racist elements in the culture were fighting a rearguard action. This, however, did not stop many Americans from longing for a simpler past when people still knew their place. In regard to the cinematic Afghanistan, what distinguishes Huston's film from Frankenheimer's *The Horsemen* is this element of unvarnished, nostalgic racism. While some critics view *The Man Who Would Be King* as an allegory "of a whole culture that began to view exploitation and plundering as a moral imperative,"[10] others see a more sinister side to its tragicomic posturing. If *The Man Who Would Be King* was meant to be simply an ironic jab at imperial pretensions, then Huston's extensive changes to Kipling's story make little sense. As Sarah Kozloff has noted, "Huston seems to have gone out of his way to heighten the racial contrast that, if explicit in other works of Kipling's, is downplayed in this particular story."[11] Indeed, "one of the satisfactions of this film [is] the extent to which it justifies all racism."[12]

Almost from the beginning, we view India and later Afghanistan through the racist viewpoint of the colonizer, nowhere more obviously than in an early scene on a train, where Peachey peers at Kipling from behind a newspaper. In Kipling's story, the title of the paper is *The Backwoodsman*. But here Huston has significantly renamed it *The Northern Star*, evoking the image of illumination and civilization from the imperial north to the benighted colonies. Of course *The Northern Star* is not a civilizing light at all but a predatory gaze. And in fact, behind the noble sentiments of colonialism is a petty thief, the criminal whose crimes themselves masquerade behind the imperial discourse of cultural workers like Rudyard Kipling. In the final image of the film, Danny's moldering skull is reunited with the tarnished crown that he had lost in Afghanistan. While the truth may be that he was a plunderer and a liar, back in the heart of Empire he can become apotheosized through the rhetoric of Kipling and Huston, transmogrified from rapacious villain to tragic hero.[13]

When the high-toned rhetoric of Orientalism cannot serve, then Huston resorts to lowbrow stereotype. One of his most blatantly racist additions occurs in the same scene with Peachey on the train. Struggling inconspicuously to replace the watch he has stolen from Rudyard Kipling (whom he finds to his horror is a fellow Mason), Peachey takes advantage of the arrival of an Indian man. The pickpocket does nothing to hide his disgust with this educated, well-tailored, and English-speaking Hindu, who greets both men obsequiously. As the train rolls across the hot, dusty landscape, the two Englishmen spurn the Indian's offer of a slice of watermelon. Suddenly Peachey accuses the hapless newcomer of being a thief. Calling him a baboon, he throws him off the train and returns the watch to Kipling with a smile. Huston's passenger all too clearly resembles the stereotypical babu—a watermelon-munching caricature whose beating comes off as comedic rather than repugnant.

Racism and colonialism have long shared a sordid and bloody alliance, the former invoked to morally and scientifically justify the latter. Bastardized Darwinism and toxic doses of cultural arrogance enabled the West to dehumanize the inhabitants of whatever land they happened to be conquering at the moment. Once dehumanized, they could be disposed of that much easier. This led to a mindset that bordered on the psychopathic. The founder of the German East Africa Colony, Carl Peters, exemplified this cancerous combination of hubris and racism when writing to the Vagogo people in the late nineteenth century: "Tell the Sultan that I do not wish to make any peace with him. The Vagogo are liars and must be eliminated from the earth. But if the Sultan wishes to be slave to the Germans, then he and his people may possibly be allowed to live."[14] This is the lost world for which Danny and Peachey, and to a certain extent Huston, pine so plaintively.

The link between imperialism and racist violence becomes sharply defined the moment Danny and Peachey enter Afghanistan. There they encounter five threatening Afghans, clad in giant animal skins, with furry caps and long hair. They finger our two heroes, stealing things from them like obnoxious monkeys. Their language is, of course, unintelligible (and neither Dari nor Pashto). Nevertheless, the two Englishmen understand they are to be robbed. Immediately Peachey ponders how to turn the tables and steal their mules. By spitting a bullet into the fire, he creates a diversion long enough for him and Danny to overpower the savages. Once their foes have been disciplined with a good beating, the two stalwarts appropriate the pack animals with smug satisfaction. Throughout the scene, the Afghans are consistently rendered as animals, while Peachey and Danny's assault on them and subsequent theft of their property come off as comical and even admirable. Thanks to the narrative that identifies us with two British imperialists, Afghans appear to be the ones who present a clear and present threat, despite the fact that our heroes happen to be on Afghan land, are armed and dangerous, and have the clear intention of subverting the Afghan government (such as it is) and appropriating its resources.

Naturally such racially tinged megalomania had gone somewhat out of style by 1975. Thus Huston would claim that the Masonry shared by Kipling and Peachey in the film's initial scenes "symbolize[s] a universal connection between men," that unites people of all classes and races.[15] Danny and Peachey seem to betray this "brotherhood" by stealing the Kafirs' wealth, for which they pay dearly. But this simplistic moral equation, which has led many to conclude that this film is anti-imperialist, ignores the fact that the film makes it everywhere apparent that the Kafirs deserve to be dominated, by virtue of their brutish, almost bestial lack of culture and civilized norms.

Another of Huston's racist additions to the original story—King Ootah's victory celebration—provides ample illustration of this point. When Peachey eyes a few girls approvingly, the king generously offers his twenty-seven daughters to him. Peachey, a little overwhelmed, begs off. Perhaps, the king asks, he would like one of his thirty-two sons? Our hero can barely contain his disgust while Danny sententiously reminds him, "Different countries, different customs. Mustn't be prejudiced." Huston lampoons such progressive sentiments by then showing the Kafirs living up to their true barbarian status, playing *buzkashi* with a man's head instead of a goat carcass.[16]

The reproach is clear: Those who profess tolerance for cultural diversity are deluding themselves. Sooner or later, savages will show their true colors, casting the difference between us and them into sharp relief. While it may be an exaggeration to say that the only good native is a dead one, they should at the very least be servile underlings like Billy Fish, the Gunga Din–style soldier Danny and Peachey encounter lurking about King Ootah's castle. *The Man Who Would Be King* palpitates with contempt for other people, for all those who stand in the way of our unrestrained and puerile fantasies of absolute power. Of course, Huston does so always with a wink and a grin, if only to distract us from the fact that he's dead serious. Like some widescreen reactionary talk-show host, Huston's racist revision of Kipling's already racist story provided catharsis for post-Vietnam America's most recidivistic anxieties and paranoid fantasies—fears of change, of others, of difference, of the loss of control—in short, of complexity.

The Fascination of the Abomination

Such defensive subterfuge indicates the horror with which certain people confronted the fact of Western imperialism's setbacks in the 1960s and '70s. What made it worse was that the West had been humiliated by people whom it had spent centuries dehumanizing and exterminating. That sense of superiority had been so terribly fragile, so easily shaken. To conquer was to live in perpetual fear, as Joseph Conrad described so brilliantly in *Heart of Darkness*:

> Land in a swamp, march through the woods, and in some inland post feel the savagery, the utter savagery, had closed round him—all that mysterious life of the wilderness that stirs in the forest, in the jungles, in the hearts of wild men. There's no initiation either into such mysteries. He has to live in the midst of

the incomprehensible, which is also detestable. And it has a fascination, too, that goes to work upon him. The fascination of the abomination—you know, imagine the growing regrets, the longing to escape, the powerless disgust, the surrender, the hate.[17]

Afghanistan, like the Islamic world as a whole, had always inspired this fascination and horror. *The Man Who Would Be King* locates itself deep within that region's "incomprehensibility" in the most inaccessible region of all, Kafiristan. At the time of Kipling's writing, this area was a vast unknown, cut off from the rest of Afghanistan by virtue of its polytheistic religion. After the Afghan king Abdur Rahman invaded and forcibly converted the inhabitants in 1896, Kafiristan (Land of the Unbelievers) became Nuristan (Land of Light). Aside from reluctantly adopting Islam, the Nuristanis religiously adhered to their tribal lifestyle. Never completely mainstreamed into Afghan society, they retained their ancestral language, dress, and distinct customs.

Organized around a series of log-cabin villages in the heights of the Hindu Kush, the Nuristanis have always been fiercely independent. In fact, it was they who first resisted the Soviet-backed Communists only a month after the Saur Revolution took place. While some have viewed this insurgency as an attack on civilizing reforms that favored women's rights, Nuristani women—like their counterparts in other tribal societies—were the most independent in Afghanistan. The *chadari,* for example, was unknown in Nuristan.

In the nineteenth century, Nuristan was visited by a number of intrepid British explorers, who described their unique buildings, religion, languages, dress, food, and social customs. They, like the Nuristanis themselves, believed that the men and women of the Hindu Kush were descendants of Alexander the Great's armies. Despite such a sizable amount of existing ethnographic data, Huston's Kafiristan bears no resemblance whatsoever to the actual place or its people, despite his insistence to the contrary.[18] This may have something to do with the fact that most of Huston's film was shot in Morocco, using native Berbers and Arabs who, incidentally, look nothing like actual Nuristanis.

Our first sight of them occurs when Danny and Peachey spot a band of brigands attacking some women and children washing on the banks of a river. Their faces hidden behind African-like skull masks, these inhuman marauders give Danny and Peachey the excuse they need to start firing, using their superior technology to show that they are in Kafiristan with the best of intentions—to protect Afghan women from Afghan men (an old chestnut of many an Afghan war).

Ironically, Huston and assistant director Bert Batt (who also worked on Caine's *Zulu*) were unable to recruit local women to act in these scenes because of their unwillingness to be photographed. So they went to the nearest cities and hired prostitutes as extras, one of whom Batt kicked in the behind during filming.[19] Thus the production itself, not to mention its imagery, Orientalized Muslim women as vulnerable harem slaves and prostitutes as well as frequent and helpless victims of (exclusively Muslim) male brutality.

But Muslims are not the only sexual predators around. Beneath the murk of imperial prejudice, lust simmers, threatening to dismantle the boundaries between civilized and savage on a variety of levels. After King Ootah's victory celebration, Peachey attracts a comely native woman (in reality, of course, a Moroccan prostitute) to his bedchamber. The scene initially plays like a primal racist fantasy: the white man with an eager and willing dark woman, mute and sensuous. But when the woman takes the anticipated next step and strips, Peachey grows nervous. The two men had, after all, taken a vow of chastity in India until they should become kings of Kafiristan. Luckily Danny appears at this crucial moment and brings the encounter to a halt. After a relieved Peachey urges them both to "go seek safety in battle," the scene ends with him staring at Danny's gleaming white shirt, the woman meanwhile submerged in shadow, her face invisible.

In *The Man Who Would Be King*, even sexuality cannot overcome the undertow of racism. The temptations and dangers of miscegenation, which Danny will later ignore to his peril, are abundantly clear, with violence provided as a suitable alternative. But what Peachey really fears in this disturbing scene is not the threat of his desire for this dark-skinned woman but rather his *aversion* to her. Whatever romance exists is between him and Danny. The fear of this true intimacy, of a socially proscribed closeness that feels dangerously like homosexuality, drives Peachey into a compensatory attack on other men to prove his manhood.

For his part, Danny remains impervious to contamination from the natives, as evidenced by the arrow that fails to pierce his skin during a pitched battle. Once enthroned, he continues to wield this phallic power of the arrow until (inevitably it seems) the woman's teeth penetrate *him*. The dread of miscegenation so apparent in the film testifies to an unconscious fear of losing one's self, of being diluted or, worse, changed. As he yearns to unite with an alien culture, Danny becomes simultaneously deflowered by it.

Sikandergul represents everything that Danny and Peachey had dreamed of in India. A mixture of Greek and African styles, the city offers the first sight of lush vegetation in that barren land, with beautiful waterfalls and clean, healthy-looking citizens. And more important, the royal treasury "makes the jewels in the Tower of London look like cheap family heirlooms." (An interesting comment because the most famous of the British crown jewels, the

Koh-i-Noor diamond, once belonged to the Afghan monarch.) Having power over some jewels, however, seems somehow unsatisfying. True power always revolves around controlling land and people. Thus Danny soon declares (to Peachey's dismay), "A nation I shall make of it, with an anthem and a flag."

The man who would be king's imperial hubris is his downfall. Simply stealing from the natives is one thing. But settling down with them, speaking their language, attempting to bring order to their miserable lives—this kind of temptation can only lead to disaster. Indeed, he and Peachey have actively derided such noble sentiments throughout the film. The omnipresent danger of being changed by the Other, of being so contaminated by the natives that racial boundaries threaten to dissolve, poisons the intimacy between the two men and precipitates a lethal crisis.

Only at the last moment, after Danny's exposure and the reinstitution of racial boundaries, can he and Peachey have their rapprochement. The erstwhile king admits he blundered because he was so "bleeding high and bloody mighty." More to the point, he failed to understand, as Peachey did, that a true intimacy with the Other has a way of threatening one's ability to constitute the requisite moral lies that enable imperial oppression. This realization saved Peachey from connecting with another (a people, a woman, a culture) and from losing himself in that Other. He survives because he stays true to his oath to Danny—that is, to himself. Thus Peachey affirms himself by singing together with Danny at the climax of the film, completing his song (whose telling lyrics combine Christian and military imagery). By the time he returns to India with Danny's skeletal head, Peachey's retreat to the safety of the self is complete.

The Persistence of Orientalism

The heroes of *The Man Who Would Be King* are ultimately regressive. They yearn for a halcyon past when narcissism was untroubled by the introduction of the Other. Whether it is a woman, an idea, or a suddenly rebellious native, an object becoming a subject provokes terror.

By persisting in this solipsistic worldview, one transforms reality into mere self-reflection. For this reason, the rhetorical apparatus of Orientalism has served admirably over the centuries in providing an image of the Muslim world that both confirms our prejudices and calms our fears. Anyone with the slightest interest in the history and culture of Afghanistan knows that Huston's version bears no resemblance to historical reality (aside from a passing mention of the city of Kamdesh, an actual Nuristani town with a population of about ten thousand). His Kafiristan is as authentic as the Egypt of a 1940s

B movie. Kipling himself, despite his proximity to the Hindu Kush, was hardly more knowledgeable. The film, like the story on which it was based, presents an imperialist confection, a fantasy world of the past wherein one can escape the unpleasant psychological, political, and cultural ramifications of acknowledging defeat at the hands of developing world insurgents.

While there are and always have been other ways of viewing the Islamic world, Orientalism's narrative remains deeply seated in our culture. Thus in spite of the evidence that renders this film's portrait of Afghanistan highly unreliable, a plethora of cultural commentators in the twenty-first century could still enthusiastically adjure their readers to "understand Afghanistan" by reading or watching *The Man Who Would Be King*. Centuries of inter-textuality have only strengthened its status as objective truth. This would explain why there was so little critical commentary in the fall of 2001 about the usefulness of a Victorian narrative and an American film of the 1970s in comprehending twenty-first-century Afghanistan. Fictitious projection becomes fact if reinforced enough in the various outlets of cultural discourse, both highbrow and low. To expect, if not demand, that Afghanistan reflect Kipling's description of it is the supreme conceit of a power that does not discover truth but creates it.

As evidenced by the film's racist paranoia, Orientalism and the supposedly absolute power it represents are never as unassailable as they present themselves to be. Many scholars, including Sara Suleri and Homi Bhabha, have noted Orientalism can be deconstructed to show that "the colonizer is not monolithically powerful, nor the colonized completely powerless."[20] Kipling also made this a constant theme in his poetry and prose:

> When you're wounded and left on Afghanistan's plains,
> And the women come out to cut up what remains,
> Jest roll to your rifle and blow out your brains
> An' go to your Gawd like a soldier.[21]

While the British had cemented their power in India, they had never been able to dominate the tribes to the north, particularly the Pashtuns. The constant engagements with (and casualties inflicted by) the Afghans were common knowledge to the nervous British rulers of India.[22] English pundits and politicians trembled at the thought of Russians and Afghans joining forces. Even into the twentieth century, Afghanistan continued to serve as a foil to colonized India, a wild frontier of redoubtable savages.

These Afghans were not the buffoons of Huston's film but rather disciplined tribal warriors who engaged British forces of up to 70,000 men. Between 1848 and 1878 and between 1889 and 1898, thirty-four border wars were fought between the British and the Afghans.[23] It was the Afghans who inflicted the humiliating defeat at the Khyber Pass in 1842, with the killing of 15,000 British soldiers, leaving only a single survivor who made it back to the fortress at Jalalabad. A generation later, the next wave of British invaders met their match at the 1880 battle of Maiwand. When it was the Russians' turn, it would be the Nuristanis, the most independent of Afghans, who first struck back at the Soviet superpower, establishing their independence from the Communist regime, though at great cost. Twenty-first-century American soldiers equally found Afghan soldiers to be "tenacious and calculating" foes, who were "bolder than those [they] fought in Iraq."[24]

The omnipresence of Afghans in Kipling's opus testifies to the fear and anxiety the British felt over a very real threat. Afghanistan signifies independence in the face of hegemony—then as now. Of course this sense of Afghans as almost elemental has little to do with reality. Instead it is a projection of imperial anxieties. The Khyber Pass and Maiwand stuck in the collective imagination, leaving persistent and disturbing questions for an empire that imagined itself as absolute power and authority. If wars were to end in such an ignominious fashion, then it was up to art and, later, cinema to atone by rewriting history. Huston's film narrative fulfills this function, revealing a conservatism deeply disturbed by the American failure to achieve unconditional surrender in Vietnam as well as the success of the Vietnamese in winning even a Pyrrhic victory. Orson Scott Card, the American science fiction author, has reflected such a worldview when he called *The Man Who Would Be King* "the classic tragedy that Aristotle spoke of—so powerful that some of us can only stand to see the ending once."[25]

Afghans, and especially Nuristanis, make perfect stand-ins for the trauma inflicted by developing world insurgents in the 1960s and '70s. They and their territory have always been the wall against which great empires have shattered themselves, while of course doing plenty of shattering on their own. As Kipling wrote in "Arithmetic on the Frontier":

> Two thousand pounds of education
> Drops to a ten-rupee jezail[26]

Nevertheless, this does not stop new generations from giving it the old college try. When imperial meltdown inevitably ensues, racism rushes to the rescue. The reason for defeat, if we're to take the film at its word, is that the natives were so bestial and irrational that even when initially conquered by these altruistic British soldiers, they didn't have the decency to submit to European rule. Clearly they could neither see the beauty of the dream nor perceive the pathos in parting the plunderers from their spoils. And if heroes like Danny and Peachey failed, then maybe it was inevitable that America in Vietnam did, too. It wasn't our fault at all, the film's convoluted logic says. It was the *natives'* fault. The film thus teaches an important lesson: Don't expect the Afghans to understand when you occupy their country and force them to do what you tell them. What is both tragic and comedic about this sentiment is that today, unlike in Huston's film, it is stated without even the pretense of irony.

3 The New Great Game

Rambo III, The Beast,
and *Charlie Wilson's War*

The defeat in Vietnam was not the only political and cultural calamity to befall the United States in the 1970s. A series of epochal events in the Islamic world dealt serious blows to U.S. power and prestige and set the stage for many wars to come. The oil embargo, a protest against U.S. support of Israel in the Arab-Israeli War of 1973, hit Americans close to home with gas shortages and

The Lost Patrol: Imperialism goes awry in *The Beast.*

inflated prices, paving the way for the Japanese triumph against domestic automobile manufacturers. Several years later, the Iranian Revolution and its ensuing "hostage crisis" humiliated and traumatized the United States. Finally on Christmas Eve 1979, the Cold War heated up again when the Soviet Union invaded Afghanistan. Their purpose, according to the Kremlin, was merely to support the communist government that had wrested power from Daoud Khan in a military coup the previous year on April 27, 1978, and was now faltering before a widespread counterinsurgency.

The Saur Revolution of 1978 had not happened overnight. For the prior twenty years, Afghan men and women, educators and soldiers, had traveled to the Soviet Union to be indoctrinated in both modernity and Marxism. Many of those who eventually joined the party membership of Khalq and Parcham, the two major Afghan communist groups, were college educated, highly literate, and cosmopolitan. Hafizullah Amin, who assumed power after murdering Nur Muhammad Taraki, the coup's initial leader, was educated at Columbia Teacher's College in New York City. This was no peasant revolution.

Although the Afghan communists were educated, they had not read Marx closely enough. Afghanistan—barely industrialized and still mostly feudalistic—was nowhere near ready for a dictatorship of the proletariat. Afghans themselves made this clear immediately after the coup. In October 1978, the rugged northern province of Nuristan (the setting for *The Man Who Would Be King*) took up arms against the government. The Nuristanis proclaimed their independence in the spring of 1979, at the same time that anticommunists in Herat murdered several Russian "advisers" and their families. To quell the crisis, the Afghan authorities appealed to the Kremlin.[1] Soviet helicopters and tanks entered Kabul that winter, beginning a decade-long war that would cost Afghanistan a million lives and dispossess millions more of their loved ones and homes.

For America, still licking its wounds from Vietnam, the war with Russia presented a welcome opportunity to settle old scores. Thanks to President Jimmy Carter's establishment of a covert operation that supplied funding to the mujahedeen (the anticommunist forces), the CIA and other governmental agencies, staffed by many bitter Vietnam vets, began to get their payback. For them this was not politics but a personal grudge.

At first the Americans were content to profit from the Afghan slaughter by dumping antique firearms like the .303 Lee-Enfield rifle and World War II–era ammunition on the desperate insurgents. When the Afghans proved themselves better fighters than anyone imagined, even with primitive weapons, the CIA upped the ante and began to supply night-vision goggles, AK-47s, rocket-propelled grenades (RPGs), and eventually Stinger missiles.[2] The guerillas not only received training in the operation of their new equipment but were also schooled in military tactics. Which mujahed commander got the spoils depended on how close he was to Saudi Arabia and ISI (Pakistani Intelligence), who dished them out. An intimate working relationship with both countries was predicated on the Afghans' indoctrination in Wahhabi Islam, the Saudi Arabian root of many fundamentalist branches, and its Pakistani equivalent, Deobandism. The CIA was interested neither in how the system worked nor in the kinds of religious education that went with arms training. They simply wanted to kill Soviets. And kill they did. By the war's end, as many Russians had died in Afghanistan as U.S. soldiers had in Vietnam. This was what every hawk had been waiting for, a chance to heal the dreaded "Vietnam syndrome" while at the same time halting communist expansion.

Afghanistan became the conservative cause célèbre. As CIA Director William Casey put it, "Usually it looks like the big bad Americans are beating up on the natives. Afghanistan is just the reverse. The Russians are beating up on the little guys."[3] Ronald Reagan, Casey, and others hailed the mujahedeen as "freedom fighters," likening them both to the American patriots who had fought against British tyranny as well as to French anti-Nazi partisans.

Of course the perceived political significance of Afghanistan in the grand scheme of American empire was minor. Certainly the men in charge of foreign policy at the time had no inkling of Afghanistan's future strategic importance. But those on the sidelines quickly exploited this covert war for domestic purposes in the United States. They sought to erase the disturbing truths outed by Vietnam and to return to the American myth of civilization holding its own on a global frontier against the forces of darkness.

To this end, the cinema (like other visual media) began to ideologically frame the conflict for the masses. Jack Valenti, the former president of the Motion Picture Association of America, has said that "Hollywood and Washington sprang from the same DNA"[4] and nothing in its depictions of Afghanistan would alter that assessment. Because it was not a war that directly involved U.S. forces, Afghanistan in the 1980s was never as obsessive a subject as Vietnam in that era or the Middle East in today's films. In the initial stages of the conflict, when CIA action in the country was still secret, the only film concerning Afghans was *High Road to China* (1982), a B movie version of *Raiders of the Lost Ark* that unashamedly featured its hero bombing Afghan women from a plane. The movie itself also mercifully bombed. Once it became general knowledge that the United States was fighting a proxy war with the mujahedeen, a number of pictures, from comedies like *Spies Like Us* (1985) to the James Bond film *The Living Daylights* (1987), began to portray their heroic resistance against the communist occupiers.

Such a conflict was particularly useful for restoring American enthusiasm for the "just war" and facilitating identification with a military power that was always supposed to be used for good. For those whose egos had been primarily defined by these notions, Afghanistan became the prelude to the Gulf War, a way for America to rehabilitate its self-image after Vietnam. The most perfect cinematic expression of this policy, and of American involvement in Afghanistan as a whole, is *Rambo III* (1987).

Rambo, named after (of all people) the French symbolist poet Arthur Rimbaud, was the creation of David Morrell, a conservative writer with a PhD in literature from Pennsylvania State University. His John Rambo is the quintessential right-wing fantasy figure, an übersoldier who professes an anticollectivist suspicion of the state that he nevertheless obeys unquestioningly. Wielding his low-tech bow and gargantuan knife with prodigious skill, he is a modern-day Natty Bumppo in black headband and rippling muscles. In all three of his 1980s-era cinematic adventures, his main purpose remains the same: to get payback for Vietnam—to undo history and "win this time." The subsequent Rambo sequels, made decades after the original three films and remarkable for their much greater body count (236 killed in *Rambo IV!*), do not concern us here.

First Blood (1982) addresses the painful topic of veterans returning stateside to scorn or apathy. With Dirty Harry–like aplomb, Rambo cathartically annihilates those at home who failed to support his cause, eventually destroying an entire town. *Rambo II* (1985) taps an even deeper vein of military angst by sending Rambo back to Vietnam to rescue the MIAs there who "are not forgotten," meanwhile single-handedly slaughtering hordes of Vietnamese. The third film portrays Rambo's parallel trajectory with the CIA, tracing the trauma of Vietnam back to its source—the Russians—for a final spat of vengeance in Afghanistan. Morrell, who by the third movie was relegated to the sidelines of the franchise, writing the movie novelization, was astute enough to realize one thing about this third film: "Now we've entered deliberate mythology. Any semblance of reality has been left behind."[5]

In academic analyses of the Rambo films, scholars commonly assign a great deal of space to the first two episodes, which easily lend themselves to discussions of the conservative backlash against the antiwar movement of the 1960s and '70s. Completely transparent wish fulfillments, these films reveal the damage done to the nationalist ego of the United States after 1973. Like its predecessors, *Rambo III* seeks to bring the viewer back to the sacred space of Americanism, to the historical moment when America was beginning its wars for civilization, unassailably victorious and still largely untainted by self-doubt or moral quandary. But more so than the first two films, *Rambo*

III (like *The Horsemen*) combines this myth of how the West was won with neoconservative imperialism, the answer to the right's postwar anxieties.

One of the earliest forms of American frontier mythology is the Indian captivity genre. Its stark contrasts of savage and civilized persisted well into the twentieth century in a plethora of Westerns in which cowboys rescue white damsels from the clutches of vicious native warriors. *Rambo III* follows in this grand tradition by having Rambo's friend and mentor, the paternal Colonel Samuel Trautman, captured by Russians and savagely tortured. Like many a Western hero, Rambo enters the wilderness to rescue a captured comrade, aided by "good" Indians, in this case a band of rugged mujahedeen clearly awed by his prowess. Like the colonel, who is captured wearing a *pakul* cap and Afghan fatigues, Rambo adopts the ways of the "Indians," indicated by his use of primitive weaponry as well as his ability to beat the Afghans at a friendly game of *buzkashi*—this despite the fact that Rambo has never played the game before. A similar scene, with Hawkeye playing a game of lacrosse with the natives, can be seen in the film *The Last of the Mohicans* (1992). As in the James Fenimore Cooper tale, good Indians assist the white warrior in his quest to free his loved ones from savage captivity.

Meanwhile, the rest of the native inhabitants behave in characteristic Wild West fashion. That is, they exist primarily as a primitive backdrop against which the hero's struggle with savagery may be seen in sharper relief. The Afghan villagers are reminiscent of the hapless Mexican peasants seen in films like *The Magnificent Seven.* Their only settlements consist of scratch-gravel villages in a desert plain. They herd goats and carry water jugs on their heads. Absolutely clueless when it comes to Western ways, one man absurdly asks Rambo, "What is football?"[6] After barely any deliberation, the Afghans naturally flock to help him, including an enthusiastic young boy who is already a committed child soldier at the age of twelve. Neither Rambo nor the film deplores his condition. Instead the boy provides suitable adoration for Rambo as a cute sidekick, the only one sufficiently unthreatening with whom Rambo can have a human connection. Typical of most cinematic natives, the Afghans ride horses, carry antique firearms, and have no clue as to how to identify or operate sophisticated weaponry like time bombs and rocket launchers. In the face of so much helplessness, Rambo can easily rehabilitate the image of the American warrior and consequently of America's imperial self-image as civilizer, beacon of liberty, and champion of the underdog.[7]

Like its people, Afghanistan exhibits an essential lack of civilization and history. It always appears as a desert, devoid of cities, cars, or telephones— anything that would locate the film somewhere other than the mythic West. Although the weapons remain distinctly modern, everything else is timeless and void, like the world of Genesis before God's shaping spirit.

Ultimately neither the people nor the land are important, it's what Rambo does there that matters. The war's the thing, a war to restore the myth of American rightness that can be sacrificed to. This purpose achieves particular clarity in the scene in which Rambo struggles to the death with a Russian giant. In one brief long shot, the mortal enemies square off on a barren plateau overlooking a desert landscape that recedes into a limitless depth of field. Such an image essentially provides a thumbnail sketch of the film's ideology, of just exactly how the players of the New Great Game perceived the Afghan conflict. There are no Afghans to provide a distraction from the real story: America versus Russia, the latest act in the mythic war of civilization versus savagery on an empty frontier.

Russian savagery constitutes a recurring, obsessive theme. In beautifully choreographed shots, helicopters swoop across the barren landscape (in this case, Israeli locations) spewing death and destruction. Communist prisons resemble the murky, infernal *carceri* of Giambattista Piranesi. Deep in the cavernous dungeons there, the Soviets use blowtorches on prisoners and keep women in cages. Not only do they ruthlessly slaughter the Afghan opposition, but they also massacre mothers with their babies. Their motives for such violence are unclear. They appear to be simply indulging in imperialist savagery for the sport of it. Our hero, on the other hand, would rather be hanging out where Trautman initially finds him: in a Buddhist monastery. Rambo's motives remain distinctly nonimperialist, even apolitical. Whatever violence he commits against such monstrous villains can only be something akin to divine retribution.

Rambo III's hyperbolic mayhem allows for a scathing critique of its representation of the Afghan conflict, especially by critics on the left. Communist belligerence, so lavishly illustrated in the film, can easily be dismissed as transparent Cold War reactionary rhetoric. Such a reading has been predominant in post-9/11 descriptions of the anti-Soviet insurgency in Afghanistan. Marxist scholars and progressive pundits in the West have often cast the Russian invasion as a well-intentioned crusade to bring "female education and emancipation" to the Afghans.[8] Such writers persistently challenge the view of Russians as genocidal or even brutal, instead pointing out the mujahedeen's numerous instances of treachery, fundamentalism, and cruelty. Interestingly, their rhetoric mirrors *exactly* that of American conservative writers justifying the 2001 invasion of Afghanistan. As the story goes, Russia, like America, was not in Afghanistan for any reason other than to free Afghan women from the burqa and boost the country's collective GPA.

If the Russians' intentions were so noble, however, why then were they so fiercely resisted by the Afghans? This is never adequately explained by progressive critics, except by incorporating Orientalism into the argument.

According to such a view, the people who resisted Russian benevolence are Muslim fanatics rather than patriots resisting a foreign occupation. It is their "antimodern" religion that causes them to act so irrationally against the Red Army.

Like most accounts of the war, what the Afghans actually thought fades before the geopolitical posturing of the two superpowers and their respective ideologies. But to ascertain what Afghans felt about the Russians, all one needs to do is look at the enduring popularity of *Rambo III* in Afghanistan and among its diaspora.[9] They were (and are) drawn to the film, absurd as it is, not simply because films about their country were few and far between. Rather it was because *Rambo III* was the only film in the West to portray the Russian depredations there. For millions of Afghans, those who lost loved ones to war or their limbs to land mines, the Russians *were* the bad guys, the ones who were, in the words of the film, "wiping out a people."

Despite the source, this information is borne out by the facts. According to the Afghan historian M. Hassan Kakar, what the Russians did to Afghanistan was not war but *genocide*.[10] The Soviet forces committed numerous, well-documented atrocities, including the August 1980 shelling of Herat that killed three thousand people and the April 1982 massacre of two hundred inhabitants of the city of Tashqughan. Kakar enumerates an appalling set of Russian war crimes that include the kidnapping of women, looting and destruction of homes, bombing of civic gatherings, and sowing of land mines in agricultural areas.

Rambo III depicts all of these unflinchingly and honestly while nevertheless containing enough factual errors that it was even attacked by the conservative *National Review* for being a "moving comic-book" and a "blatant use of a current tragedy for commercial purposes."[11] The same writer chastised the filmmakers for not giving enough credit to the Afghan guerillas by "endorsing the sillier stereotypes about the fighters." Interestingly, the leftist press frequently commits the same errors, giving far too much credit to American militarism as opposed to Afghan resistance for the ultimate victory against the Soviets.

Although many on both sides of the political spectrum view the movie as a piece of Hollywood dreck, *Rambo III* is nevertheless one of the few films of any era to honestly portray the U.S. objectives in the Afghan-Russian war. Rambo's relationship with the Afghan boy inadvertently reflects that of the CIA operatives (motivated by short-term revenge) who supplied the mujahedeen with weapons. Content to equip men whom they saw as simpletons with the means to sow mass destruction, they gave no thought to the future of the country once the Russians left. Like Rambo, they were there to settle a grudge with the commies, who had held America's warrior image hostage for far too long. By freeing the colonel and defeating the Russians with a proxy army, Rambo and his Vietnam vet spies in the real world could heal themselves of the stigma of being victims and, worse, of being wrong.

Curiously, neither the film nor the conservatives who eagerly embraced its message ever seemed to consider that defeat was not an illness to be healed but rather a lesson to be learned. For them the issue of paramount importance was that Rambo as Vietnam vet no longer be seen as a child-killing, psychopathic thug (that's what the Russians are) but as a noble savage, a defender of the downtrodden.[12]

It seems paradoxical to locate a film that is really about the Vietnam War in the Afghanistan of 1987. But the mechanism in operation here corresponds to one earlier used by the Western genre to allegorize Cold War anxieties of the 1950s and '60s. The only difference is that by the end of the century, U.S. imperialism has moved to new frontiers, from obsessive dwelling in the mythic past to a more tentative spectrum of dominance in the present.

Rambo III prophesies just how tentative this dominance will become by its complete disinterest in the complexities of the conflict, mimicking a larger political neglect that would sow the seeds of the Taliban ten years later. War, as envisioned in the film, is not really about the suffering of Afghans, or about their need for independence, or about religious freedom. Instead, its meaning centers on, as we have seen before, regeneration through violence. By framing the war as a cosmic grudge match, all thought of politics or economics can be relegated to the bleachers. War becomes cleansing, purifying, mythic, and heroic. The film sees the world through a glass darkly, its reflection mirroring only our most nationalistic image of ourselves and the most ready-made excuses for our own imperialist brutality.

This brand of narcissism has long endured as a leitmotif of American political mythology. So wrapped up in its own pain and turmoil, the conservative American consciousness as typified by Rambo cannot possibly see the reality of Afghanistan or the inevitable chain of events that will lead to 9/11. Even when Rambo glimpses this reality, he studiously avoids drawing any conclusions from it or making any emotional attachments to it. On his arrival in Afghanistan, he sees a modern chamber of horrors—the makeshift hospital, the bombed-out villages, the child soldiers—vignettes looted from the pages of *Time* magazine, images of a war that an American audience had been watching for almost a decade. What then is Rambo's response? Sympathy? Anger? Sadness? As it turns out, none of these. He merely says, "I'm not a tourist." But of course he *is* the consummate tourist on a predictable package tour of the opposition's atrocities.

With a little reflection, Rambo's complete absence of empathy with what is happening to the Afghans should raise an alarm. But there are other pertinent danger signs, a series of incredible omissions of context and complexity. Our cinematic tour guides have no interest in showing us the modern cities of Afghanistan like Kabul, Kandahar, or Herat. Neither do they give any indication that thousands of Afghan communists aided the Russians in their invasion and occupation. Only one reference to jihad, an oblique statement of the mujahedeen's commitment to fight for "land and God," indicates that Islam may be a motivating force behind the insurgency. The Arabs who aided the mujahedeen—people like Osama bin Laden—remain invisible. The same holds true for Pakistan, the country that more than any other created much of the internal distress in Afghanistan by arming and training successive waves of fundamentalist guerillas from Gulbuddin Hekmatyar's murderous soldiers to the fanatical Taliban.

Tourists see only what they want to see. Their visits tend to be extremely superficial, focused on staged experiences of tradition and local color, without ever having to encounter the locals on their own terms. In such a way, Rambo tours Afghanistan, following his own agenda, and abruptly departs when his objectives are finished. "Can you not stay?" the Afghans ask him. "I've got to go," he grunts, though never explaining why.

With the Russians defeated, America cared nothing for Afghanistan or Afghans. As CIA chief in Pakistan Milton Bearden put it: "Did we really give a shit about the long-term future of Nagarhar? Maybe not. As it turned out, guess what? We didn't."[13] The film mirrors this sentiment, its sympathy for the people who had suffered so much from America's proxy war simply a ruse to rally support for another anticommunist jihad. It was a hypocritical and horrifically ill-advised strategy. Such pathological shortsightedness during the war and subsequent to it led to the instability that came afterward. By 1993, four years after the Russian war ended, the U.S. government had frozen all foreign aid to Afghanistan. A year later, Mullah Omar and his merry band were on the move.

This was not only a betrayal of the "gallant people of Afghanistan" to whom the film is dedicated but also the cause of two new wars and countless deaths. Land mines still litter the countryside to this day, as do the blasted shells of Russian tanks. By the turn of the millennium, there were more guns per capita in Afghanistan than in any other country. The major exports were opium poppies and desperately cheap labor for the surrounding nations of Pakistan and Iran. The Taliban was born, the Buddhas of Bamiyan were demolished, and Osama bin Laden settled down to train a new generation of Islamic militants.

Rambo III elucidates this clear-cut cause and effect in its own ham-fisted way. All of the things that are invisible to Rambo (and to his audience), blinded by ideology and the pathetic need for nationalist self-esteem after Vietnam, are precisely what led to later disasters for the United States abroad and at home. Because those in power did not care, they did not notice the extent to which radical Islam (stimulated by Saudi Arabia and Pakistan) was permeating the once relatively moderate Afghan nation. By refusing to see the various factions of mujahedeen as anything other than primitive simpletons, incapable of running a modern state, America convinced itself that a peaceful resolution to the Afghan civil war was impossible. And by ignoring the costs of the vicious wars that it helped escalate and sustain, the United States allowed a generation to be born without hope or help, peace or promise.

The Road to Kandahar

A year later as the Russians were preparing to withdraw, a new film debuted on the Afghan conflict. Based on a play written by William Mastrosimone (who also wrote the screenplay), *The Beast* (1988) is a variation of John Ford's 1934 thriller *Lost Patrol*. In both films, a group of soldiers becomes lost in the desert, soon falling prey to an implacable Muslim enemy. *Lost Patrol* describes them as "sneaky Arabs" and "dirty, filthy swine." *The Beast* eschews this unsubtle approach for a view of Afghans complicated by a healthy dose of post-Vietnam malaise. Unlike Ford's band of Brits, *The Beast*'s Russian tank crew is lost not only in the midst of a vicious wilderness but also within the labyrinths of a senseless war—and their own brutality.

Things start going wrong when the Soviets lose their way after annihilating an Afghan village and committing a slew of war crimes, including running the tank over a mujahed as his family watches helplessly. Constantine Koverchenko is in the driver's seat during this atrocity and, strangely enough, becomes the hero of the film. He's a bespectacled, rebellious young man of the Mikhail Gorbachev era who's open-minded enough to befriend Samad, the only Afghan member of the tank crew. His commander Daskal, on the other hand, is a brutal, battle-hardened Stalinist who hates Samad as much as he does all other Afghans.

A local group of mujahedeen whose village the Russians have just destroyed sets off in pursuit of the tank. Their leader is the charismatic Taj, who vows revenge on the barbarous communists. As the tank struggles to find the road to Kandahar, the mujahedeen engage in a cat-and-mouse game with the Soviet lost patrol, waiting for the right moment to use their ace in the hole: an RPG that will destroy the enemy vehicle with one shot.

Inside the tank, paranoia reigns. Daskal becomes convinced that Samad is in cahoots with the rebels. The last straw comes when the Afghan dares to pray beside a river. The commander shoots him in the back and departs while Constantine, enraged, threatens to report this as a war crime (despite having committed a few of his own). Fearing an official reprimand, his fellow crew members strand him in the desert. Luckily, Constantine's conversations with Samad have taught him some things about Afghans, including the practice of giving hospitality to all strangers who ask for it, even if they are enemies. Thanks to his cross-cultural dialogue, he narrowly averts a swift execution at the hands of Taj and his men by invoking this time-honored code of ethics.

The embittered hostage soon repairs their damaged RPG and joins forces with the insurgents against the men who left him to die. When the tank falters into a rugged mountain pass on its way back to the Kandahar road, Constantine, Taj, and the other Afghans destroy it in the film's climactic firefight. The Russians surrender, but although Taj demonstrates his humanity by releasing them, Afghan women chase after the Soviets and beat them to death with stones. Horrified, Constantine rejects Taj's offer to join the mujahedeen and returns to his own side, thanks to the convenient presence of a Russian helicopter.

For filmmaker Kevin Reynolds (who directed Kevin Costner vehicles like the successful *Robin Hood: Prince of Thieves* and the notorious flop *Waterworld*), *The Beast* was a critical highpoint that nevertheless fared poorly at the box office. After a brief run at some film festivals in New York, Toronto, and Cleveland, it was pulled from distribution, largely because the studio felt no one would want to see a war picture that "didn't involve Americans or take sides."[14] Of course, the film does involve Americans and it does take sides—but only subliminally.

The Afghan war and the era of glasnost finally permitted Russians and Americans to bond, allowing them to recognize one another in Constantine's heroic (if not treacherous) switching of sides. Now that the United States and the Soviet Union have both had their respective Vietnams, America can afford to be sympathetic, especially as it watches the Berlin Wall tumble down. As long as the Russians are morally defeated and stand squarely against the kind of communism represented by the World War II vet Daskal, they will be portrayed with complexity and dignity.

When one considers that Kevin Reynolds also scripted the notoriously silly anti-Soviet film *Red Dawn*, it's clear that political circumstances have drastically changed. The Red Army no longer serves as the pure, unadulterated villain of the earlier film but instead becomes a complex assortment of good guys and bad guys—a perestroika crowd with a hard-liner in charge, not so much unlike Oliver Stone's *Platoon.* Frequently this motif of a "band of brothers," using war to overcome their prejudices and differences, helps to cinematically solidify nationalist identity.[15] Letting Russians take the place of Americans in the war story manifests what only a few years before would have been a dangerous admission of commonality.

Indeed, Rambo would be appalled amid such moral ambiguity. Luckily, these Russians who feel like Vietnam-era soldiers, lost in a war they never made, are not given a free pass. The ethics of their Stalinist leader, like his tank, are revealed to be dangerously off track. The film stresses this metaphor consistently, most notably in an extreme long shot in which the tank rolls past, almost infinitesimally small and overwhelmed by white desert. The surrounding wasteland is so devoid of character that it could be essentially anywhere and everywhere. Such imagery universalizes the Afghan war, inviting one reviewer to sourly note, "Analogies to Vietnam are invited."[16]

But it's not so much analogies to the war that are important as the morals drawn from them. The Russian lost patrol, as it turns out, has strayed into even more dangerous territory than the typical revisionist Western, which seeks to efface American atrocity by redefining the true American as victim rather than aggressor. For it becomes apparent by the film's conclusion that no stable boundary exists between victor and victim, good and evil, and, worst of all, us and them.

A comparison between *The Beast* and *Rambo III* helps clarify this potential for destabilization. In both films, the turning point for the heroes, Rambo and Constantine, takes place in a vast cave where they encounter their enemies in dramatic confrontations. If one looks closely, it's clear that the same location (Israel's Bell Cave) was used in both films. Such mirroring highlights the contrasting ideological responses to Vietnam. For Rambo, the cave provides an opportunity to indulge in a slaughter fest of throat-slitting and archery, unleashing his fury on the Russians who (through a proxy army) first defeated him. In the universe of Rambo, Afghans are coded as good guys and Russians as out-and-out villains. Killing them ends not only the war but also the discussion as to who is right or wrong.

Constantine has no such chance at regeneration through violence. Vastly outnumbered and completely vulnerable, he has been reduced to nothing, abandoned even by his own comrades. In such a position, he grows dependent on others—or in this case on the Other. With them, in that liminal space of the cave, things start to happen. Taj and Constantine share food, learn to communicate in each other's language, and become united through a common purpose.

This is not how it's supposed to happen. In the usual Indian captivity story, "the hunter confronts an Otherness, represented by the wilderness and the Indians, that threatens to assimilate him into barbarism. Through vengeance, he finds his identity—as a white, civilized, Christian male."[17] But in *The Beast*, no reassuring burst of self-validating violence occurs as it does for Rambo. Constantine's eyeglasses, a symbol of his old identity, are crushed. Without them he can now see an ill-defined but subversive borderless world, where common ground can be found between cultures and enemies, soldiers and insurgents.

This narrative resembles that of many other "Vietnam Westerns."[18] In these revisionist films, the native becomes the avatar of authentic American virtue, as opposed to its victim. This certainly explains the portrayal of Taj as Afghan (or Indian) hero. Early on, an itinerant Sufi identifies the mujahed leader as David, battling the Soviet Goliath, surely a clarion call for sympathy and identification. A noble savage, Taj is fearless, heroic, compassionate, and clever. Alone among the Afghans, his morality and honor remain untainted through the film. His character perfectly illustrates the most sacred social customs of tribal Afghanistan (*pashtunwali*): honesty and integrity, extending hospitality to friends and strangers, nurturing friendships, safeguarding family honor, and keeping one's oaths.[19] A paragon of decency, Taj forbids his men to commit cold-blooded murder or loot the corpses of Russian soldiers. To the very end, he extends the hand of brotherhood to Constantine, hoping that the two of them can permanently join forces. In some ways, it is Taj, more than Constantine, who is the true hero of the film—a sentiment that came easy while America was backing the fundamentalist mujahedeen against the Russians.

But to their credit, Reynolds and Mastrosimone do not show Afghans simply as peasants and rustic freedom fighters but also indicate the existence of sophisticated, urban intellectuals like Samad who supported the communist revolution. The most complicated character in the film, Samad illustrates in his little bit of screen time the kinds of complexities in Afghan society later explored by 2007's *The Kite Runner*. In a fireside game of chess with Constantine, he explains his motivations for joining the tank crew:

> I love Afghanistan. We're a flea on the tail of a bear. We must join the twentieth century. When Afghans accept that, I will be there. Knowing technology and Russian.

Of course this assumes that modernization in Afghanistan was previously impossible without Soviet military intervention, which was certainly not the case. Nevertheless, the film still presents Samad as one of a large class of socially mobile, progressive Afghans who can "reconcile dialectical materialism and Allah," as he puts it. That such words could even issue from an Afghan's mouth would be unthinkable in any of the films that came before. To portray the existence of an educated class contradicts Orientalist paradigms of timeless primitivism. So, too, does the very existence of the film's "Kandahar road" that the Soviets seek so desperately. When they find it, the camera offers a view through their binoculars at a paved road on which a truck drives by on its way to a city. Viewing Afghanistan in *The Beast* provokes a kind of cognitive dissonance, conditioned as we are to accept a view of Afghanistan's devastation as primeval and essential and not simply the product of Russian aggression and civil war.

Unfortunately, *The Beast* falls short of subjecting the mujahedeen themselves (or their American sponsors) to such a critical view—despite the fact that it was they who later caused 50,000 civilian deaths in Kabul alone during the early 1990s. With good reason, journalist Kathy Gannon called the new government formed by mujahedeen commanders (and U.S. clients) Hekmatyar, Rabbani, and Massoud, "the biggest collection of mass murderers you'll ever get in one place."[20] To countenance the savagery of the Afghan resistance would naturally have tarnished America by association. And so, despite the seemingly progressive emphasis on cultural cooperation, *The Beast*'s analogy to Vietnam ultimately neutralizes American culpability for its own war crimes. It could do so within the context of a number of Vietnam films from *Apocalypse Now* to *Platoon* and *Full Metal Jacket* that described the ways in which a "bad war" had poisoned the kindest of hearts and the best of intentions. In such an environment, atrocity appears almost foreordained. It's somehow understandable that Constantine runs over a man with a tank, slowly torturing him to death, as it is when Daskal shoots an unarmed man in the back and poisons drinking water. Both hero and villain have become beasts, the crimes they commit not simply the product of moral choices but rather the regrettable yet inevitable effects of an "unjust war." Such wars have the property of making good people bad, of confusing boundaries that in a "good" war are crystal clear. Without the well-established distinctions between good and evil, civilization and savagery, Constantine becomes (literally) groundless, suspended in the air in the film's final scene.

The Beast's captivity narrative gone awry indicates the extent to which American cultural identity had become as lost and off track as the Russian tank in the Afghan desert. To face the future, the United States had to face an Afghanistan (and the developing world as a whole) far removed from the simplistic imperialist nostalgia of earlier films. It had to face the possibility of not simply dominating but instead negotiating.

The idea is almost too horrible to contemplate and sends Constantine back to his Russian comrades in a final flight from the reality on the ground. In the closing moments of the film, he comes face-to-face with the real Afghanistan, the repository of imperial nightmares, where the Khyber Pass and the Sharbat Gula stare linger to haunt us. Finally, the film taps the deepest level of fear, the place where defiance and resistance must be acknowledged. Taj appeals to God and gets instead an avalanche of irrepressible violence. Sherina, the wife of the mujahed murdered by Constantine and his tank at the beginning of the film, resurfaces in its climax to claim her vengeance. She does what the men could not, bringing down the tank and battering the Russians to a pulp, one by one. Returning from her gory task, she greets Taj with a malicious smile, her face covered in a new and terrible veil of blood.

Today, conservatives and liberals alike prefer to view Afghan women as largely helpless victims of societal oppression. They are, in short, the captives of American frontier mythology, waiting to be rescued by a new generation of Indian killers. But if anyone is held captive here, it is Constantine and the besieged imperialism he represents. The shadow of Vietnam and Afghanistan, of My Lai as well as Maiwand, has reached into the present, confusing the civilized and the savage, showing us the heart of darkness lying in ourselves. We run over people with tanks and massacre civilians. We do these things.

At the same time, the enemy has proved himself and herself to be our match: to be able to resist our technology, our resolve, our righteousness. The thought, for many, was unbearable, as was the idea that savagery was a common denominator on both sides of any conflict.

And so *The Beast* provides an exit by dredging up Orientalist stereotypes. Beneath the facade of Taj's nobility, it shows us the truth about him and all the other Afghans: the truth that is an unveiled woman, bathed in blood. This projection of inner savagery allows Constantine to once again be good, to return to the civilization that was always inside him, part of his DNA. The Russian's ordeal ends at that moment, when borders are redrawn, boundaries reinstated, and dialogue dropped.

The identity of the eponymous "Beast" finally becomes clear with this revelation of the bloody killer in the final scene, foreshadowed by the film's epigraph (from, of course, Rudyard Kipling's "The Young British Soldier" quoted in chapter 2). Through intertextuality, the film links Sherina to her equally savage sisters who (in Kipling's imagination) slaughtered an older generation of empire makers. Here, then, is the "essence," the "true face" of Afghanistan. With great relief, we once again encounter the age-old enemy that gives no quarter and deserves none. To reimpose frontier mythology frees us from the dreadful apprehension of moral, let alone military, failure.

Such an escape, however, would only lead to future captivities. In 2004, conservative ideologue Robert Kaplan wrote in an essay he titled "Indian Country" that "in the days of fighting the Indians, the smaller the tactical unit, the more forward deployed it is, and the more autonomy it enjoys from the chain of command, the more that can be accomplished." What was accomplished was made clear that same day when reports surfaced of U.S. Special Forces having killed an eighteen-year-old Afghan boy, Jamal Naseer, after torturing him by beatings and electric shocks in a secret detention room.

"In Indian country, you want to whack bad guys quietly and cover your tracks with humanitarian-aid projects," a general tells Kaplan.[21]

The road to Kandahar is paved with such intentions.

The Killer's Gaze

Flash forward twenty years to the sequel of the New Great Game, set in an Afghanistan even more devastated than the one Rambo and Constantine knew. Like *The Man Who Would Be King* of a generation before, *Charlie Wilson's War* debuted at a time when the war was going badly for the United States. "Mission Accomplished" had given way to an "enduring freedom" in Afghanistan and Iraq that by all accounts would go on indefinitely—with Bagram Air Base serving as "the centerpiece for the CENTCOM Master Plan for future access to and operations in Central Asia."[22] The year 2007, when the film was released, was "the deadliest for U.S. and NATO-led forces in Afghanistan since the Taliban regime fell in late 2001," with the Taliban and al-Qaeda aggressively engaging the foreign troops there.[23] In the process, the United States and NATO killed four hundred Afghan civilians in what President Hamid Karzai called "careless operations."[24] The Third World insurgents who had so traumatized the neoconservative minds of the Vietnam era were back with a vengeance. In one of the most politically disaffected climates in recent memory, *Charlie Wilson's War* arrived to inspire the American public to stay the course.

Based on the hagiographic best seller of the same title, the film chronicles the dissolute Democratic Congressman Charlie Wilson's attempts to help the "gallant people" of Afghanistan against the Soviet juggernaut. A lovable rogue in the same mold as Danny Dravot and Peachey Carnehan, Wilson (played by the all-American Tom Hanks) and his CIA fellow traveler Gus Avrakotos aid the mujahedeen out of the goodness of their hearts and the righteousness of their cause. The real Avrakotos was also present in Greece in the 1970s to enable a military dictatorship that distinguished itself by rolling over students with tanks (incidentally the same tactic used by the Russians in Afghanistan in *The Beast*).[25] In Afghanistan he supported terrorist bombing and assassination as well as endorsed a Pakistani system of awarding a bounty for each Soviet belt buckle.[26] Naturally, the film declines to offer this information.

Instead, *Charlie Wilson's War* spares no effort in lauding the CIA and its achievements in Afghanistan. For anyone with a modest acquaintance with the history of CIA operations in and around the country, however, such a narrative seems disingenuous, to say the least. The gallant people aided by the CIA in the 1980s were soon being waterboarded by their erstwhile comrades in the new war on terror. Not too surprisingly, the first U.S. fatality in the latest Afghan war was a CIA "interrogator" in Mazar-e Sharif. Seven years later, CIA-led death squads killed two hundred people in the space of a few months, according to a United Nations report.[27]

The CIA was not the only beneficiary of cinematic whitewashing. The title character himself, previous to the Afghan war, had supported the brutal Somoza regime in Nicaragua. Although the film makes Wilson out to be a compassionate freedom fighter, it fails to mention that he also championed Gulbuddin Hekmatyar, the most ruthless and fundamentalist of all the mujahedeen commanders. Later in life, Wilson became a six-figure-a-year lobbyist for the same Pakistani dictatorship that later helped install the Taliban. But in *Charlie Wilson's War,* the hero appears motivated not by a will to power or lucrative sinecures but by a sincere and selfless urge to aid those in need. Mike Nichols, the director, has said that the "main thing about Charlie and what his story expresses is that a person can make a difference."[28]

This gloss ameliorates the film's unrepentant imperialist nostalgia and conservative-inflected militarism (also crucial elements of *The Man Who Would Be King* and *Rambo III*). As opposed to these earlier films, Nichols's cinematic incursion makes its apology for war in Afghanistan by appealing to the schizoid rhetoric of American liberalism, which postures compassion while still enabling economic and military devastation. Thus, *Charlie Wilson's War* is replete with congressmen and CIA spooks who bemoan the implementation of what Arjun Appadurai has called the "anti-Marshall plan" that abandoned Afghanistan in the 1990s.[29] These stalwarts instead try to persuade clueless bureaucrats to fund schools in the war-torn nation. Unlike other Americans, they really care about the people. When Charlie Wilson visits a refugee camp in Peshawar, he can barely contain his shock while overhearing tales of Russian atrocities (which happen to be true). Similarly, hungry Afghans scrambling after sacks of rice stir his sympathy and righteous indignation. Yet how does he show his sympathy? Does Charlie Wilson allocate millions to build schools there, improve the drinking water, or donate food and medical care? Of course not—because if he did, it would demonstrate he cared about Afghans. Instead, he arms them to be used in a proxy war to kill Russians. The audience interprets this as sympathy—because we are thoroughly bound up in the killer's gaze.

The deleterious effects of this identification with power are especially evident in the display of Russian atrocities, meant to illustrate the rightness of Charlie Wilson's cause. During a scene that features the helicopter bombardment of Afghan civilians, the camera remains firmly fixed within the Russian cockpits, never on the ground where it might catch the reaction shots of Afghan villagers. Victims do not matter to the killer's gaze. Consequently, these scenes eerily resemble *Apocalypse Now* and other documentary footage of Vietnam War air attacks, where the camera's viewpoint is always that of the attacker. Such a seemingly unconscious device creates a synthesis of killers' views that becomes our own.

For all of Wilson's deeply expressed sympathy with the Afghan cause, Chalmers Johnson has noted that "Wilson's activities in Afghanistan led directly to a chain of blowback that culminated in the attacks of September 11, 2001 and led to the United States' current status as the most hated nation on Earth."[30] In his review of the film, Johnson makes his case by reflecting that "there is not a single instance in which the [CIA's] activities did not prove acutely embarrassing to the United States and devastating to the people being 'liberated,'" while also noting that "[t]he billion dollars worth of weapons Wilson secretly supplied to the guerrillas ended up being turned on ourselves."[31] This is the very definition of the term *blowback.* The film chooses to ignore such contextualization, however, primarily because Tom Hanks, both star and producer, "just can't deal with this 9/11 thing."[32]

That barely suppressed trauma manifests itself in the film's opening scene, in which a silhouetted Afghan in a *pakul* cap and *shalwar kemis* prays beneath a starlit sky and crescent moon—the very picture of old-school Orientalist exotica. Suddenly, the silhouette rises, picks up an RPG, and fires it straight at the audience. This terrifying return of the repressed is the only honest moment in the picture, a visual shorthand for the film's main theme: America "fucked up the endgame" (as Charlie Wilson puts it in the film's conclusion) and thus allowed the Taliban and other terrorists to turn their weapons on America when the commies rolled out in disgrace. Mike Nichols remained reluctant to blame the shortsightedness of the intelligence community, rationalizing that "you don't know the consequences of any act."[33] Even with twenty years of hindsight, he cannot admit that the covert war in Afghanistan was wrong, that it perpetuated a conflict that killed a million Afghans, devastated their agriculture and economy, and took a people who were moderate in their religion and made them prey to fanaticism.

Perhaps more than any other film, *Charlie Wilson's War* demonstrates the ways in which cinematic representations of Afghanistan have been used to justify continued aggression there. As the CIA agent puts it, "We always go in with our ideals and we change the world and then we leave." The obvious implication is that this time the United States should stay in Afghanistan with its lofty ideals, that war could be used constructively, just like in the good old days. If so many people didn't still believe this old canard, the whole thing would be laughable. Maybe that's why reviewers labeled *Charlie Wilson's War* a comedy.

If there is a common denominator in all of these Hollywood films, it would be their obsessive resonance with that curiously American blend of racism, imperialism, and misogyny: the frontier myth. Afghanistan fades into a palimpsest beneath this mythic framework of desert plains, lone riders, native tribes, and the merciless struggle for definition between the civilized self and the savage other. Cultural imperialism works this way: refashioning the world in the image of whoever has power. As soon as the United States had actually conquered the Native Americans, it began to project its dreams of unconditional surrender and racist frontier war on a global scale. "We," of course, were always the cowboys, while "they" were the Indians. Thus John Ford, the great auteur of the Western, set *The Black Watch* (1929), his first full-length film in sound, not in North America but in Afghanistan, with Myrna Loy starring as an Afghan princess in love with a British soldier. Throughout the 1930s, a number of Afghan "Rule Britannia" adventures followed in its wake, including *Lives of a Bengal Lancer* (1935), which stars Gary Cooper as a British officer squaring off against Afghan torturers, and *Wee Willie Winkie* (1937), a Kipling tale transformed into a Shirley Temple vehicle. The fact that *Lives of a Bengal Lancer* has the dubious distinction of being "definitely the favorite film" of Adolf Hitler suggests the possible links between Orientalist discourse, Western films, and genocidal policies.[34]

From a cursory perusal of Richard Slotkin's exhaustive volumes on the frontier myth, it seems safe to say that American nationalism functions a great deal like any other religion. Along with its sacred symbols, spaces, and images, it also subscribes to a variety of myths that seek to explain the origins of America as well as set the norms for self-identity in the national context. Although the Western genre does not provide the only set of archetypes (the Horatio Alger rags-to-riches tales would be another example), it helps articulate, more than any other narrative, how America views itself in the world.

Myths tend to be constructions by a particular group in power to naturalize their worldview as the only ideology that is normal, moral, and sane. Thinking in mythic terms tends to blind individuals from perceiving the complexities of a world that really does change from place to place and from one era to the next. Worse, by identifying one's culture as the cosmic good, myth simultaneously demonizes whoever stands in one's way, right or wrong, no matter what the context. In short, the purpose of mythic thinking is to nullify critical examination and self-reflection. Myth has a way of preventing alternate points of view. And it has a way of perpetuating conflict.

In American film's representations of Afghanistan, this mythic way of seeing suffuses the real place and its people. The "real" Afghanistan becomes subsumed in the cosmogonic narrative of American civilization triumphing over primordial savagery. American audiences are channeled into the same old narrative with themselves as the only characters. Over time, with people of many eras, religions, and races portrayed in a similar way, values become facts and myths become objective, even scientific, truths.

Not surprisingly, the popularity of Westerns waned precisely at the moment when U.S. triumphalism was called into question during the height of the Vietnam War. The final scenes of *The Man Who Would Be King* and *The Beast* replay both the trauma of Little Big Horn and Vietnam itself, with imperial power struggling against its defiant and still dangerous subjects. But just as the genre began to sink beneath the weight of its ideological baggage, it transferred its basic conventions to science fiction films like *Star Wars* (with George Lucas citing *The Searchers* as a major influence) as well as a rising tide of neonoirs like *Chinatown* and *Taxi Driver* that located the Wild West in the modern urban jungle.

By offering Afghan versions of captives and savages, the films discussed prevented Americans of all stripes from seeing where the real drama in Afghanistan was: not in the romantic Hindu Kush or at a *buzkashi* match but at much more modern and prosaic locales like Kabul University or the Haqqania madrassa in Pakistan. Momentary reflection soon gave way to nostalgia for simpler times when racism and imperialism could wreak havoc without ever having to say they were sorry. And in the wake of that nostalgia rose many a rough beast, its hour come round at last, slouching toward Kabul to be born.

PART 2

The Burqa Films

4 Land without Images

Kandahar

With the Russians gone, the mujahedeen armies soon began jockeying for power over what remained. Promptly abandoned by the world community, Afghanistan was left to descend into the anarchy of civil war. Fundamentalism metastasized into a plethora of ethnic armies, now intent on using their salvaged Kalashnikovs in the service of racial hatred. What had once been a tribal federation of Pashtuns, Panjshiris, Tajiks, Hazaras, Uzbeks, Nuristanis, and many more soon disintegrated into a spiraling whirlpool of factions and

The Abstraction of the Desert: Nafas (Nelofer Pazira) en route to Kandahar.

counterfactions, supported by various world powers eager to take their turn at playing the New Great Game.

The cost of the Russian resistance was almost incalculable. The country itself plunged into a dark age, with a million dead and countless others scattered across the world as refugees, five million of them living in Pakistan and Iran. By 1990, with 44 percent of Afghanistan's population dislocated, Afghans had become the largest refugee population on earth.[1]

Six years later, those who remained had little spirit left for fighting. When a group known as the Taliban, a term that means "students of religion," came to power, many Afghans—especially Pashtuns—enthusiastically supported them in the hope they would end the fighting. According to legend, the Taliban's initial success involved rescuing children kidnapped and sexually abused by warlords and their soldiers. Riding in on Datsun pickup trucks and equipped and indoctrinated by Pakistan, the Taliban rapidly defeated the numerous factions of former mujahedeen. After almost twenty years of fighting, it was something of a relief to drive on a road without getting shot at.

And yet many Afghans felt that the Taliban were essentially another invading army of foreigners, in this case ethnic Pashtuns who had been born and raised in Pakistan (albeit mostly in refugee camps), indoctrinated there in Wahhabist madrassas, and then unleashed on their ancestral country. Once in power, however, the Taliban proved to be a match for the depravity of their fellow fundamentalists. Continued famine, disease, and staggering unemployment along with their campaigns against women, ethnic minorities (notably the Hazaras and Tajiks), and the Afghan cultural heritage took Afghanistan from bad to worse.[2] At the beginning of 1997, less than a year after the Taliban took power, the country had become a Grand Guignol stage set—a desolate spectacle of bullet-ridden ruins and human misery. The Taliban fought bitterly in Mazar-e Sharif and Herat, causing thousands of deaths on both sides. People were bombed, buried alive, raped, and forced into marriages with mullahs. Thousands of children died of exposure to cold. Polio raged in the refugee camps.[3]

Despite these horrors, the world had more or less forgotten about Afghanistan. Some feminist groups campaigned against Afghanistan's "gender apartheid," which had forced women from work and made the *chadari,* the traditional Afghan covering for women, compulsory. President Bill Clinton, a supporter of the Taliban (having invited a delegation of them to America to seal a pipeline deal), ignored their concerns, bombing the country only once to distract Americans from Monica Lewinsky's blue dress. A few years later, the Taliban detonated some bombs themselves at the Buddhas of Bamiyan, Afghanistan's most precious archeological site.

Yet while more international outrage was expressed over the destruction of the Bamiyan Buddhas than the human death toll, concerned organizations and individuals did continue to champion the rights of Afghans and draw attention to their suffering. One of them was the Iranian film director Mohsen Makhmalbaf. "The Buddhas of Bamiyan were not destroyed," he wrote. "They collapsed out of shame." To rub the world's neglect of Afghanistan in its face, Makhmalbaf began work in 2000 on what would be his sixteenth full-length feature film and greatest international success, *Kandahar* (also known as *Journey to Kandahar*). By the time it was hitting screens worldwide, Afghanistan was "enduring freedom" from yet another invading force: the United States of America.

Winning not only a prize at the Cannes Film Festival but also UNESCO's Fellini Award in 2001, *Kandahar* went from being considered a "baffling and ponderous" work pre–September 11, to being named by *Time* as the best film of the year after the World Trade Center was destroyed.[4] Suddenly Makhmalbaf's cinematic guilt trip had become a *Let's Go: Afghanistan* for armchair pundits and cineasts worldwide, including the United Nations General Assembly and President George W. Bush, who screened it at the White House.

September 11 transformed the film into something more than politically conscious entertainment. It became a lens through which to see the "real" Afghanistan, to make sense of this country that America and its "coalition of the willing" was invading as a first stop on their war against the nefarious "axis of evil." Due to circumstances quite beyond its control, *Kandahar* became something "useful" to the newest player of the great game. This usefulness was not simply a happy stroke of luck, however, but a necessary by-product of Makhmalbaf's cinematic construction of Afghanistan.

Tales of the Grotesque and Arabesque

To tour Afghanistan with Mohsen Makhmalbaf is to make a long day's journey into Oriental night. The threat of approaching darkness is ever present, an onslaught that spells death for the sister of Nafas (Nelofer Pazira), a Canadian Afghan woman who has undertaken a quest to stop her sister from killing herself at the next solar eclipse. In the meantime, the sun remains so oppressively ubiquitous that Nafas calls it her "worst enemy." And yet, despite the near absence of darkness, the dearth of interior sets, and the avoidance of any night scenes, this is the darkest of films. After a harrowing journey, Nafas fails in her quest. Trying to blend into a wedding party to avoid detection, she is unmasked, and we see her face for the last time, knowing she will not reach her sister to stop the suicide. A curtain—in the form of the *chadari*—literally falls over her last glimpse of the sun, slowly vanishing into shadow.

Before Nafas completes her futile journey, she encounters a host of benighted and degraded human beings. These include her ghoulish tour guide Khak, a child whose name means "dirt" (not a popular or even probable name for an Afghan). After being expelled from a Taliban madrassa, the boy joins Nafas on her trip, stopping along the way to loot some skeletal remains. Along with the child, *Kandahar*'s Afghanistan plays host to numerous other bizarre or grotesque figures, including an African American mujahed with no medical expertise moonlighting as an old-fashioned country doctor, a healthy array of bandits, teachers who turn their pupils into psychopathic religious zealots, a man who uses his wife's burqa to measure a pair of prosthetic limbs for her, and Hayat, a con man and thief who steals from NGO hospitals and inadvertently leads Nafas right into a Taliban checkpoint.

Under their oppressive regime, it is clear Afghanistan has become a vast mental asylum where not only the inmates but also the land itself has gone mad. Darkness has descended over the country like the *chadari*: stifling, self-effacing, absolute. It impacts every facet of Afghan life, attacking the people like a plague. Mourners in dark veils decorate the landscape like brittle flowers, eruptions of black in the blazing glare of desert. Far above, Red Cross helicopters parachute artificial legs to land mine victims. The legless, black-turbaned men hobble and limp toward these metallic limbs, floating gracefully through the cloudless sky. One man collapses before he can reach his prize, smearing his face in the dust. The worst of it all is that the extras are not acting. Their legs are really not there as much as the land mines—which we never see—are.

In terms of physical environment, we glimpse only what we are meant to discover. Part of this is due to what Mehrnaz Saeed-Vafa calls a "cinematic version of hejab" in which Iranian concepts of privacy prohibit "exposing personal and private spaces."[5] *Kandahar*, like many other Iranian films, projects the inner space of the characters onto the landscape as well as the characters' system of social relations. Getting into Afghan homes or heads is not an option for a culture that, unlike the West, does not encourage exposure to complete strangers of the private and especially the familial.[6]

And so instead of portraying Afghans in humanizing, domestic settings, the film situates itself in the bleak and public spaces of refugee camps, squalid villages, and barren deserts. To do otherwise would flout viewer expectations. In nearly every media account, whether it is film, fiction, or news, Afghanistan represents negation. It is absence.[7] Within such a perceptual framework, Afghans and abjection are synonymous. All of them appear pathetic, maimed, starving, thieving, dying, despairing, deceitful. As desolate as their lives, the land itself bears no trace of fertility or beauty. The representative Afghan child loots corpses, lies, and trains to be a religious zealot. The cast of adults includes land mine victims, brigands, and polygamists. Not a single one of them offers much help to Nafas. Instead such characters exist primarily to draw attention to their hapless suffering. Among them the women are clearly worse off, secluded behind the *chadari,* helpless and invisible, bearing their scars in secrecy.

Makhmalbaf's *Kandahar* is a grotesque and arabesque nightmare of terror, horror, and mystery. As in Edgar Allan Poe's fiction, the concepts of grotesque and arabesque animate the film's narrative, providing its themes and its imagistic wellspring. When Poe and other nineteenth-century writers used the terms *arabesque* and *grotesque,* they were not simply evoking the exotic or disgusting. Art critics used such terminology when referring to designs (usually derived from Islamic art) that "violated" the natural order.[8] Because Muslim art was prohibited from depicting human images, it frequently incorporated organic shapes into geometric patterns, blending the abstract and the concrete. For Islam this did not mean dematerializing the natural world, nor did it mean despiritualizing the heavenly one. Rather it reflected the Qur'anic understanding of the universe as a divinely ordained contiguity between the spiritual and material. In the Muslim worldview, God cannot be separated from his creation. The world is not "fallen." From the moment of creation, God has remained always in charge, without rival. Thus for Muslims, the natural always simultaneously implied the spiritual, as opposed to the Western, Christian understanding that drove a wedge between the two.

For neoclassicists, however, this Muslim blending of the two spheres went against their metaphysical grain. The designs they termed *arabesques,* the style of "blended forms," were both repulsive and attractive. It indulged the occasional fancy for the fantastic while at the same time disturbing an aesthetic that posited a strict separation between the "orderly God-ordained world" and the demonic.[9] For the Enlightenment thinker, the arabesque and grotesque serve no worthwhile purpose. Rather they hint at dangerous, liminal states of being in which two worlds collide. As these forms fuse into each other, their separateness dissolves into the maelstrom. For Poe, the fear of death involves the growing apprehension that this subjective state is pure illusion and delusion—a folly that precedes the final dissolution into unity.[10]

In this absolute state—an impending and irrepressible reality—no language exists to distinguish objects from one another. All is one.

The Muslim insight that ninety-nine attributes fuse into a single God stands in opposition to a secular humanistic worldview that exalts the self as sole arbiter of truth. To this self, its opposite (unity over separateness, permanence over change, tradition over technology, and tribalism over self-interest) must be feared, palliated, and repressed. Then as now, the Muslim world was selected as a repository of modern dread. And Afghanistan, the site of fierce Muslim resistance to Western invaders, became in the popular mind the most depraved, most grotesque, most shadow-gripped of all the world's dark places.

How strange that the metaphysical preoccupations of an Iranian film seem to be precisely those of the modern West, whether it be secular or Christian. Yet if Makhmalbaf frames his fear of Afghanistan with such seemingly Western tropes, it should come as no surprise. The Muslim world, simply because it is our Other, is not, as it turns out, really other at all. Iran and the modern world are not incompatible, as much as political pundits would make us believe otherwise. In fact, the Islamic Republic itself is a thoroughly modern (or even postmodern) concept. The worldview of modernity has as much a foothold among intellectuals there, if not more so, as it does in the very Western and American Bible Belt. The boundaries between Iran and the West remain as illusory today as they were a millennium ago when Shia Persia was teaching the Catholic West how to do algebra, geometry, and Greek-style philosophy. If Iran can look at Afghanistan in the same way that Belgium looked at the Congo, then perhaps it is not civilizations that clash but something else within them or beyond them.

In spite of such commonalities, however, *Kandahar* adheres to a distinctly Iranian worldview, its Afghanistan a place where Iranian nationalism can reflect upon itself: the status of its women, its enforcement of hijab, its imperial nostalgia (as well as its designs for the lost lands of the Persian Empire), its relationship with radical Islam, and its role in perpetuating the Afghan civil war. For example, the majority of Afghans in the film stem from a single ethnic group: the Hazaras. With their commonalities of language (Persian) and religion (Shia Islam), they form the most Iranian-like ethnicity in Afghanistan. Yet their differences are obvious, from their style of dress to their Mongolian features. As part of the enormous refugee population living in Iran and supplying the country with cheap labor, Hazaras are not simply Afghans but the dark double of Iran itself.

As stated previously, the Islamic Republic does not exist in a cultural and political vacuum, U.S. sanctions notwithstanding. Rather Iran and especially

Iranian cinema play a highly visible role in the international world of art. For the economically beleaguered country, it remains absolutely essential that its films, if they are to enjoy any financial success, be produced for consumption on the world market. In effect what this means is that they must be made competitive in the European and American cinema festival circuit. Film festivals exert an enormous influence over Iranian production, creating a "set of concerns that gradually and retroactively affect the film production and distribution process."[11] This translates to a careful tailoring of stories and images to appeal to Western audiences' preconceived notions of the "authentic" Iran (and in this case, Afghanistan). Azadeh Farahmand has said that in Iran, "certain filmmaking formulas are unreflectively adopted to aim for international success."[12] This is part of a larger effort on the part of the Iranian government to foster diplomatic and economic ties with other countries, especially the United States, through cultural products.

Many of these films are produced in part by foreign (usually French) companies. Any politically sensitive issues that might offend Western viewers tend to be carefully excised in the cause of higher profits and greater distribution. Escapism rather than political activism becomes the order of the day. Such works encourage exoticism because Western viewers expect a "tour" of Iran, a sense that they have traveled somewhere quite different from their own backyards, full of spice and color. Filmmakers find it more commercially viable, then, to eschew still lifes of commonality between West and East for landscapes and figures that stress folk traditions, titillating Islamic subjects like polygamy and veiling, and rural settings where often impoverished locations contribute to a sense of the East as essentially primitive.[13] Naturally the Iranian community in the West tends to sharply criticize these films for depicting highly biased and selective images that emphasize the grotesque, repressive, or abject.[14] Many of the filmmakers who buy into this formula for success encounter scorn in their own country for being people who "make films for foreigners."[15]

In the case of *Kandahar,* however, we have an Iranian making a film not about his home country (done admirably well in *Gabbeh,* his most successful film before *Kandahar*) but about neighboring Afghanistan. There was little subsequent criticism in Iran or in the world community itself over how Afghans were portrayed in the film. The only objections came from voices in the Afghan diaspora, which not surprisingly objected to *Kandahar'*s portrayal of "a country full of grave robbers, con artists, and thieves."[16] Makhmalbaf has repeatedly stated that his aim in making the film was to draw attention to the sufferings of a country that has suffered for so long under a foreign yoke.[17] Similarly, Nelofer Pazira confirmed that the director was "frustrated that even people living next door, like in Iran, did not really know much about Afghanistan."[18] Their later collaboration in humanitarian projects in Afghanistan as well as Makhmalbaf's creative and financial support of Afghan cinema testifies to the sincerity of their intentions.

Despite such goodwill, the Afghanistan of *Kandahar* fits firmly within Orientalist discourse, typified by paintings like Antoine-Jean Gros's *Napoleon at the Pesthouse at Jaffa* (1804). In this work, as in *Kandahar,* the landscape lies under a pall of disease and misery. Muslim physicians stand by helpless, impotent in the face of bubonic plague. But all is not lost. Light streams from an unseen source, illuminating Napoleon, hands outstretched in a Christlike gesture of power and compassion. His miraculous touch heals all infirmities. He is, by his own admission, "the true Muslim," able to solve Egyptians' problems with the divine sanction that has been denied them. As art compounds conquest, imperialism (in the words of Roland Barthes) "evaporates, engulfed in the halo of an impotent lament which recognizes the misfortune in order to establish it only the more successfully."[19] This suffering provides a necessary prelude to war: a humanitarian crisis of epic proportions just waiting for someone with the power to intervene.

The Disorienting Orient

Unlike any movie before it, *Kandahar* seeks to define the Afghan experience. The film's neorealist approach is particularly suited to such a task, as well as its identity as an Iranian film—a film made by *them,* not us. Because their country borders on Afghanistan, the Western viewer surmises, Iranians must possess a more authoritative view of life on the ground there. The fact that they speak the same language and share the same religion seems to substantiate this premise. This vantage point of greater proximity—both culturally and geographically—presumably allows the film to bring the "real" Afghanistan and its sufferings to light. But in many ways, *Kandahar* wears an aesthetic veil itself, a fiction hiding beneath the burqa of documentary.

Unquestionably there are things that are "real" in the film—real Afghans with real land mine scars, real refugee camps, real starving Afghan kids, real Afghan women in real *chadaris* singing real songs in real languages. The Afghan-Canadian Nelofer Pazira, whose attempts to contact a friend suffering under the Taliban inspired the film, is a "real" Afghan who nevertheless speaks "our" language, who understands Afghan culture and yet can distance herself from it. An evidently nonprofessional actor, Pazira as Nafas is the authentic native informant par excellence—both insider and outsider, a reverse image of Rudyard Kipling's Kim. Thus Robert Fisk, one of the most renowned commentators on the Middle East, can enthuse that "*Kandahar*'s power came from the fact that they were real people. Nelofer Pazira is a Canadian (-Afghani) journalist . . . the Imam teaching the children how to use the Kalashnikov, that is what he does, the boy who collects jewellery from the skeletons of people who die in the desert, that's actually what he does."[20]

And like real life, the narrative of *Kandahar* follows a nonlinear path, with no driving inner conflict or substantial resolution. Nafas, the Afghan with Western eyes, does not change in the course of the picture. Nor does Afghanistan itself change in any way. The two remain fixed categories. This changelessness naturally plays into viewers' expectations, conditioned as they are by Orientalist discourse and its essentialist view of the Islamic world.

Curiously, the film's countervailing tendency to surrealism also has the ultimate effect of manufacturing authenticity. Makhmalbaf's skill in setting up the perfect cinematic image is obvious as soon as the film rolls, presenting an eclipse surrounded in blackness accompanied by the drone of Persian classical music. For the rest of the film, these stark and startling images of suffering and horror take on, in an almost perverse way, an exquisite element of beauty. They resist the narrative structure so powerfully that in effect the story becomes mere blank space beneath prosthetic limbs and black *chadaris,* propelling *Kandahar* to its final twilight. Like a dream, atmosphere and feeling congeal into portentous symbols, erupting from the artificiality of narrative into the surreality of subconscious truth. This was, after all, the original aim of surrealism: to delve into the radioactive depths of the unconscious mind where, in a new language of melting clocks, shadowy streets, and amorphous color forms, the old and hidden truths could finally come forth in an aesthetic and epistemological epiphany. Surrealism posits a direct relationship between general and particular, abstract and concrete, metaphor and reality. To see the images of Afghanistan—both grotesque and arabesque—is thus to see Afghanistan itself—to peer into it with the penetrating power of both analysis and inspiration.

While the "real" or natural elements of the film are no doubt there (the people and landscape they inhabit), they have been recombined into an obvious work of art. In this sense, then, the Afghanistan of *Kandahar* is not natural, nor is it "real" but rather a construction, a man-made object. Its view of Afghanistan can never present the entirety of that place, despite the camera's depth-of-field penetration into the landscape, but only a carefully choreographed tour of certain sites, selected not randomly but deliberately for both manifest and latent reasons.

If Kandahar explores Afghanistan's suffering, it does so only through this process of aestheticization, its artfulness mediating the experience and isolating us from the pain with which we are supposed to identify. We can look at Afghans and intuit their terrible situation, yet it does not touch us. While Afghanistan's poverty cannot be denied, it nevertheless can be rendered beautiful or at least entertaining. Set against the hypnotic soundtrack and stark loveliness of the landscape, even the poorest of Afghans emerge, especially when clad in *chadaris,* as aesthetic objects.

Makhmalbaf himself understood this when he said, "When you look at these women wrapped in their burkas, there is an esthetic harmony on the outside, but on the inside, under every burka, there is suffocation. It's a strange contradiction."[21] For the Afghans themselves, this kind of retreat into art is unavailable because, being poor, they are without power. They cannot transmogrify their reality. They must simply live in it.

By living in a real place as opposed to a work of art, Afghans can see quite clearly what remains practically invisible to the rest of the world: the historical context of their suffering. In the world of art, however, this context must often take to the back burner in lieu of arresting images and metaphoric dialogue. With the origins of Afghan poverty thus effaced, the essential quality of Oriental backwardness becomes tautological. Worse, the film does not dare to suggest a chain of cause and effect between the poverty of the figures on the screen and the affluence of those watching them and munching popcorn in the air-conditioned theater.

That connection between the poor and the rich, between those who are objects and those who are subjects, those who are seen and those who watch, continues to be the most important and yet most discreetly mystified of realities. As Julia Thomas has pointed out, visuality "is not the tool of an anterior society or ideology, but a mechanism that *produces* as well as represents culture to itself, constituting its relations of power and difference."[22] *Kandahar* obscures these relations with its pretense of being a cinematic mirror of reality. Like the colonial postcards that Malek Alloula analyzes in *The Colonial Harem,* "it has erased the traces, and above all the direction, of its mise-en-scene," and thus "can successfully keep this mirror trick (tautology), so that it presents itself as pure reflection, something it definitely is not."[23] Furthermore, this pure reflection projects itself to "a *public incapable of questioning its truthfulness,*"[24] a public that has never visited Afghanistan and knows that country only through the mediation of people who are not themselves Afghans.

One such cultural mediator in the film is Tabib Sahib, the doctor Nafas encounters on her journey. This African American living in the middle of the Afghan wilderness commands the respect of the viewer as well as the view itself. As a Westerner, he has expert, privileged knowledge about Afghans—things that are beyond their ken. He knows, for example, the difference between hunger and disease. He knows that Khak is untrustworthy. The doctor's motives, on the other hand, cannot be impugned, because he originally came to Afghanistan to fight the Russians and then fought with the various factions against one another in the civil war. A battle-weary veteran, the former mujahed has become an ascetic Sufi healer, despite his lack of a medical degree. This last point matters little, however. After all, as he puts it, "the basic medical knowledge of a Westerner is far beyond what they know."

Tabib Sahib's character masks the West's true intentions as much as his ersatz beard obscures his identity as civilized man. "Weapons are the only modern thing in Afghanistan," Tabib observes. What he does not observe is that those weapons, far from growing out of the Afghan soil, were supplied by the very Western powers that he represents. These weapons and their use against and distribution to the developing world have—perhaps more than anything else—allowed the West to *become and remain* the West.

Aimé Césaire wrote that "no one colonizes innocently . . . that a nation which colonizes, that a civilization which justifies colonization—and therefore force—is already a sick civilization."[25] The point here is that while Afghanistan has never been colonized, it has been the consistent target of imperial aggression for two hundred years. How curious, then, that the film presents Tabib Sahib as the one civilized character despite his possession of a gun and his self-professed involvement in one war after another. But the greatest of ironies lies in the true identity of the actor who plays Tabib Sahib, who in real life is Hassan Tantai, also known as David Belfield, a fundamentalist assassin wanted by the FBI for the murder of an Iranian diplomat in 1980.[26] In this real-life interplay of murder and masquerade, we have a far more fitting metaphor for Western involvement in the affairs of Afghanistan and beyond.

Viewers first encounter this "doctor" in a scene in which he easily diagnoses a Hazara woman's hunger despite the fact she claims to be ill. Forced to consult with the woman behind a curtain, draped there at the command of the Taliban for propriety's sake, he uses her child as interlocutor. The doctor then asks the woman to approach the curtain so he can examine her. This curtain, as symbol of the Taliban, effectively turns her into a series of body parts, the "real" woman being concealed. The ragged hole through which he sees bears a great resemblance to the film's initial image of the eclipsed sun seen through the "caverns of the burqa." In the end, the curtain actually aids the doctor in reducing the woman into separate objects that he can examine at a safe distance.

Feminists have long noted the Western media's tendency to carve women's bodies into titillating fragments to be displayed in advertising and film.

Through the editing process, Tabib's body is shown far more frequently, as observer, than is the body of the woman he is observing. We look at her from his point of view, even transcending it temporarily to see both of them, an observer of the observer and observed, a "transparent eyeball" surveying the scene from a command position.

The Afghan woman, on the other hand, is in no position to present herself. She appears as a conglomeration of disjointed parts, largely voiceless and fragmented, never able, in the words of Chandra Mohanty, to "rise above the debilitating generality of [her] 'object' status."[27] She cannot do so while the doctor holds the power of vision. His eyes, highlighted by a pair of rimless spectacles, convey this exalted position as Western observer, sage, and healer.

Eric Egan has observed that in *Kandahar* "those Afghans who are allowed to speak do so at a local and seemingly inconsequential level," while "[it] is left to the 'foreigners' to comment on the 'real' issues."[28] Nafas, for her part, consistently draws attention to her status as a Western observer, despite her Afghan heritage. Not only does she repeatedly withdraw the *chadari* from her face (a topic that will be discussed in greater detail later), but she also plies Khak and Hayat with American dollars and speaks English as often as Dari. In this way, Nafas can make a claim for objectivity—an ability to see Afghanistan from both an internal and external point of view; in short, the way it really is. Tabib can speak to Nafas like an equal because they both appear to transcend culture; she is an Afghan living in the West, while he is an African American Muslim in the East. In many ways, they are both liminal representations, outsiders and insiders whose protean identities convey a sense of privileged authority.

Ironically, Nelofer Pazira, the actress who plays Nafas, did not dare to return to Afghanistan on her initial journey. Only in the film does she cross the border in an act of suicidal folly. To blunder through the Afghan desert alone with a wad of American cash and a tape recorder on a journey to the Taliban stronghold is not just an act of hubris. It is also colossally stupid, considering that even in the United States women are on their guard while traveling alone. Her attempt in Afghanistan indicates the superior position that Nafas represents, a position that the film never really questions. Rather, it instead singles out for attack the obstruction of that commanding surveillance.

In a typically Orientalist way, Makhmalbaf presents Afghanistan, the Taliban, and other representatives of Islam and tribal values as a vexing issue that requires a solution from the outside, presumably from the audience and the powers they represent. The source of Afghanistan's travails (as far as the film reveals to us) appears to be something intrinsic to the Afghan nation: a geographically defined, genetically dictated tendency toward chaos and atavism. The Taliban are simply the latest manifestation of a darkness that lies within Afghanistan, the disorienting Orient of Western and Eastern viewer alike. This darkness, precisely because it mirrors the lack within the imperial gaze, the frustration of its self-mandated omniscience whether American or Iranian, cannot be presented except as a paradoxical image of absence and presence.

Naturally enough, a tiny, easily concealed machine whose nickname is identical with that of an airplane's flight recorder represents the industrialized world of the West. Nafas's "black box," a tape recorder she holds throughout the film, not only provides the justification for her narration but also serves as the audience's collective ear. That no one usually hears a plane's black box until after a fatal crash is certainly not a fact lost on Makhmalbaf. For all of Nafas's technical superiority, she becomes quickly lost in her home country, disoriented in a journey toward a place that she never sees.

Edward Said described Gerard de Nerval's Orient as a "quintessential Oriental world of uncertain, fluid dreams multiplying themselves past resolution, definiteness, materiality."[29] It serves equally well as a description of Makhmalbaf's Afghanistan. Nafas's journey, far from being a compassionate survey of Afghan suffering, provides the opportunity for self-discovery through a nightmare world of people and places objectified for self-reflexive speculation. At the same time, one can read such an excursion as "the production of knowledge as power and with the representation of the Orient and its inhabitants as static, unchanging, incapable of change."[30]

When Nafas runs away screaming after Khak loots a skeleton, we are left to ponder whether it is a sense of moral outrage or disgust that prompts her reaction. Perhaps she simply recognizes that she bears the genetic material of the people surrounding her, their blood tainted (like hers) with a seemingly irredeemable primitivism. Whatever the reason, Nafas, on the way to Kandahar, has reached the heart of darkness. The land of her birth has become uncanny and inexplicably foreign thanks to the Taliban, though we are not really told what it was like before their rise to power or how it came to be this way. In such a disturbingly strange and static world, Nafas consistently loses her way.

The most salient characteristic of Afghanistan, aside from its grotesqueness, is this atmosphere of disorientation. During the film, the landscape and its people constantly challenge Nafas's ability to exercise her Western power of seeing. She complains at times of not being able to read her companions. "I can't say what he's thinking," she says of Khak as they stumble through the desert sands. At the Red Cross hospital, she says of other Afghans, "I can't see their faces to know how they feel about me."

The native informant has reached a dangerous place where her power and self-assurance have suddenly grown tentative. Nafas seems always to be going in the opposite direction of any other travelers on the road. Suddenly immersed in a state of nature, she tries desperately to battle against an oncoming current of primitivism and cultural disintegration. Long before her cinematic journey, T. E. Lawrence would write: "The abstraction of the desert landscape cleansed me, and rendered my mind vacant."[31] His words have their visual analog in the image of Nafas superimposed against a desert background, with a caravan of camels parading into her veiled head and out the other side.

In this internal culture clash, Nafas confronts her Afghan Other, against which she can set herself and the modernity she represents all the more forcefully. Nafas narrates to her sister that she is giving "her soul to the journey. So I can give you reason to live." And tellingly, she records her desire to "discover hope for [her sister] from their dreams"; that is, the voices she captures on her "black box." How this will benefit her sister exactly is not revealed. But in regard to Nafas's self, her entrance into this disorienting surreality not only bestows hope but also grants affirmation. It is only after confronting the Islamic unknown that the outsider looking in can establish herself as its antithesis.

The ramifications for those actually living in the dreamworld, the Afghans, are simple: They cease to exist as human beings, variable and complex, and rather become set pieces in an imperial drama of cultural and self-discovery through negation. A veiled Prometheus, she brings to light through her Western-enhanced vision an Afghanistan that, like the formless void of Genesis, waits for the life-giving *nafas,* or breath, of a higher, civilizing power.

Unfortunately something stands in the way of that power, something all encompassing and threatening: a sartorial act of resistance to imperial ways of seeing and knowing that we call the veil.

Kandahar Unveiled

Above everything else, *Kandahar* is a film about the Islamic veil. The film's forty-four-page script mentions it more than fifty times as "the burqa." Nafas herself repeatedly draws attention to it by donning and doffing her *chadari* in nearly every scene. Unlike any other piece of apparel, the burqa appears in dialogue and scene descriptions and as a character's name. The script describes veiled women time and again, in clusters of black mourners and in blue-, yellow-, and white-clad wedding parties. The first Afghan women shown at the refugee camp quickly veil before the camera's intrusive eye. Even the poster advertising the film features a group of veiled women in the desert. Possibly more than any film ever made, *Kandahar* is a meditation on the West and the East's fascination and obsession with the veil.

This fascination, at least in Europe and America, has had a long and persistent influence on the way that the Muslim world is both portrayed and understood. Christian polemicists like Dante frequently characterized Islam not as a faith but as a sexual perversity, obsessed as they were with Muhammad's polygamy (while ignoring the likes of Abraham, King David, or King Solomon). Other writers and poets portrayed a wildly sensuous world of voluptuous flesh, polygamy, and female submission. Many artists painted a variety of exotic nudes they called odalisques (*odaliq* originally meant "chambermaid") in one titillating harem scene after another.

Alas, harem actually means "both the area of the home in which women dwell and the women of the family, the word connoting sacredness and inviolability."[32] Thus grandmother's bedroom becomes eroticized into a pornographic peep show, the "*locus* of an exotic and abnormal sexuality . . . a microscopic Middle East, apotheosizing the two characteristics perceived as essentially Oriental: sensuality and violence."[33] This became the "authentic" Orient, the Orient that can be conjured in a Masonic hall or a Disney movie—the Arabian Nights confection of curled-toe shoes, flying carpets, and scantily clad heroines in veils.

As Malek Alloula puts it, "There is no Orient without the hookah."[34] Such a vision of the East is only possible through a constant reinforcement in culture. Subsequently, these stereotypes and clichés establish themselves, through the normalizing discourse of Orientalism, not as value-laden judgments but as authentic components of a true picture. These fantasies only became problematic later in the nineteenth century when Europeans came face-to-face with the genuine article. Muslim women, as it turned out, did not replicate their counterparts in Western wish fulfillment. Instead of being naked, these women were in some places completely covered from head to toe by a veil that has become the very symbol not only of women in the Islamic world but of Islam itself.

In contemporary Islam, veiling falls under the practice known as *parda*, a term that means literally "covering." It is the same word used for curtains or drapery. Just as in the home, the Muslim "covering" ostensibly maintains the integrity of the household—its privacy and separateness from the public sphere. In Afghanistan under the Taliban, women were forced to wear the *chadari*, the head-to-toe veil often worn in villages but rarely in the capital of

Kabul. In previous years, many Afghan women outside of the sophisticated urban elite had worn the garment, and those who did not often wore the chador, the headscarf or shawl traditionally associated with modesty and religious piety.

Although many writers have consistently labeled Afghan women as victims of a tribal culture, oppressed into passivity and silence, Afghan women, should one deign to ask them, often have their own ideas about wearing the chador. One such woman when interviewed said, "We do these things out of love and respect for our husband and our family. . . . We are not oppressed as Americans would believe."[35] As M. Catherine Daly has concluded after conducting numerous interviews with Afghan women living in America, "wearing a chaadar is more than ideal female behavior; it is an acknowledgement of the general support for the attitudes, values and beliefs of Islam and Afghan culture."[36] Less fortunate Afghans who have not had the opportunity of emigrating from Afghanistan to America—women like Sharbat Gula—have even defended the chadari as "a beautiful thing," which they choose to wear.

For the West, however, there can be no separation of public and private; the more exposure the better. Walls have been dissolved to form cubicles. Bustle skirts have given way to low-cut necklines. Reality TV shows consistently dissolve the boundary between public and private. Therefore, the Islamic practice of parda has been singled out by many writers as "an abomination," "gender apartheid," and "victimization." What makes it so disturbing is its direct challenge to the Western need for exposure. The veil not only proclaims the presence of the woman without revealing her to view, but it also alludes to the religion she represents as essentially unwilling to become transparent, culturally and politically. As Franz Fanon wrote, Muslim woman is "she who hides behind the veil,"[37] as does her religion itself. Here the authoritative gaze of modernity cannot penetrate.

An object that does not exist objectively, the Islamic veil becomes the fetish whereby "the Orient reveals itself, reveals that there is an Orient, a place, a culture, an essence that needs to be grasped, known, and apprehended."[38] Psychology defines a fetish as a neurotic response to an infant's apprehension of sexual difference, its purpose to "disavow the perception of difference."[39] In traditional Freudian circles, the fear of castration initially generates this fetishism. But from an epistemological viewpoint, this difference does the castrating by directly challenging the self's autonomy as arbiter of reality. By acknowledging that something stands outside the self's solipsistic narrative, it calls that narrative, and the identity it represents, into question. Such questioning amounts to an immediate admission of defeat.

Neuroses usually stem from psychological shocks to the system. The more stress and anxiety, the greater the inflammation of neurosis. Thus Faegheh Shirazi has charted the use of the veil in American pornography, noting how the more aggressively the Islamic world resisted Western intervention the more the veil became a symbol of oppression and victimization rather than sexual titillation.[40] While being the very essence of this veiled victimization, *Kandahar* also attempts to penetrate the veil, to make the hidden reveal itself with the clarity of a dissection. The first scene of the film begins this process, with the sun eclipsed in a field of blackness, an eye being slowly blinded. Suddenly, as if to palliate the horrible image, Nafas reveals herself and speaks. Our first sight of her is a point-of-view shot in which we, as the Taliban, expose her to our gaze. In order to represent their repressive power, the film must portray the Taliban as this power of unmasking, of visual penetration.

But that power almost immediately compromises itself by revealing yet another mask: an impassive, emotionless face of an actress who is not an actress. The masks appear as impenetrable as the layers of an onion. Inscrutable and indecipherable, the abyss of the woman's face not only mirrors the self but also reveals the abyss within the self, defined by its negation: not female, not void, not difference. A conviction of the masculinized, modern gaze thus emerges that at all costs, "they should remain different, because I should remain the same."[41] Thus viewers in the more liberated societies of Iran and the West can vicariously imagine domination over women by seeing, with the Taliban, women as truly other.

A later scene at the Red Cross field hospital indelibly displays the degree of that otherness. After a number of grotesque vignettes, a man appears whose wife has lost her legs to a land mine. He has finally arrived for her long-awaited pair of prosthetic limbs. They are clumsy contraptions of metal and wood that look impossibly uncomfortable. The man, not surprisingly, feels sure that these legs will not fit his wife. Undeterred by the doctor, who insists they are just her size, the man pulls out her wedding dress (a *chadari*) and casts it over the legs. Beneath the cloth lie the ersatz limbs, disembodied and lifeless. This is the secret: The people beneath the veil aren't real. When the camera dwells on hands trying on bracelets and bangles, applying nail polish, these body parts are always subsumed by the black hole of the burqa. Are there human beings beneath?

Certainly we see the film's protagonist there often enough. But Nafas only unveils to reveal her identity as Westerner and to reassure us of our ability to see. She exposes her face time after time, in front of Khak, Tabib Sahib, Hayat, the doctor named Monika, always when she must beg for them to help her find the way to Kandahar. "I'm a woman on my own," she says, lifting the garment, "I can't hurt you." Seeing beneath the veil enables the viewer to reduce these "aggregates of prohibition, mobile extensions of an imaginary harem whose inviolability haunts [us]."[42] Out of this anonymous, *chadari*-clad sea, form slips through our perceptive grasp like quicksilver. Unveiling in this context becomes a tool to separate what is unified, to resist resistance and satiate desire. It is, by its very nature, opposed not only to the Taliban but to Islam itself, for it seeks to represent the human body at all costs, to set that body up as a sacred sign for absolute knowledge and power.

And while it may seem that oppressed women can only benefit from such rhetoric, Nafas's words immediately after unveiling bear repeating: "I can't hurt you." As long as she secludes herself beneath the veil, she remains a threat, a mysterious danger. Only when we see her can we rest secure. To drive this point home, Makhmalbaf has Tabib Sahib say, "For woman, hope is the day she will be seen." If Tabib can be believed, an Afghan woman's only hope is to become what Western women are: objects of the male gaze. Only by being seen can she acquire not only identity but also salvation. The fear persists, however, that even after unveiling the woman will still be hiding behind yet more masks. Characterized by its exotic mystery and endless duplicity, she and the Islamic world she represents are labyrinths of subterfuge.

At the beginning of hostilities with Afghanistan, there were a number of sources in the American media that harped on the Afghans' dissembling nature. One can never depend on them, went the "expert" analysis. They are always changing sides, always ready to switch loyalties—which is just what you would expect from barbarians.[43] Naturally, America's inclinations to support and then attack Saddam Hussein or ban the sale of weapons to Iran and then covertly supply it with arms, for example, are conveniently forgotten. The point is that Muslims, and Afghans in particular, are liars.

Just look at all the liars in *Kandahar*. Nafas consistently misrepresents herself as an Afghan citizen and eventually joins a wedding party, pretending to be related to both groom and bride. Khak, her guide for part of the trip, claims to know the Qur'an despite his illiteracy, a fact he hides (not too well) in school. He insists on the value of a ring he steals from a skeleton only to simply give it to Nafas later. Hayat, the Hazara man who offers to take Nafas to Kandahar, is clearly a thief, which he explains with a lie, and lies about how he came by a pair of prosthetic limbs. At the end of the movie, he, too, gets beneath the burqa, dissembling not only about his relation to Nafas and the wedding party in question but about his own sex as well.

Afghan women, from what little we see of them, are also deceptive. One of the most pathetic images of the film shows the women Nafas initially travels with stopping off at a roadside merchant's stand to buy makeup and jewelry—

forbidden, of course, by the Taliban's application of Sharia. What is interesting about this scene, aside from its criticism of the Taliban's version of Islam, is that it portrays the women seeking to mask themselves even more beneath the veil. After all, makeup is deceptive at heart. It augments and transforms nature, signifying women's ability to alter their appearance, to mask their "true" self. But just as women appear infinitely deceptive and impenetrable, these veils attest to an essential secret. In the film's final scene, a number of them hide things beneath their *chadaris,* taking advantage of the freedom that garments give to conceal. In the non-Afghan mind, the very nature of the veil is duplicitous. The more the concealed remains invisible, the more we insist on its absolute importance, its centrality to our power and under-standing. The more it eludes, the more we pursue it, even into the "caverns of the burqa" itself. This is how the movie ends. The Taliban capture Nafas and force her to unveil in order to speak her name. We return full circle to the initial moment when we, as the Taliban, unmasked her.

But if the viewer's gaze seeks to truly assume the "subject position" of com-mand, then simply seeing Nafas's face one last time holds little importance. Because we know by now that no matter how many women are unveiled, an essential mystery remains: what goes on beneath the flesh that they so easily mask, down deep in the silence of their inscrutable minds. This is why it is essential for the camera to assume Nafas's point of view: her eyes from beneath the *chadari* screen, staring at the setting sun, the source of vision fading to black. This culminates the film's perceptive project, gaining us complete control through identification with the woman (and the faith she represents), revealed now completely in this act of ocular possession. We're inside her head; we see the world as she sees it. The final obstruction to a fantasy of total power has been breached. We are both the Taliban that unveils and that which is veiled. We are man and woman, and we see both positions. We are total power. Afghanistan has served its purpose. There is nowhere else to go: Fade to black and roll credits. And yet we still have not reached Kandahar, where the Taliban has its stronghold, where the sister waits for death. We have not reached it, still hidden, still invisible, still beyond our yearning grasp.

Such a discussion does not fall merely in the range of the philosophical or aesthetic. During moments of conflict, with battle lines drawn, it becomes especially important for power to manage the problem of the Muslim veil. First of all, women must be seen. How else can they be controlled? As Franz Fanon wrote about the French antiveiling campaign in Algeria, "If we want to destroy the structure of Algerian society, its capacity for resistance, we must first of all conquer the women: we must go and find them behind the veil where they hide themselves and in the houses where the men keep them out of sight."[44] The United States, once it decided to invade Afghanistan in 2001, likewise claimed it was doing so to free Afghan women from the burqa, to liberate those women who were "cloaked in danger," "all wrapped up with nowhere to go," and "tearing at the veil." The problem was how to sell this to the American people.

Happily, a number of films appeared at that very moment to serve this end. While well-meaning efforts designed to spotlight the so-called gender apartheid of the Taliban, these films played to American elites seeking a foothold in Central Asia. Most who watched the news at the time can remember the horrific scene of a woman, clad in a *chadari,* shot in the head in the middle of a soccer stadium. First shown in the spring of 2001, it was originally filmed by RAWA, an Afghan feminist organization, and later became part of Saira Shah's documentary *Beneath the Veil.*

Shah, the daughter of Idries Shah, an Anglo-Afghan writer and expert on Sufism, had journeyed to Afghanistan to expose the atrocities of the Taliban. While largely ignored before September 11, the film afterward became the most "recognizable symbol of Taliban barbarism."[45] By replaying this ghastly clip on CNN and harping on "the burqa factor," those in power were able to drum up support for the war among even the liberal intelligentsia. Like many a grand crusade—one thinks of Homer's *Iliad*—the invasion of Afghanistan began as an attempt to rescue a damsel in distress from the Taliban, who had been oppressing women for years in plain view. What most failed to notice was a Physicians for Human Rights report that noted that 90 percent of women in areas not controlled by the Taliban also wore the *chadari.*[46] At any rate, Shah's film was called "invaluable war propaganda" by conservative writer Martin Kramer, who claimed it was crucial in forming a more wide-ranging "domestic coalition" to execute the newly christened war on terror.[47]

Similarly, *Kandahar* offers an equally compelling story line for American authorities: a "simple, direct" film that is "a call to attention and accountability" as well as a testament to the dangers of so-called Islamic fascism.[48] The film presents a country so debased that only a (military) miracle can solve its problems. The most potent image of that country's depravity, naturally, is the *chadari* itself. *Kandahar* was labeled "the ultimate burqa film," where "no aspect of the *chadari,* practical or aesthetic," remained unexplored. As such, it was, like Shah's film, "useful in war," a purpose conservatives thoroughly approved of, as it effectively duped the public into supporting a war that writers like Kramer foolishly and prematurely declared "mercifully short."[49]

Kandahar's treatment of the *chadari* made it not only compliant with U.S. military interests in Afghanistan but played into Western anxieties over the power of Islam as well. Makhmalbaf aestheticized his Iran's Islamic other into a surreal burqa of images that simply reinforced negative stereotypes about Afghanistan. This process of altering begins with how the film names the Afghan veil: not as the *chadari,* which is a Dari word, but rather burqa, an Arabic one. With his insistence on the use of the term *burqa,* the director draws a distinction between his culture, which also uses the term *chadari,* and that of the Arabs. This would be a keen insight if it portrayed the Afghans as people who had been effectively "colonized" by the extremist theologies of Wahhabism and Deobandism through the likes of Osama bin Laden and fundamentalist Pakistani clerics.

But Makhmalbaf eschews such contextualizing for the purpose of essentializing Afghanistan. Inexplicably differentiated from Iranian culture (with which they nevertheless share a common language and literary tradition as well as various modes of dress, cuisine, and art), Afghans can now assume a position of ignoble savage against which Iranians can negatively posit their collective identity. At the same time, the language of alterity that Makhmalbaf employs, with its concurrent images of the veil, surrealism, and debasement, serves to bolster not just the imperial consciousness of Iran but also that of the United States.

The Quiet Iranian

If there is a veil to be penetrated regarding this film, it is that between Makhmalbaf's ideology and his aesthetics. Clearly, the former dominated his early cinematic output. As a firm believer in the ideals of the Islamic Republic (Makhmalbaf was jailed and brutally tortured by the Pahlavi regime), he initially called himself a "Muslim artist" charged with revolutionary zeal to create an "Islamic cinema."[50] When the revolution came, Makhmalbaf supported it wholeheartedly, his early films being the product of "a devout religious and revolutionary zealot with an ardent belief in the righteousness of Islamic ideology and the ethos of the new theocratic regime."[51]

The Iranian American film critic Hamid Dabashi finds a great deal to criticize in the director's early films and writings, especially the prominence of religious extremism and his devotion to politics above and beyond art for art's sake.[52] Makhmalbaf himself, in an interview with Dabashi, judged his earlier works in a similar fashion: "In the first period, truth is defined by religion, and in the second, it is defined by, let's say, social justice. In the end they're one-sided. Absolutist." Since the 1980s, his philosophy has matured, as evidenced by the increased quality and complexity of his work. Now, he says, his interest lies in "the multiplicity of perspectives."[53]

By the time *Kandahar* was filmed, the director had moved enough away from his youthful extremism that he could deliver some well-deserved jabs at Islamic fundamentalism. As an artist, he is motivated by a social conscience that extends beyond Iran's borders. His compassion for Afghan women is heartfelt. His focus on Afghanistan's suffering seems sincere. He has aided many cinematic projects in Afghanistan both creatively and financially. His film studio has apprenticed many a young Afghan filmmaker. Afghans like Nelofer Pazira have praised him for providing an opportunity to highlight the suffering of Afghanistan—largely ignored by the world community—though Pazira herself did a far better job in her own film *Return to Kandahar* (2003), an insightful documentary for Canadian television that included all of the history, context, and complexity so lacking in narrative films of the region, whether Western or Eastern.

While filming *Kandahar,* Makhmalbaf himself insisted that he was not making a political film, that instead his purposes were purely "humanitarian." It is seldom that a film director explains in any detail his reasons for creating a particular work. Usually the best one can hope for is a few bland sound bytes and a couple of anecdotes about the cast for the DVD special features menu. Happily in the case of *Kandahar,* we have something far better and insightful: a thirty-four-page essay (published as a small book in Iran) called "The Buddha Was Not Demolished in Afghanistan; He Collapsed Out of Shame," which Roxanne Varzi has called more moving and effective than Makhmalbaf's film.[54] At the same time, the essay evokes the older Makhmalbaf, described by Dabashi as someone "[w]ith absolute conviction, and totalitarian tendencies."[55]

When examining the situation in Afghanistan, Makhmalbaf (along with many Western writers) personifies the country as a woman. "Not a beautiful girl who raises the heartbeat of her many suitors," he says, but more like "an old woman," who just drags you down with her troubles.[56] Like other foreign pundits and powers, Makhmalbaf takes it on himself to save this woman. He begins by citing statistics, listing the staggering number of Afghan deaths due to war and starvation since the Russian invasion: two and a half million. "The total number of people who were killed and left Afghanistan equals the entire Palestinian population," he notes.

His compassion is sincere, but it is based on aggregates. For all his cinematic attention to authentic detail, Makhmalbaf sees Afghans as a multitude, as "loads of lame men," the dying "covering the streets like carpets." They are "populations," "sects," "tribes," but never people. In this way, his thinking corresponds to that of the ideologue who sees movements and forces, only rarely glimpsing the individual human beings who make up such collective bodies.

Afghans, for Makhmalbaf, are indeed invisible, just like their country is on the world stage. Afghanistan, he writes, is "a country without an image." We cannot see it on the news because the Taliban refuses to let journalists in. Neither do they allow films to be produced that can reveal Afghanistan to us. In his essay, Makhmalbaf sets out to tear down this veil, to give Afghanistan a face by providing what his film does not: a historical context.

As soon as the director begins his history of Afghanistan, the link between his aesthetics and his ideology becomes clear. This imageless country, Makhmalbaf writes, first came into existence when, in a fit of folly, it declared its independence, right around the same time America was declaring its own. But Afghanistan never got off the ground like the United States because, Makhmalbaf insists, Afghans are simply not capable of ruling themselves. It is not just that they have always been "cattle breeders," embroiled in a "perpetual tribalism." They are also "trapped in a valley with geographical walls," each tribe "the natural prisoner of a culture stemming from a mountainous environment and cattle-breeding economy." In Afghanistan, "belief in tribalism is as deep as those valleys." Geography dictates and is mirrored by cultural backwardness.

Iran, on the other hand, has always been characterized by its status as a civilized nation. In its modern incarnation as the Islamic Republic, Iran allows no room for tribalism. Rather, the various ethnic groups, which do not even speak the same language, are united in a national brotherhood where bias due to ethnicity is unknown. Iran is also fortunate enough to have oil and has thus been able to make the successful transition from an agricultural, traditional tribalism to a modern, industrial nation.

"Perhaps," Makhmalbaf insinuates, "if Afghanistan had not separated from Iran 250 years ago, it would have had a different destiny based on its share of oil revenues."

Afghanistan, the former "Iranian province," has clearly made a moral blunder. In daring to break from Iran, it continues to pay the price for its present suffering. That price is the inability to "evolve" and "move beyond tribal rule." It has "failed" to achieve an "Afghan sense of nationalism." It is "a museum" of primitive tribalism, which, frustratingly, no tourist gets to visit. The cause of all this lies not beyond Afghanistan's borders but deep within the Afghan psyche. With the persistence of a genetic trait, backwardness defines them as much as their bleak natural landscape.

Thus modernity cannot take root in Afghanistan. King Amanullah tried to reform them in the 1920s, the director tells us. His reforms in many ways mirrored Reza Shah's in Persia, when the *shalwar kemis* gave way to the Brooks Brothers three-piece suit. Of course, as in the case of Iran, such reforms were not, like Kemal Atatürk's, suggestions but commands. Reza Shah began an "antiveil offensive" in 1936, when police were given the power to forcibly remove women's veils.[57] Similarly, Amanullah's policies were enforced through ukase rather than education. The Russians tried the same thing decades later and failed just as miserably.

But Makhmalbaf does not equate the failure of Amanullah's modernization with his ham-fisted implementation. Rather, he blames the "cattle-breeding tribes" that resisted modernization because (in a wonderful illustration of circular reasoning) they were cattle-breeding tribes. With such inbred recidivism, the king's attempt at pulling Afghanistan out of its moral debasement only served as "an antibody to stimulate traditional Afghan culture making Afghanistan so immune to it that . . . modernism could not penetrate the culture in a more rational form."

Makhmalbaf's solution to this problem is simple. Iran must begin regarding its next-door neighbor as an "economic and cultural opportunity." And Afghanistan must finally assume its true place in the modern world by providing "cheap labor" to Iran. Here we have the former Islamic radical's answer to Afghan suffering: They should relinquish the cultural and economic self-sufficiency that they have fought to protect for themselves and their children these past hundred and fifty years and should submit to the wrath of the free market and the global economy. With this accomplished, Iran will have effectively reannexed its lost province.

The only problem is that others have beaten Iran to it. Most notable among them is Pakistan, which Makhmalbaf correctly identifies as responsible for training and financing the Taliban. He discusses the conflict over the Afghan-Pakistani border, a contrivance of the British Empire that has caused at least as much conflict over the years as that between Israel and Palestine. The purpose of Pakistan training the Pashtun Taliban is patently obvious to Makhmalbaf: "to have covert control of Afghanistan and stop the Afghans from demanding the cession of Pashtunistan," an area bordering the two countries that is ethnically Afghan and also happens to take up half of Pakistan's territory.

With Pakistan running the show, Iran's dreams of "cheap labor" to stimulate its economy are confounded. Largely this has to do with Iran's ignorance, Makhmalbaf explains. Unlike Pakistan, Iran sees Afghanistan as "more of a threat than an opportunity . . . to make a lucrative investment." And since it is manifestly clear that Pakistan is doing nothing to help Afghans, it is time for people who speak their language and share their culture and (in some ways) their religion to step in and help their tribal cousins to find a new path. Afghanistan needs to be rescued by the only people who really know how.

Makhmalbaf would have to be at least subconsciously aware that this kind of rhetoric has been heard before in Afghanistan in the 1840s, in the 1970s, and in the present day. In none of these circumstances have the Afghans proved as pliable and docile as foreign governments might wish. Nor have they shown any inclination to compromise their soul as a people in order to join the new world order of either global capitalism or communism. They have secluded themselves behind a number of veils that Makhmalbaf demands be removed. What is hidden must be exposed in order for it to be controlled. Such resistance in the face of overwhelming savagery and impossible odds must be broken. To further this end, he presents the "ultimate burqa film," its subject a place where (in the words of the screenplay) "everybody here's a threat or an opportunity."

"Did the Taliban bring the burqas or did the burqas bring the Taliban?" he asks. Of course, the director of *Kandahar* has already decided that the burqa *is* Afghanistan. It is the sign that marks Iran's Islamic other. If Iranian women wear the hijab, their law imposes at least a reasonable one, not the monstrous burqa that hides that which must be seen. If the Islam of Iran condones polygamy, one should not speak of it but instead point the finger at Afghans who marry absurdly young, for survival's sake, and turn their homes "into harems." If Iranians can marry each other just for the weekend in order to enjoy state-sanctioned sex, this is not hypocrisy. But Afghan marriage, which seals the identity of their tribal culture, amounts to nothing more than "buying a woman."

The *chadari* is not simply the sign of Afghanistan's cultural and religious debasement. It is also a sign of Afghan identity. As such, it is, and always will be, a threat. "Perhaps," Makhmalbaf thus intones, "someone has to forcibly rid her of the burgha, so she'll realize that . . . she can choose for herself." This is just what you would expect from a sincere, concerned soul who has only the best interests of Afghanistan at heart—in order to make it fit for domination.

This revealing essay makes it clear how the United States was able to use *Kandahar* to bolster its own invasion. Makhmalbaf's film is the harbinger of a new age of globalized imperial rhetoric, where modernist ideologies of the transcendent, from liberal democracy to radical Islam, prove themselves equally compatible (and subordinate) to the forces of oppressive capitalism. In such a post-Orientalist discourse, the supposedly clashing civilizations, the West and Iran, are equally capable of utilizing the age-old language of culture war in the name of empire. In the twenty-first century, the West no longer has a monopoly on Orientalism. It is now a floating signifier in the free market of ideas. As such, its manifestations can be readily employed to suit the needs of any number of powers that share the common language of ambition. If, as Ziauddin Sardar and Merryl Wyn Davies claim, "cinema is the engine of empire,"[58]—specifically an American kind of empire—then the de facto setting of cinematic representation appears to be an imperial way of seeing, no matter which civilization happens to be providing the frame of reference.

If Afghanistan is indeed a land without an image, then *Kandahar* does not rectify the situation. Instead it "relegates the Afghan people to background objects of curiosity, depriving them of independent action and voices, consequently stripping them of human dignity and emotional force."[59] Veiling Afghanistan in a diaphanous *chadari* of depoliticized and dehistoricized surreality, the film refuses to face the truth that is nothing more than that stare of Sharbat Gula from beneath her own *chadari*.

Ultimately, *Kandahar,* like all imperialist art, is about fear. "Oh God," Makhmalbaf cries at the end of his essay. "Why have I become so powerless, like Afghanistan?" This is the end result of his journey to Kandahar. To represent them, he must represent himself. To control them, he must reveal his need. To believe in his cause, he must create characters in the place of people. And when it is all over, the people, in all their suffering and hopeful resistance, are still there. This is the image that, at the end of *Kandahar,* burns into our eyes with the white heat of the implacable sun.

5 Afghan Gothic

Osama

Prologue: Women in the Wild East

The cover of Edward Said's *Orientalism* bears what is possibly the most unpleasant image to ever grace a scholarly tome: a reproduction of Jean-Léon Gérôme's painting *The Snake Charmer*. Its primary focus is a naked boy, his body encircled by a sinuous snake, performing for a motley group of cutthroats, presided over by a gray-bearded man in a green turban. Lounging

Street of No Return: Osama (Marina Golbahari) flees the Taliban.

against an exquisitely decorated but chipped wall, the old man stares at the boy intently.

This pedophiliac image makes a fitting illustration for a book in which Said explores the ways that the Muslim world has been stereotyped as (among other things) an exotic land gone to seed, where every Western sexual taboo can be transgressed. At the same time, as evidenced by the fully armed and solely male spectators, it is a man's world where untrammeled violence and sexual aggression are automatic, almost genetic parts of the cultural makeup. Like the figures set against it, the mosque wall is "stamped with otherness,"[1] the symbol of a religion both baroque and alien that encourages just the sorts of things that civilized society abhors: polygamy, holy war, stoning for adultery, and so on. It is therefore no accident that the boy, with bare buttocks facing us, stands on a prayer rug.

This image of the Muslim world has become so pervasive over centuries of use that it passes for real knowledge about a place that most people in Europe and America have never visited. It insinuates itself into art, both highbrow and low, in books, music, bubblegum cards, popular editorials and academic articles, and, especially, the cinema. In *Reel Bad Arabs,* Jack Shaheen has cataloged the dreary list of Arab white-slave traders, bandits, perverts, and terrorists that haunt the reels of Hollywood's dream machine. From films like *Abbott and Costello in the Foreign Legion* to Disney's *Aladdin,* the world of Islam has been consistently portrayed either as a fantasy land of Arabian Nights adventure, where every wish can be gratified, or as a squalid desert just waiting for the messianic touch of progress. Shaheen can find only a handful of films that portray Muslims with any degree of sensitivity or complexity.[2]

The remarkable consistency of this stereotyping inspired John C. Eisele to christen a new genre in film: the Hollywood Eastern. According to Eisele, the "eastern film genre" has an extremely long shelf life in cinematic history, stretching at least as far back as the 1905 Georges Méliès film *The Terrible Turkish Executioner.* Its thematic elements are familiar to anyone: "abduction and enslavement (of women) in a harem or imprisonment (of men) in jail; identity twists; and the depiction of the East as a place of both terror and redemption for sins."[3] As the Wild West grew more politically correct, with a plethora of revisionist films in the 1960s and '70s depicting black cowboys, white men gone native, and compassionate and heroic Indians, the Wild East became even more barbaric, especially after the 1973 Arab-Israeli War and subsequent oil embargo.[4]

Ever since, for every *Rendition* or *Syriana* there have been a couple dozen *True Lies* and *Rules of Engagement* in which real American heroes shoot down Arab terrorists like George Armstrong Custer given a second chance at Little Big Horn. Fortunately, Afghans escaped much of this negativity because they were not Arabs and had the good sense to mount a jihad against communism in the same period when anti-Arab hysteria was reaching its highest point in the two decades before 2001. As a consequence, films like *Rambo III* and *The Living Daylights* portray Afghans sympathetically, but their appearance and actions are still very much in keeping with wild Eastern stereotypes.

Certain "truths" emerge in the context of this genre, set pieces that distill the Muslim world to Western viewers. They are akin to the archetypal images typically seen in the press: the veiled woman, the bearded mob burning flags, the crowd shots of kneeling worshippers at the mosque, the turbaned, scowling imam. This is not to say that these visual motifs are not reflective of real life in these places. But by isolating them from the vast sea of images that make up the Muslim world, media discourse creates a narrative that relies on omitting any complexity or diversity, in short anything that might help humanize people in Afghanistan or elsewhere for Western audiences.

Of all the stereotypical premises for adventure in the Wild Eastern, the one most relevant to a study of the cinematic Afghanistan is the sheikh subgenre. The reference, of course, is to the phenomenally popular hit of 1921 that made Rudolph Valentino a superstar. The plot revolves around a barbaric Arab chieftain who abducts a civilized, Western woman. Forced to wear Arab dress, the woman quickly becomes absorbed in the new culture, even falling in love with her captor as she domesticates his savage side. This free-spirited adventuress is in turn tamed by the machismo of the sheikh, who in an unlikely plot twist turns out to be European, thus sparing the audience from the thought of miscegenation.[5]

Female abduction is, of course, a mainstay of American pulp fiction and film, and an essential component of Easterns as well as Westerns like John Ford's *The Searchers,* in which saving helpless women and genocidal frenzy go hand in hand. Hollywood women seem to be forever in need of rescue, and naturally men with firepower or at least brute strength volunteer for the task. Such a far-reaching narrative lends itself quite easily to the justification of invasion, as the Soviet Union and the United States both found out in, respectively, 1979 and 2001. "The fight against terrorism," First Lady Laura Bush said, "is a fight for the rights and dignity of women."[6] Who, after all, can resist a damsel in distress, especially when she is a little girl forced to wear a burqa and marry a perverted mullah? Certainly not the audience of *Osama.*

The Afghan Horror Picture Show

The U.S. invasion of Afghanistan in the wake of the September 11, 2001, attacks appeared, at first, to be devastatingly efficient. The Taliban, who had previously been supported by the United States through funding to Pakistani

intelligence, were quickly, almost effortlessly supplanted by former mujahedeen guerillas, now known as the Northern Alliance. After a terrifying
aerial bombardment that was a test run for Baghdad in 2003, the Taliban
were quickly routed and Kabul occupied by yet another foreign power that
claimed, as had the Russians in 1979, that it was there to protect the Afghan
people from terrorists. The year 2001, which began with the Taliban destroying Afghanistan's greatest cultural icon, the Buddhas of Bamiyan, ended
with the apparent destruction of the Taliban itself. When the smoke cleared,
the Afghanistan that emerged was every bit as desolate as that cliff face in
Bamiyan. Out of the ashes came a gothic film that was one of the first Afghan
cinematic productions in nearly fifteen years.[7]

Its director, Siddiq Barmak, grew up in a culture that had only just recently embraced the cinema. The first Afghan film, *Ishq Wa Dost* (Love and
Friendship), was made in 1946 in conjunction with Huma Film Studios, an
Indian production company. *Ishq Wa Dost* shows its Bollywood roots with a
hearty dose of songs, dancing, love triangles, and beautiful girls (all of whom
were Indians, not Afghans). Afghan cinema subsequently languished due to
lack of state funding until the 1960s, when Barmak was a youth. After the
Afghan Film Organization was created in 1968 with American backing, film
production proceeded at a rapid pace. Historical epics like *Rabia de Balkh*
(1974) and romances like *Mujasema Ha Mekhandan* (1976) shared screen
space with hordes of Holly- and Bollywood imports. When the communist
coup occurred in 1978, the new government quickly transformed the cinema
into an organ for state propaganda. By the time the war with the Russians
was over, however, there were more pressing concerns for Afghans, like survival. Only three films were made between 1986 and 1996, when the Taliban
took power. The last of these was *The Summit* (1992), a war story about the
mujahedeen. Barmak estimates that the entire history of Afghan cinema in
the twentieth century amounts to about forty films.[8]

The twenty-first century, on the other hand, saw Afghan film become an
international sensation with the 2003 release of *Osama*, transforming its star,
Marina Golbahari, from a beggar to a celebrity. Eventually winning a Golden
Globe and numerous film festival prizes, including the distinction of being
the first Afghan film ever screened at Cannes, Barmak's *Osama* has become
in many ways the definitive film on Taliban-era Afghanistan, a definition
of what the country was, is, and could become. As art and as propaganda,
Osama was the most sophisticated Afghan film ever made and the only one
that Western audiences had ever seen. It is a testament to the horrors of war
and fanaticism, a cinematic jeremiad that invites its viewers into a New Great
Game that has become a nightmare.

It also firmly fits the Hollywood Eastern mold. The story concerns an un-
named young girl who masquerades as a boy in order to find a job. Under
the Taliban's harsh laws, women had been forbidden not only to go to school
but also to work. And so the girl's mother, a nurse by profession, must resort
to subterfuge to care for her patients. But even this does not alleviate their
desperate situation. In the miserable atmosphere of oppression and desperate poverty, the mother finally begs an old friend of her husband to employ
the girl (now with a boy's haircut and clothes) in his tiny shop. Almost immediately, the Taliban compel her to attend school, where she endures what
passes for education with Afghanistan's rulers: Qur'an memorization and
military training. Her classmates, seeing right through her disguise, taunt
her until she is discovered by the authorities. In a travesty of justice, they
forcibly marry her to the same repulsive mullah who runs the school. The
film ends on her wedding night, which is nothing more than a brutal and
mercifully offscreen rape.

Osama is essentially a horror movie. Its monsters, though not supernatural,
are terrifying just the same. The kind of insane mob so familiar to viewers of
Universal's *Frankenstein* attains an even greater shock value here, its members
attacking the girl at school with a mindless, bestial ferocity. Even the children
are damned in Afghanistan, religious robots primed by fundamentalism to
hate women. Indeed the film's narrative bears many gothic hallmarks, most
notably the lone heroine trapped in a shambling ruin, menaced by religious
fanatics and sexual predators. It almost sounds like an Afghan adaptation
of Matthew Gregory Lewis's notorious 1796 novel *The Monk*. Both *Osama*
and *The Monk* have at their center a white-hot rage against the machine
of religious hypocrisy. "The sleep of reason produces monsters," Francisco
Goya wrote, and nowhere does this better apply than Afghanistan under
the Taliban.

Originally, Gothicism emerged as a gadfly to the self-righteousness and
optimism of the Enlightenment. Peering deep into the human psyche before
psychology was invented, Gothicism created a natural history of humanity's
inner demons. *Osama* offers a terrible illustration of what happens when
those inner demons get some fresh air.

We are never told where the Taliban came from, how they came to power,
why they are in Kabul—all of the things that would provide the film with
some political, cultural, and historical context. Rather we are immediately
immersed in a world gone insane. From the initial scene, we discover that
basic civil liberties like free speech and the right to assemble are not toler-
ated, that those who transgress will be locked up in chicken coops. We see
weddings broken up, women chastised for showing their feet and ankles in

public, and people rousted from work to attend compulsory worship. We even witness foreign aid workers and journalists executed for nothing more than wanting to help the Afghan people.

The sadistic Taliban stand out from all the other Afghans. They wear large turbans, color their eyes with kohl, brandish machine guns, and drive Toyota pickup trucks. They look like savages, primitive nomads who happened to time-warp into a modern arsenal. There is no mercy among them, especially for women.

The terrorizing of women parallels the indoctrination of male youth. Barmak's treatment of the Taliban madrassa differs from Mohsen Makhmalbaf's portrait in *Kandahar*. There, Makhmalbaf inserts an over-the-top scene with a boy wielding the Qur'an in one hand and a machine gun in another, ready to dispatch enemies of the faith. Barmak opts for reality over surreality, showing children who are not simply mindless killing machines in training but hapless innocents, preyed upon by unscrupulous men. The scenes depicting them at study emphasize their conformity, their white turbans acting as badges of identity. But some of the children entertain no illusions about what they're doing there. When they are marched to the school, the girl's friend Espandi suggests that Osama bin Laden is going to train them for war. Another says they are going to prison. In a sense, Barmak suggests, they are both right.

The school certainly looks like a prison, with a foreboding narrow gate and castlelike walls that stretch high into the sky, blotting out even the comfortable familiarity of the bleak landscape beyond. When the girl attempts to prove her male identity by scaling the lone dead tree in the courtyard, her climb takes her briefly past the walls into a blank sky that leads nowhere. She cannot escape from the school, nor can she elude the mob of boys who ceaselessly taunt her, delighting in her vulnerability. When she is finally exposed, a terrifying sequence ensues in which the Taliban command the boys to arrest her. The children tear after her, howling like wild animals. Trapped and cornered with nowhere to hide, hemmed in on all sides by junior fanatics and the scabrous school walls, the girl is caught and condemned.

Although viewers almost immediately identify with the helpless girl in the foreground of the movie, it is hard to ignore the background of the film: a once beautiful city of flowers, trees, gardens, thriving businesses, modern high-rises, and exuberant crowds now a dead zone of barren and unremitting rubble. Barmak's film plays like "Yentl in Hell," and Kabul looks the part. In *Osama*, the history of Afghanistan is written in the ruins.

One can see the influence of *Lawrence of Arabia* here, the first film that Barmak ever saw.[9] Just as in David Lean's film, *Osama* opens the viewer's eye to a desolate panorama of (urban) desert. From the very first sequence, which portrays a demonstration of women clad in blue burqas, the camera's depth of field extends far beyond the protesters to include the hills of mud-brick homes behind them and the mountains beyond. The women in their baby-blue garments descend from the brown bleakness like a stream of tears, only to be flushed from our view by the Taliban's hoses, *chadaris* soiled and drowned in the filthy mud.

The monochrome of dust overpowers vision. The shell-battered, bullet-ridden walls are the same color as the earth over which they teeter. In this desolation, silence reigns. People move through Kabul's streets like wraiths, men hauling carts like beasts of burden, women scurrying by furtively, afraid. The city has become a graveyard of opened tombs and shrouded corpses who have forgotten they should be dead.

We have seen ruins in films before, from the small scale of Tara in *Gone with the Wind* to all of New York City in *Beneath the Planet of the Apes*. In the end, there's nothing really horrible about them because you know they are matte paintings or models. They're not real. Even the postwar Vienna of *The Third Man*, with real ruins and rubble in plain sight, is still somehow pleasant to the eye, thanks to director Carol Reed's expressionistic use of chiaroscuro.

Ruins, in fact, have been an artistic staple in Western art for centuries. Edgar Allan Poe's blank-verse poem "The Coliseum" sketches out the relationship between ruins and romanticism. In the poem, ruins serve as vehicles for meditation on the fragility of human hopes as well as on the hubris of empire. Their attraction lies in their ability to exalt human achievement while at the same time putting humanity in its place.

The Colosseum itself became a tourist mecca in the nineteenth century for sensitive, artistic types who found its vegetable decay not only aesthetically beautiful but also spiritually inspiring. Percy Bysshe Shelley viewed its over-grown walls as stand-ins for the struggle between individuals and implacable time.[10] For him, Roman ruins were sublime repositories of spiritual energy against which the poet could assert himself even in the face of his inevitable extinction. Shelly understood that, as Christopher Woodward has written, "ruins do not speak; we speak for them."[11] In the face of their meaningless-ness, we create a meaning from their terrifying raw material.

Osama's Kabul provides the twenty-first-century analogue of that most famous Roman ruin, Pompeii. Its homes are just as devoid of any decoration, even of windows, roofs, or doors, except for the occasional pair of misshapen clapboard shutters. And it is certainly as silent as the older town and as color-less and monotonous. The only difference seems to be that even though the eruption has passed, some of the buildings still smolder. Such destruction terrifies all the more in that its source was not some natural disaster but other human beings. Sigmund Freud said it of Pompeii, but it equally applies to Kabul: "What had formerly been the city . . . assumed an entirely changed appearance, but not a living one; it now appeared rather to become petrified in dead immobility. Yet out of it stirred a feeling that death was beginning to talk."[12]

Barmak visually expresses the same sentiment. In *Osama*, there can be no romanticism among Kabul's ruins. Unlike Makhmalbaf, Barmak's occasional surrealism does not transmogrify horror into beauty. In his film, the ruins and the prisons are one and the same, with Afghanistan a vast road going nowhere, an existential horizon that dead-ends in all directions. He develops this in a series of shots that make up a collective thumbnail of Afghanistan's past, present, and future. The first of these takes place in the hospital, a bombed-out building with naked walls pitted with bullet holes. The door, an impossibly distant vanishing point, is dead center in a perspective shot that renders the hospital an empty void, framed on one side by a brown plastered wall and on the other by a colonnade of brown and baby-blue shafts, the same colors employed in the women's demonstration. After the Taliban arrive to arrest a foreign aid worker and some others, the patients and their families flee. The crowd quickly disperses, leaving a lone boy to hobble agonizingly after them. A polio victim, his legs are misshapen, his body contorted. The boy's movements leave no room for detachment. He is no actor; this is no special effect. He simply represents a country that has abandoned its children to disease and to stark emptiness. The same colors of brown and blue make a substantive link between citizens and city, Afghans and the Afghan landscape. Both have been annihilated, blown apart. The people are the ruins. We never see the boy reach the exit.

In a later, similar shot, the girl flees from a Talib patrolman, who eyes her suspiciously as she hurries home in her father's clothes after her first day stirring milk at the store. Cradling a melon and some naan, she scrambles down a long dirt road into a tunnel of blank mud-brick walls. When the turbaned Talib emerges at the mouth of the alley, he completes a terrifying, surreal image akin to painter Giorgio de Chirico's mysterious, empty street and its running girl pursued by shadows. The only difference is that here the shadow has a form.

Just in the nick of time, she reaches her door and bars herself in. But she has lived long enough in Afghanistan to know that there is no safety in her home. After the night and its gunfire, she awakes to what Westerners deem a completely neutral noise: the sound of automobile traffic. But in Afghanistan, cars don't take people to work or play, they transport Taliban who come to imprison or shoot them. In that one horrible scene, we can see and hear the chasm between her world and ours.

Occasionally the sense of claustrophobic destruction opens into larger, more horrible vistas. When the girl and her mother return home chaperoned by a friendly man, their bicycle ride takes them through an even deeper space of desolation. Smoke rises like punctuation marks over the rubble. Along the way, they come across no street traffic, not even pedestrians. There are also no phones, no electricity, no motors, no antennas, nothing. Not even a single modern-looking building remains intact. They might be the only human beings left alive after the apocalypse. In the distance, the mountains of the immense Hindu Kush brood at the farthest extent of a vast nothingness.

At the end of the film, the girl takes a similar ride into the smoke of obscurity, this time on the back of the mullah's wagon, into the countryside. Past the city limits, the land is as bleak as the buildings. Barren, skeletal trees writhe from the dirt into an icy winter sky. Sharp breaths mist from the travelers' mouths, frosting the air. Soon the girl will be locked in the mullah's house, invisible, as good as dead. The forlorn, scraggly road stretches to the cold mountain horizon of emptiness.

This image of Afghanistan as a primeval void seems natural enough, especially when history fades into the dusty background. *Prehistoric* is not an especially positive term in our culture, and places like Afghanistan seem to beckon our help in reshaping their history, which appears at least to viewers of *Osama* as being practically nonexistent. But as with *Kandahar,* when we see Afghans as changeless and ahistorical, we legitimize whatever we do to them as civilizing and liberating.

Nevertheless, to portray Afghanistan as a rubble heap is not necessarily to essentialize or debase it. It's obvious here, as opposed to Makhmalbaf's film, that at one time there were grandiose public buildings in Kabul, now in ruins. Barmak provides just enough visual context to situate the narrative in time, placing it in a familiar world of oxygen tanks, pickup trucks, and machine guns. These things are realities as much as the destruction on display. Afghanistan, clearly, has been debased not by some innate cultural savagery but by the ravages of war, its echoes tattooed in bullet-ridden walls.

In *Osama,* war is not simply a palimpsest or a backstory. It is a character— but not in the usual way as seen in combat films. The narrative allows no room to glorify the heroism of the battlefield, to wax poetic about the brotherhood of soldiers or the sacrifice of a generation. The audience experiences war through the eyes not of those who fight it but of those who survive it, at the moment when the smoke clears. The quiet is not peaceful; it is macabre. The sun does not dawn on a new day of hope. Instead it barely illuminates a barren landscape where female children, who cannot work, are nevertheless sold into sexual slavery. The rubble does not stimulate the aesthetic sensibility; it merely looks ugly. A war story, Barmak seems to say, is always a horror story.

Negative Space

Osama may be in part a lament for the horror of past wars, but it also provides a compelling justification for the ongoing war on terrorism. There is no question that the Taliban were (and are) a deeply inimical, dangerous force in Afghan society that acted like DDT on its cultural, spiritual, and emotional life. But in the aftermath of American bombardment, the film's narrative brings closure. Like a typical Hollywood vehicle, focused on conflict and its hackneyed resolution in redemptive violence, Afghanistan's problems begin in *Osama* with its Taliban villains and end (offscreen) with the onslaught of the U.S. military. The burqas have been withdrawn and justice restored. After viewing the film, Americans can rest assured that they have put their three-hundred-billion-dollar military budget to good use.

Barmak's film enjoyed a critical success unlike any Afghan film before or after. Westerners of all stripes embraced the narrative of Taliban cruelty—from White House hawks to Feminist Majority pacifists. Like horror movies with their damsels in distress, *Osama* followed the formula of narrative films like *Kandahar* and documentaries like *Afghanistan Unveiled*. With its sympathetic female lead, it pitched the Afghan conflict as a war for sexual liberation against the fanaticism of Islam. Was the U.S. invasion right or wrong? Did it do more harm than good? Did innocent people get bombed? Were feminists cynically manipulated by warmonger politicians? Who cares, Jane Smiley wrote in the December 2, 2001, *New York Times Magazine*. The end justified the means, because "the Afghan women took off their burkas."[13] The U.S. military agreed. On February 1, 2005, Marine Corps Lt. Gen. James Mattis was caught on camera emoting on the joys of liberating Afghan women: "You go into Afghanistan, you got guys who slap women around for five years because they didn't wear a veil. You know, guys like that ain't got no manhood left anyway. So it's a hell of a lot of fun to shoot them."[14]

Lila Abu-Lughod has challenged these "projects of saving other women," claiming they "depend on and reinforce a sense of superiority by Westerners, a form of arrogance that deserves to be challenged."[15] By saying that Afghan women need to be saved, she writes, one claims that they need to be saved *from* something. To bring Muslims up to our supposedly lofty level necessitates a cultural overhaul often portrayed as a black-and-white conflict: the struggle for women's rights over traditional Muslim mores. Thus the conflict between the West and the Muslim world primarily revolves around the question not of democracy but of *sex*.[16] In other words, the goal is for *them* to behave in every way like *us*. On this point, liberals and conservatives agree wholeheartedly.

While *Osama* does not portray Islam itself in an overtly negative way, religious observance seems to be what the Taliban does as opposed to the common people, who appear to worship only when they are forced to. We are never shown a scene in which the female protagonists of the story practice their faith. By identifying the male villains with Muslim religious activity, Barmak by extension links oppressed women with a secular world that is far less threatening to Westerners. In this way, the film presents Afghan women as outsiders in their own culture in order to facilitate our identification with them. To expand upon Eisele's classification of the genre, the end result is not simply a reassertion of traditional values but more what David Spurr calls an "affirmation of colonial discourse . . . which justifies the authority of those in control of the discourse through demonstrations of moral superiority."[17] The girl, like all heroines in "sheikh" films, becomes one of us, not one of them. We can then save her for ourselves; that is, for the civilization that we represent.

The need for this affirmation appears to stem from an unconscious realization that the imperial discourse of American power in the Middle East is at its most compromised in fifty years. Women, especially when cloaked by the *chadari,* embody Islamic intransigence, resistant to the penetration of Western culture and values. Muslim women themselves in many countries and circumstances clearly recognize this, deliberately adopting the hijab to align themselves ideologically and visually to anti-imperialist resistance. Yet many Western feminists insist that this gesture ultimately deprives women of power. But perhaps it might be more accurate to say that such a gesture deprives Western, secular feminism of its own totalizing authority. Gayatri Spivak has written that feminism "must recognize that it is complicitous with the institution within which it seeks its space."[18] The prevailing ideology of empire often prevents those in the West who wish to speak for Afghan women from realizing that the Afghans themselves are capable of speaking from within their *chadaris,* or without them. As a consequence, sympathetic activists do not allow Afghan women to be heard but put words in their mouths, words that often inadvertently stem from a sovereign subject of which feminism, in this case, is merely a part.

The advantages of such a cultural project should by now be obvious, not least of which being its ability to enable a union between the economic and military forces that currently control the United States (no matter who's in office) and their ideological and political enemies, from left-wing feminists to Iranians. If Afghanistan is to be exploited one way or the other, it makes sense to manufacture it into a commodity image (a veiled victim) that can gain currency on the global market, something that can be bought and sold across religious and cultural and political boundaries. The intrinsic meaning of Afghanistan no longer matters. Rather, its importance lies in its ability to provide labor, raw materials, a metaphoric setting for adventure, a buffer state, a chance to claim more ideological ground for a cause, or a place where one can make a fortune. If Afghanistan is indeed a woman, her worth depends on whatever, or whomever, is watching and buying.

The Western Harem

Barmak understood that Westerners would see *Osama,* that indeed they had to in order for it to be successful. And so the narrative was modified to fit their expectations. Any artist in the marketplace understands how this works. Entertainment media exist not so much to increase our awareness but to confirm our suspicions. The first scene reveals this dynamic by introducing us to Afghanistan through the viewpoint of a Western photographer, later executed by the Taliban. The girl's friend Espandi speaks directly (through the photojournalist) to us, taking American dollars from our hands to reveal Afghanistan to our eyes.

But there are other indications that the director does not simply conform his narrative to pander to U.S. interests. Unlike *Kandahar,* in which the patriarchal and imperialist designs of one country coincide with another's, *Osama* reveals a complex dialectical struggle with the Eastern film tradition as well as the whole of Orientalist discourse. Sometimes sabotaging its own propaganda, the narrative becomes a contradictory and hybrid work of art that reflects the struggle of its creator to navigate, like Afghanistan itself, a treacherous path between what it wants to be and what others need it to be.

This tension becomes apparent as soon as the film begins. Its first image of Eastern women unveils not the stereotypical harem slave or oppressed, voiceless shadow but a mass demonstration of women. That their faces are invisible behind the *chadari* is not nearly as important as their obvious ability to organize, carry signs, and demand change. Their sheer numbers are frighteningly potent. The way Barmak films it, they resemble an implacable blue tide, stampeding past the camera like a force of nature, as terrifying as they are themselves terrified. When a Talib places a woman in a cage at the close of the scene, she lashes out at him with her fists. This first sight of powerful Afghan women threatens the expectations of the typical Western viewer. As the film proceeds, women become progressively cowed and eventually imprisoned in the mullah's harem, barefoot and pregnant. And yet the protest remains in the narrative, a destabilizing vision that only an Afghan would have dared to film.

The scene thus functions as a critique of the media's convention of dwelling on mass demonstrations in the Islamic world. Time and again, news programs treat viewers to Hamas parades, flag burnings, and the like, with the inevitable crowd shots of bearded young men bouncing up and down and shouting at the camera. Never do we actually grasp the material or historical reasons for their protest. Neither do we ever see women participating. Rather, these stereotypical mob shots reinforce the Orientalist view of the Islamic world as threatening, irrational, monochromatic, and patriarchal. Here, however, the women protesters confront not just the Taliban but also their fellow Afghans and the West. They, like Sharbat Gula, do not emerge from "under the burqa." They don't have to, being quite vocal even when beneath it. Unlike Makhmalbaf, Barmak does not fetishize the *chadari*. For Afghans, who live behind the larger cultural veil, whatever frisson the film provokes does not come from images of the *chadari*. Rather it is the girl's donning of male dress that provides the narrative's dramatic tension. The suspense in *Osama* revolves not around her invisibility but around her exposure to the male gaze.

At the same time, this gaze is not as one-sided as it appears. The girl is not simply seen; she sees as well. Although her boyish haircut and clothes enable her to crash an all-male prayer session at the local masjid and earn desperately needed food for her family, her gaze becomes truly subversive only when she gets to school. Here she learns to read the Qur'an, to don a turban, and to take her place among the boys as an equal. More important, she can see inside the closed walls of their world, mingle freely at recess with the other boys, climb trees and scamper around. For the first and only time in the film, as the girl watches the other boys at play, she smiles. Her cross-dressing has enabled her to taste the forbidden fruit of male bonding. Barmak gives us the moment in a close-up, the background of boys unfocused against the dusty walls. In a moment of stasis and of equilibrium, the girl's own gaze links her to action outside the frame, the world of men, as invisible as women beneath the *chadari*. Her smile is tentative and enigmatic, because we can only guess at what she is seeing. In that liminal instant, all action freezes and we are left to contemplate a person who is, albeit briefly, freed from culture as well as biology to assert her own identity.

The ambiguity of her position cannot last. Despite the grandmother's soothing words, the girl cannot walk under a rainbow; men and women cannot trade places. In the end, it is the girl's own biology, her menstrual period, that betrays her. When the mullah says, "*Dukhtar ast!*" (It's a girl!), it is not as much a statement as it is an accusation, a death sentence. And yet, even in the midst of total defeat at the film's conclusion, comes a parting shot of defiance: the caged girl skipping rope, free from the *chadari,* still in her short-cropped hair and father's clothes.

The emotional trauma of seeing her married to the mullah initially crowds out this parting image. And yet it signifies the most powerful theme of *Osama:* that Afghan women, and all Afghans by extension, will maintain their own inner freedom in the most oppressive environment. Only the girl's interior world of imagination, play, and dream can ultimately provide the antidote to the Taliban's brutal regime. This invisible place within the self can never be veiled or jailed. Within its walls, she still possesses the power to be both child and adult, woman and man, aggressive and meek, and know the peace of freedom from necessity.

This is not exactly how we would imagine the damsel in distress of the Hollywood Eastern. Muslim women are usually portrayed in Western art as extremely passive. All one has to do is look at any number of nineteenth-century seraglio paintings to see a vision of Muslim women as voluptuous and inert, waiting for a male to actuate them. The work of Jean-Auguste-Dominique Ingres provides the most obvious example. In one of his most famous paintings, *The Turkish Bath* (1862), he presents a symphony of flesh, with women of all races cavorting in a sensuous mass. Some are playing music, others braiding hair, still others simply lying about, fondling each other in a near swoon of ecstasy. All of them are young, even girlish, and beautiful, not individuals so much as bodies to be possessed by watching. The tondo frame of the work reinforces the image of voyeurism, as if one is staring at them through a keyhole or a pair of binoculars.

This nineteenth-century peep show presages the scopophiliac nature of film. Laura Mulvey's groundbreaking essay demonstrated that the cinema structures its views of women around voyeuristic and fetishistic ways of looking.[19] To look at women in Ingres's paintings as well as Hollywood film is to see through the male gaze, to be coerced into identification with a vision that objectifies women into spectacle. Rosalind Coward writes that "Voyeurism is a way of taking sexual pleasure by looking at rather than being close to a particular object of desire . . . and Peeping Toms can always stay in control."[20] *The Turkish Bath* stands as the most blatant visual metaphor for this system of voyeuristic control. It distills a fantasy, a dream of not what could be but what should be. Observing women without being observed conveys power. The voyeur himself is veiled and uses that veil to establish his controlling position. What he sees, or wishes to see, are women who have no ability to look back. At the same time, he creates himself by looking at them, by making them the center of his attention. Their presence enables him to dissolve himself in them. This is the perversity of his desire, one that is carefully concealed by absenting himself from the picture. We do not see the Peeping Tom gazing through the keyhole. Rather, we become him in the smoke-and-mirrors game that we call objectivity.

Fatima Mernissi, a Moroccan author who herself grew up in a harem, has analyzed what she calls the "Western harem" through a close reading of Ingres's work. By doing so, she discovers a startling difference between Western and Muslim views of women. Whereas Western works like *The Turkish Bath* glamorize female passivity, Muslim harems involve "sex-wars during which women resist, disturb men's schemes, and sometimes become masters."[21] The obvious example for Mernissi is Scheherazade, a woman who "commands words, not armies, to transform her situation . . . a symbol of the triumph of reason over violence."[22] Curiously, upon her translation into Western literature, Scheherazade is deprived of this active power. Edgar Allan Poe solves the problem of her subversive voice by brutally murdering her in his 1850 story "The Thousand-and-Second Tale of Scheherazade." Whereas *The Thousand and One Nights* relates a dialogue between men and women in which women tell the stories and provide the viewpoint, Poe and later writers invert the equation to keep men's sovereign position.

This dramatic difference between cultures was not lost on Barmak. He exploits it to the hilt in *Osama*'s central event, the moment when the girl penetrates as deep as she will go into the private world of men. In this scene, the boys have gathered in the school's hammam, its bathhouse, to listen to a health lesson. Inside the murky chamber, a single shaft of light streams from the ceiling, revealing the assembled children, white towels wrapped around their waists. Here the boys are instructed in the fine art of washing their genitals in the Islamic way. The more the boys attempt to clean themselves, the more they are overpowered by the gloom of the dank room as well as the potbellied mullah indoctrinating them. Repeating the same lines over and over, he fondles himself behind his towel and beneath the water. The frightened girl attempts to hide, blending into the dark, drab walls.

In Muslim culture, the sexually segregated hammam is a sanctuary, a place where women can let their hair down, gossip, and relax. *Osama*'s bath scene, on the other hand, is fraught with tension as boundaries are dangerously transgressed. The female intrudes in male territory, witnessing an initiation ritual focused on the penis. Her difference is an anatomical truth that the Taliban consider to be a sign of inferiority or a danger in need of domination. Only now can she see exactly what separates men from women: nothing mysterious or erotic but, rather, a shabby and simplistic rite of passage.

At the same time, the bathhouse scene dwells not so much on phallocentrism as it does on perversion and pedophilia. This sanctuary, this place of cleansing, has been turned into a voyeuristic show for the perverted mullah, who is a dead ringer for the gray-bearded spectator of Gérôme's *Snake Charmer*. Here the Taliban lets its own hair down, and we finally get to see the reality behind its self-righteousness. The girl watches the spectacle aghast. Eventually, of course, the mullah spots her and commands that she disrobe and bathe herself. Leering at her just barely prepubescent body, he groans with pleasure and asks her if she would like him to wash her feet. Despite the Taliban's proscription against homosexuality, he continues eyeing her unctuously, exclaiming that she looks like "a nymph." When one of the boys asks him what he means, he says that nymphs are "boys who look like girls in heaven." The more these men attempt to display their religious purity, the filthier they become. This perverted mullah not only discovers her sexual identity but also finally forces her into "marriage." Thus the girl pays the penalty for daring to walk beneath the rainbow, to see through the male gaze and penetrate the other sex's inner sanctum. She is not simply put in her place as a result but locked there and then raped, the penultimate scene of the film showing the mullah bathing as he did before. The reluctant child bride meanwhile lies offscreen, invisible—just like the Taliban want.

Now the erotic fantasy of Ingres can finally give way to the sordid reality of sex as power. The child "odalisque" cannot possibly be viewed any longer as sexually seductive. Alone and terrified, she can only be a victim to the predator's stare, not an accomplice. At the same time, by actively transgressing, the girl reveals herself as an active human being instead of the passive caricature of the harem slave that Mernissi notes does not even exist in the Muslim world. Throughout the film, the girl maintains her ability to penetrate and to resist.

Throughout this crucial sequence, Afghanistan enters into a complex dialogue with its Western spectators, as Barmak inverts Ingres's *Turkish Bath* fantasy. In the film, it is the woman who assumes power, who watches. Even more threatening, she exposes the male voyeur. For it becomes painfully obvious that the dirty old man instructing them is the male gaze itself, watching the boys as she watches him. In this spartan environment, no artifice or beauty can hide the cold, calculating stare of the sexual predator. As the morally corrupt mullah is exposed, so, too, is the West and its increasing eroticization of the female child, a natural result of the quest for the perfect passive woman.[23] Thus the girl turns a mirror on the previously invisible male gaze, an act so disturbing that she must be punished in the harshest way at the film's conclusion. But the damage has been done. The film has dissolved the boundary between gaze and object of the gaze, spectator and art, the West and Afghanistan, to reveal a liminal space wherein the two can finally see as they are seen.

Lost in Translation

Before Afghanistan appears in *Osama,* before the story even commences, an epigraph appears on screen, white letters on a black background. The Farsi characters look exotic, graceful, while at the same being completely unintelligible to the average American. Happily, subtitles are provided. They say: "I cannot forget, but I can forgive—Mandela." This quote is not to be taken lightly. It not only sets the mood but also defines the whole purpose of the film. In the light of this, *Osama* can be taken as a kind of Afghan Holocaust remembrance, an evocation of the past and its horrors to remind Afghans and the world of what must never happen again.

There's just one problem. That's not what the Farsi really says.

What it does say is this: "Oh God, I would rather side with those who put the world over their religion, than those who put their religion over the world." Obviously it bears no resemblance to the translated English. This is because the author is not even Nelson Mandela but Ali Shariati, the Iranian ideologue of the Islamic Revolution.

The meaning of this quote in relation to the film is not nearly as important as the fact that it is not the quote translated. A vast difference exists between the two, unresolved by our supposedly dominant position as spectators. For unless we enter into the linguistic world of Farsi, we cannot understand the self-referential meaning of the words on the screen. This is, and always has been, the most threatening characteristic of the Islamic world and of Afghanistan in particular. They do not relate to us; they refuse to be assimilated into our language. Time and again, Afghans have rejected imperial incursions, both culturally and by force of arms. Despite our imprecations, they have no need to unveil themselves to us. Rather, they invite us, as Barmak does, inside the veil itself. Viewers who cannot read Farsi simply assume that the subtitles are accurate reflections of the words above them. By doing so, they themselves are unveiled as both dependent on the mediation of another culture and limited in their ability to perceive that culture's point of view. Just as these two languages are incommensurate, so, too, is the interior experience of the film's reality from that imposed on it by a hegemonic audience.

Film is translation. It is the abstraction of an abstraction, the mimesis and the illusion of vision. Far from reflecting reality objectively, films by their nature transfer us from one discursive field to another.[24] Like Western discourse, film universalizes its particular subject position by identifying mass audiences with a single camera's point of view. To speak filmic language is to identify one's self with a specific way of seeing that has been naturalized by our near constant participation in mass media culture. This way of seeing abhors complexity. Hence the sharp chiaroscuro of most Hollywood productions that obsessively crosscut between good and evil, ugliness and beauty, tragedy and comedy, self and other. On the screen, these absolutes can not only be identified but also possessed, in the viewing of simple tautologies and contradictions, self-evident truths and lies that are constantly reenacted with the force of myth.

Osama at times drives a wedge between these antipodal categories, and by doing so it creates a new space of contingency where meaning is not universal and absolute, but rhetorical. Here, on the border between Dari and English, a new hybrid language can be spoken between the two parties with which they can contest each other's ways of seeing. Neither side stands privileged over the other by cultural omniscience. In such a place, old boundaries dissolve, rendering the other familiar and altering the self.

People in the West often have a rather naive understanding of their counterparts in the Third World. That they can be generalized at all under such a term reveals both the power and the vulnerability of imperialist rhetoric. The fact, of course, is that the Third World does not exist. It is a phantasm. Similarly, Afghanistan, as we conceive it, also does not exist. Far from being an actual place, it is more a series of images and ideas that we have assembled, sometimes blissfully unaware of their source, origin, or actual meaning. Knowledge on Afghanistan remains especially scant in America. Thus, viewing the film provides a great deal of information that an audience would be hard pressed to define as fact or fiction. When we see the Afghanistan of *Osama* or *Kandahar* or any other film, we believe in it, but only because it tells us what we already know—or what we want to hear. The rest tends to be ignored.

One of the most disturbing things about watching *Osama,* or any film about Afghanistan, is realizing just how dependent we are on others to interpret the world for us. Our relationship with the news media is a prime example. We trust them to report what is, not how they perceive it to be. But how are we to know which is which? Can we trust a film like *Osama* to translate the experience of living in Afghanistan into something we can understand?

Reviewers of the film in the United States certainly had no doubts, largely because of the persistent belief that when one views "Third World" films, one gains some "authentic" insight, gets a handle on how things really are "there." Unfortunately, this point of view ignores the fundamental nature of film as a process of translation, especially when used to represent a culture different from one's own. This process always involves, like any translation, the internalization of the other so that it can be rewritten in the language of the familiar.[25] We, as spectators, supply meaning to this Afghan film's cinematic signifiers. That is, we translate its strange and exotic imagery into our own visual and cultural language. Such translation, however, like knowledge itself, is "deeply inscribed with the politics, the considerations, the positions and the strategies of power."[26] An "imaginary geography" is created where, as Edward Said noted, the Muslim world is portrayed not as it necessarily is, but as it ought to be.[27] Consequently, this produces a total way of seeing, an informational filter that paradoxically seeks what is most familiar (itself) in what is foreign.

To put it another way, *Osama*'s narrative, replete with Orientalist set pieces, tells us what we already know: that Afghanistan is a damsel in distress, desperately in need of rescue. For Bert Cardullo in the *Hudson Review,* the film can be viewed, therefore, as a clarion call to "exorcise oppression," not just to recount it.[28] Pointing out how Barmak portrays "the unspeakable poverty, astonishing backwardness, and brutal inhumanity" of the region, Cardullo lays the blame squarely on "Taliban government" and "Islamic law," terms that he uses synonymously. Alas, little has changed since the fall of 2001. On the contrary, he assures us, "casual repressiveness . . . seems sewn into the very fabric of Afghani society." Of course, Cardullo never mentions that the U.S. government and its allies were more than happy to subsidize the Taliban's casual repressiveness when it benefited them to do so.

Instead he quotes an interview with filmmaker Samira Makhmalbaf (the daughter of Mohsen Makhmalbaf) at the 2003 Cannes Film Festival:

> The Taliban were not simply a group who ruled in Afghanistan for a few years and then were gone. They're in the minds of people, in the culture of Afghanistan and of so many other Central Asian countries—it's not like an external wound you can dress. It's deeper. It's like a cancer.[29]

Calling a group of people, no matter how despicable, a "cancer," opens a Pandora's box of vile impulses. Cancer is not something to be reasoned with, or understood. Instead we only attempt to exterminate it, always with the best of intentions. In making his point about the "Taliban mindset," however, Cardullo fails to mention that Samira Makhmalbaf has elsewhere written that "The Taliban are the group around the fascist Bush in the democratic society of America. Bin Laden is a Talib. Bush is a Talib."[30] To do so would once again force us to confront the cancerous mindsets we ourselves hold dear. Clearly, something has been lost in the translation.

Such an utter lack of self reflection or critical capacity would be absurd in any other circumstance. But this is the Islamic world, after all. The issue at stake is not what divergent meanings Siddiq Barmak or Samira Makhmalbaf might wish to express but how to translate them in a politically expedient manner. Cardullo's grasp of the situation in Afghanistan, as mediated by *Osama*, reflects a solipsistic process that seeks confirmation of what it already believes and wishes to justify. In a sense, it is like a religious faith, but one deeply embattled and paranoid. Such an ideology "testifies to something amiss within society, since a society that was not threatened would not need ideological defenses."[31]

Osama was allowed to succeed where other films on Afghanistan have not because it delivered a familiar image. When the subaltern speaks, it is sometimes a ventriloquist act. Other cultures are just as subject to our representational schemes as we ourselves are. They, in fact, have little power to contradict such representations when our visual language amounts to the lingua franca of cinematic expression. Barmak's first film experience, as stated previously, was not an Afghan production but *Lawrence of Arabia*. The assault of Western ways of seeing on the rest of the world through aggressive marketing of its films creates a circle where everyone becomes caught up within the dominant culture's Orientalist paradigms. In order to be heard in such an economic and political environment, you must tell them what they want to hear.

In the beginning of *Osama*, hordes of women march through the streets of Kabul, demanding the right to work. They cry, "We are hungry! We need jobs!" At the same time, they hold signs that say, "We are not political." Their asseverations notwithstanding, it seems quite obvious that when you take to the streets en masse in *chadaris* to shout at the Taliban, you are most definitely being political. To openly admit being political, however, means that one is aggressively pursuing a policy of self-determination, a tactic frowned upon by the West. Thus when talking about the Afghans as victims of horror, a cagey Barmak told an interviewer, "We won't touch now who was behind all these things, who was involved in this dirty little game in the region, but I would like to invite all people to give something, to make a new action against all this terror and horror, against all tragedies, totalitarian regimes, who makes this horror."[32]

The director knows very well "who was behind all these things, who was involved." But to name names would alienate the very people to whom the film is pitched. Rather than provoke self-righteous pity, it would condemn. Speaking truth to power does not make it easier for your nation in the short term. Especially not when these people occupy your country with tens of thousands of soldiers.

Politics has long shaped Barmak's creative output. When the communist regime controlled Kabul, he went to Moscow from 1981 to 1987 to study film. There he was influenced by the likes of Andrei Tarkovsky and Tengiz Abuladze.[33] Returning to Kabul, he made films like *The Stranger* (1986), which portrays a prerevolution Afghanistan where tribal values lethally clash with exploitative landowners, their policeman lackeys, and bumbling American tourists. An interesting film in its own right, it somehow manages to find fault in both the boorish values of the West as well as the backwardness of Afghan society. Inexplicably, the film was banned for being too critical of the government.[34] Nevertheless, it is difficult not to view *The Stranger* as a Marxist critique, despite the director's disavowal of the communist regime. This might explain Barmak's highly ambiguous attitude toward religion, oscillating from resigned tolerance to active dislike. Whether Barmak was a communist or not, he was forced to mimic its ideology. Otherwise, *The Stranger* would not have been made. The situation with *Osama* was no different.

Although Barmak's film allows for divergent readings of its narrative, one should not overstate their presence or potential. It's possible to deconstruct practically any story and use it to subvert itself. What's more relevant is to discuss the ways in which a dominant reading is either overtly sustained or challenged by a work of art, especially when that work is being used to justify military intervention. If Barmak opens up a destabilizing space where Western visuality might be challenged on an almost subliminal level, he also follows the Western program of Taliban demonization and historical decontextualization.

In an interview, the director stated that the Taliban "want to cut the past, because then people can lose their identities. If they have no identity, they must accept the new identity."[35] This extremely perceptive statement holds true for Barmak as well as for his political opponents. His film presents a fantasy of consensus, of simplicity. Effectively ignoring the ethnic and tribal rivalries as well as the atrocities committed by Russians and Northern Alliance soldiers (along with the part the United States played in both), *Osama* creates an Afghanistan that does not exist. This one-sided depiction of the Taliban is the film's greatest flaw.

At the same time, it can be seen as symptomatic of an art medium that is Manichaean in its very nature. This is, after all, Hollywood film as adapted by Afghanistan. Just think of Judah Ben-Hur and Messala. Or Dorothy and the Wicked Witch of the West. There are no gray areas in those conflicts. Neither can there be for an Afghan who does not have the luxury of objectivity. Afghanistan is a war zone where no one is allowed to be an innocent bystander. Barmak, like everyone else in his country, became ensnared in the political turmoil of his native land and was forced to take sides. By happy circumstance, he found that the enemy of his enemy could also be his friend and audience. The Taliban are the villains in *Osama* precisely because they have too many enemies—so many that even the United States and Iran, the strangest of bedfellows, can join forces to condemn them.

While I have discussed the ways in which the political climate of the United States influenced *Osama,* Iran also played an important part in the film, though completely behind the scenes. In fact, according to James Meek:

> Barmak could not have made *Osama* without Mohsen Makhmalbaf's help; the Iranian director invested thousands of dollars of his own money in the film, lent Barmak his Arriflex camera and encouraged him in the sending-out of the film treatment, which eventually resulted in money from Japanese and Irish producers.[36]

This makes perfect sense when one remembers that politically the Taliban are aligned with Pakistan, Iran's great rival in the most recent indigenous phase of the New Great Game. Barmak has been unequivocal in stating which side he takes in this conflict, mentioning in one interview that Afghanistan is part of Iran's "cultural space."[37] Tajiks, who speak Farsi (as opposed to the Pashto of the Taliban) and make up the Northern Alliance, are culturally tied to Iran. Barmak, himself a Tajik, also chose a Tajik girl to star in his film. These political affiliations, like the Farsi script of the opening frames, are invisible to the Western viewer, a context that is largely untranslatable to our own cultural experience. And yet it fundamentally affects the entire production.

Certainly Barmak and other Afghans have reason to hate the Taliban. But it is more difficult to understand them, something Barmak never attempts to do in the film. By doing so, his side, the Northern Alliance, might be exposed for all its flaws. It was this group, made up of a variety of ethnic and political factions, that devolved into a morass of internecine violence after the Russians departed the country in 1989, eventually laying waste to the capital city and creating the urban destruction that *Osama* chronicles. Commanders turned into warlords and gangsters while the country disintegrated into feudal anarchy. Drug running was rampant. Corruption and banditry made it nearly impossible to ship goods on the country's perilous roads. Warlords kidnapped and raped children with impunity.

When Mullah Omar and his guerillas hanged one such warlord from the barrel of a tank, they were welcomed by some as liberators. Finally there was a faction intent on restoring law to Afghanistan, though a fierce and fundamentalist law it was. Certainly their religious mania did not discourage the American government from inviting them to the United States and taking them on a tour of Mount Rushmore while trying to negotiate with them for Unocal pipelines deals. Nor did it discourage Pakistan, which had finally given up on the fanatical former mujahed Gulbuddin Hekmatyar. By October 1994, Pakistan enabled its Talib clients to capture a munitions dump with 18,000 machine guns, dozens of artillery pieces, and many vehicles, jump-starting their conquest of Afghanistan.[38]

It did not take them long to graduate from liberators to extremist tyrants. While enjoying the support of many Afghans at first, especially their fellow Pashtuns, the Taliban met greater resistance in the North, among the Tajiks and others. They were especially vicious to the Hazaras, not only an ethnic minority but also religiously Shia. Once the Taliban gained control of most of the country, their attacks on minorities intensified along with the application of their oppressive laws.

During this time and afterward, few attempted to make sense of who the Taliban were and why they committed such atrocities on the people and cultural heritage of Afghanistan. One of the few was the British journalist Robert Fisk, who saw the Taliban movement as a kind of unconscious imposition on the Afghan homeland of the harrowing conditions of the refugee camps.[39] David B. Edwards provides a more complex analysis of the same phenomenon, noting that throughout the 1970s and '80s most of Afghanistan was in the midst of an identity crisis, thanks to the incursions of foreign armies and party politics, whether Islamist or Marxist. In the refugee camps, the ancient tribal authority, the ethical codes that had defined society for centuries, eroded in the face of Islamic party dominance of aid and weapons. To subjugate women became for these exiles a way to impose control in a world without order and without honor, a way of clinging to the traditional "gendered ideals of personal integrity" in the face of bewildering interference from a host of outsiders.[40]

Unfortunately, such crucial insights into the psychological dynamics of the Taliban are completely absent in the film. This is not to say that such knowledge should elicit sympathy. The Taliban committed a host of atrocities that no amount of understanding can excuse. But to resolve conflict and prevent it in the future requires transcending the urge to demonize one's enemy and to find some way in which both sides' desires can make sense to each other. In *Osama*, however, a viewer can never understand the Taliban. You simply want them gone, exterminated by Lieutenant General Mattis and his boys. And in their place? The same bunch of narco-terrorist warlords and thugs who made even the Taliban seem like an improvement.

Marina

In spite of its propagandistic tone, *Osama*'s politics cuts both ways. It is obviously a film that in some ways rampantly supports Western intervention. But in the background, you can see the larger space of the circle, the one that shows women taking to the streets, beating their captors, keeping their minds free from tyranny. In its narrative, average people survive under conditions of unspeakable hardship, using subterfuge and community to hold on in the face of starvation and despair. Even when no questions are asked, if you listen, if you look into the deep space of the rubble, you hear the questions just the same: How did it happen? Who's responsible? What can we do about it?

Marina Golbahari, the film's star, embodies the answers to those questions. The ruins speak through her, brimming in her eyes with the tears that seem to come so readily. When Barmak found her, according to a much-repeated story, she was begging in front of a store near, appropriately, Kabul's Cinema Park. Her first words to him were, "Your charity."

There are perhaps sixty thousand children like her in Kabul.[41] Desperately poor, they forage in garbage dumps, lie in the dust all day for a few coins, and eat the refuse from restaurants. Golbahari was from a family of eight, living in a single cramped room in a relative's house in Kabul. After the departure of the Taliban, she began to attend school to learn basic reading and arithmetic. In Naofumi Nakamura's remarkable *Marina* (2003), a Japanese TV documentary that chronicles the making of *Osama*, the young girl's screen test reveals a dirty, bedraggled child who counts to ten and sings a song about beheading Russians. One immediately sees that mysterious quality in her eyes that struck Barmak. Her gaze is soulful, full of premature knowledge and pain. At twelve years old, this person already knows what suffering is. When he asks her about her experiences during the war (her house was bombed and a wall collapsed on two of her sisters, killing them), she begins to cry. The tears are painful to watch.

Barmak quickly hired her and made her his star. Her pay was $7 a day, with her invalid father (who had been imprisoned and tortured by the Taliban) receiving an additional $100 a month for a year or so.[42] The film was shot in winter over a three-week period, in often freezing conditions that entailed stopping the day's shoot in order to warm up Golbahari's frostbitten hands and feet by plunging them in an open flame. Immediately before each scene, Barmak had to recite her lines to her. Then, to prepare her for the shot, he would sometimes employ cruel method-acting tactics. During the filming of her marriage to the mullah, for example, the documentary *Marina* captures a moment when Golbahari giggles after seeing makeup applied to her face. The director begins to fume at her, demanding she think of her father's wounds, her sisters' deaths. With the girl in tears, the camera started rolling.

Originally titled *Rainbow, Osama* was rewritten by Barmak when he took on his young lead. Like the Kabul around her, Marina's history and her intense personal suffering are the palimpsest to the narrative, transcending it. Her instinct is so true because Barmak's story mirrors her own experiences. Within the person of Marina, a parallel narrative clearly manifests itself in *Osama,* the Kabul that was, the Kabul that is, the girl who was destroyed, and the girl who has survived. Marina is all of them, playing not only herself but also a whole gender and nation.

In one remarkable scene of Nakamura's documentary, this identification with a nation's sufferings becomes most apparent. It comes during the filming of the girl being mobbed and chased, right after the mullah has exposed her. We see Marina running from them, hemmed in on all sides. The way *Osama* shows it, she is helpless, terrified, a victim. But for one brief second during the filming, a boy jostles her, roughly. She reacts by shoving back, far harder than he, her face contorted with rage. It is not acting. It is reacting—not only to a boy but to a whole history of abuse and misery. For a split second, she transforms herself into the aggressive woman that haunts the dreams of Muslim men. It is the true face of Marina Golbahari, who has lived through war and who, like Sharbat Gula, is not afraid to return our gaze. For those who rush to call Afghanistan a "failed state," Barmak posits Marina's eyes. In this way, a beggar child suddenly acts, in every sense of that word, on a world that is in many ways responsible for her suffering.

The last image of the film shows Marina skipping rope in jail. Is it a dream, a flashback? Or is it a moment of revelation, a last parting glance of the film's mandorla-like space? It is no accident that Barmak set this scene in the notorious Pul-e-Charkhi prison in Kabul. It was here that thousands upon thousands of political prisoners met their deaths from the Saur Revolution into the present day. Here a fictitious character becomes a flesh-and-blood girl who transcends her cage by dragging us in there with her. In that moment we discover a new language, a grotesque and arabesque mélange of Western and Eastern, privileged and impoverished ways of seeing that pose an even greater challenge to systems of domination than Poe's apprehension of total unity. In such a rhetorical environment, dialogue and debate become necessary conditions rather than threats to be avoided at all political, cultural, and spiritual costs.

If Farsi and English, East and West, frame the film's narrative, then to deconstruct the film is to expand that mandorla, that intracircle space, to the circumference of both circles—to see the pockets of resistance that lie immanent in a gesture, a word, a piece of crumbled wall. Then we can expand it even further to include ourselves, to see how our action or inaction has contributed to the ruins, the rage, the religious hunger. Finally, in some ineluctable moment of infinite regression, we might be able to view, out of frame or focus, a moment of identification, a transition from guilt or blame, arrogance or pity, to a common humanity whose definition can and must be mutually negotiated. No one film can take you this far. The best it can do is point you in the right direction. *Osama*, sometimes in spite of itself, does that.

PART 3

Border Crossings

6 The West Unveiled

In This World

We live in a world of borders, barriers, and walls. New states continue to proliferate, splintering from larger ones, all eager to share in the splendors of nationalism. Since the events of September 11, 2001, Westerners have developed an increased need to demarcate themselves from the rest of the planet. Paramilitary organizations in the United States patrol the U.S.-Mexican border, eager to prevent an "invasion" of illegal immigrants. Pundits applaud the Israeli construction of a wall in occupied Palestine to fence in the Arabs. Eastern Europeans build similar walls around Romany neighborhoods. Spaniards in the North African enclaves of Ceuta and Melilla live behind barbwire fences. Borders are everywhere subjects of vicious, even genocidal disputes: in Kashmir, in Pakistan, in the Sudan, in Lebanon, in Korea, in Palestine.

On the World Market: Enayat (Enayatullah) at the mercy of human traffickers.

As new nations are created and new walls erected, millions upon millions of people are robbed (by human or natural disaster) of their states and their homes, their livelihoods and their identities. Among the refugees in the world, the greatest population by far comes from Afghanistan. In 1990, even before the rise of the Taliban, almost 42 percent of all refugees were Afghan.[1] Between the years 1979 and 1992, more than a fifth of Afghanistan's population—more than six million people—were driven from the country.[2] Since the U.S. invasion, many Afghans have returned, despite the country's lack of political stability. Even so, a million Afghan refugees remain in Pakistan today. They live in places like Shamshatoo camp, near Peshawar.

Writing about this camp in the *New York Times Magazine,* journalist Peter Maass described its heart as "a nameless crossroads of nameless roads."[3] Here, close to fifty-five thousand Afghans of every ethnicity endure the misery of displacement in houses made of mud. The camp is notoriously unsanitary. As one journalist reported, during one three-month period a child died nearly every day from "bacteria-related dehydration."[4] While having numerous amenities, such as sixteen schools, several medical centers, and even electricity, Shamshatoo remains a place where children work twelve hours a day at a carpet loom to feed themselves. There is no security there. Police provide protection for the inhabitants—but only for a price. Their brutality is commonplace. There are no locks and no doors. The only privacy women can get is by wearing the *chadari.* Food is rationed and blankets and mattresses distributed—but often only to those who can afford to bribe the Pakistani distributors. Those who cannot are beaten with sticks and driven from the line.[5] It seems inconceivable that such a life would be an improvement on where they came from. And yet many camp residents, when interviewed, have insisted they would rather stay in Pakistan than return home to a country still plunged in lawlessness, poverty, and war.

Afghanistan is more than a place; it is a global situation, like all wars, a seismic catastrophe that shatters and scatters all in its wake. One injustice spawns an entire brood. The violence never seems to reach an end point. Rather, it metastasizes in Pakistani madrassas where Afghan refugees flee for a modicum of learning, only to be indoctrinated in Islamic fanaticism. To understand Afghanistan—to encompass its tragedy completely—one must gaze past its borders and see this vast diaspora, the aftermath of successive conflicts with Russians, with one another, and with Americans. In such a place, the rage can swell up like an ocean squall. Robert Fisk, a British journalist quite sympathetic to the plight of Muslims around the world, was attacked at Shamshatoo not long after the October 2001 invasion of Afghanistan. Seeing a Western face, the families of people slain by American bombardment vented their frustration and grief, nearly killing him. Neither he nor his assailants could escape the war they all thought they had left behind. And neither can the West continue to elude the seismic aftershocks of Afghanistan's "endless war." This is the great message of Michael Winterbottom's 2002 film *In This World*.

How the Other Half Moves

The impetus for the film was, according to the director, a news story he read about fifty-eight Chinese refugees suffocated in a metal container on a ship traveling to Britain. Winterbottom and screenwriter Tony Grisoni saw this as symptomatic of a global imbalance that demands rectification:

> You have millions of people in Pakistan working for a pittance. They see on someone's TV people with mobile phones, the technology that connects everyone. . . . They live in a world dominated by ours, but they have no access to it because they do not have any money. As long as that situation continues, there are going to be people who would like their fair share.[6]

The end result of their efforts to document the plight of these economic refugees is the most harrowing and subversive road movie ever made. The story begins in the Shamshatoo camp, where we meet the family of Enayat, a young man whose father decides to send him to the West for a better future. He enlists the help of Jamal, an Afghan boy from the camp who can speak English and act as interpreter along the way. From the moment the two depart, they are thrust into the most vulnerable position of all: that of stateless, illegal immigrants who must depend on mercenary people-smugglers and their own nascent street smarts to survive.

After bribing a border guard to let them into Iran, they fall into the hands of perverted traffickers and unscrupulous border police who, after stealing most of their possessions, drive them back to the Pakistani desert and abandon them there. Thanks to Enayat's precaution of hiding money at the bottom of his shoe, they have enough to return and this time successfully make it to the Iranian border with Turkey. From there they cross the mountains at night, alone in the brutal elements, with police firing at them in the darkness. Once in Istanbul, they work in a factory for the privilege of living in seclusion and squalor until they are loaded into a metal trailer and shipped across the Mediterranean.

For forty hours, they squat in absolute darkness, slowly suffocating. There is no way to escape and no one to hear their cries for help. By the time the Afghans reach Trieste, Enayat is dead, and Jamal must make his way to England on his own. After working in Italy selling trinkets, he steals a purse and buys a train ticket to France. Placed in a refugee tent camp, Jamal meets Yusef, a young man who hopes to return to England where he managed a restaurant before being deported. The two escape the tent camp and secrete themselves beneath a tractor-trailer loading into the Channel Tunnel. Arriving safely in London, they begin work at Yusef's restaurant. Jamal calls Enayat's father and tells him the news that Enayat is no longer "in this world." The film ends with a shot of Jamal seeking solace in a mosque, its last image the walls over which Jamal whispers a desperate prayer.

The narrative sways far off course from the usual road movie. The formula for this particular genre is a relatively recent one, evolving out of the American Western and its sweeping tally of conquered landscapes. Certainly Jack Kerouac defined the modern road/buddy story with his novel *On the Road* (1956), which takes the romantic quest of the cowboy and transplants it to the modern highway. Inspired by this work, a bumper crop of road movies appeared from the late 1960s onward, from *Easy Rider* (1969) to *Thelma and Louise* (1989). What all these films have in common is what the road signifies to its travelers. In the words of songwriter Paul Simon, they have "all gone to look for America." At the end of the road, they always find, in some sense, an empowering awareness of who they are and what their life means. Along the way, they flout social conventions, assault boundaries, and restore the meaning to what appeared to have been a pointless world, all through the simple process of motion. Especially in Kerouac's novel, speed is power, and the ability to move is as important as the traveler's ability to see in ways that no one else can. In such asphalt-paved vision quests, the road-movie heroes peer past the veil of prosaic norms to experience life as it truly is.

Such romance has been a staple of travel writing for centuries. It evokes a deep-seated anxiety about modernity and its inherent process of destabilization. To travel from the center to the periphery entails the search for a new permanence within flux. Such a journey simultaneously confronts the transition from history to histories, from West to world, and at the same time maps those histories and world in such a way as to render them once again familiar and controllable territory. The unknown becomes known in a ritual that creates the observer through giving him or her something to observe.

In most road movies and travel accounts, however, movement and self-knowledge remain one-sided enterprises. They appear not to be available to those who are under observation. Through travel, a vision projects itself into other parts of the world that cannot project this vision back. Thus when Edward Said discussed the Napoleonic cataloging of Egyptian history and culture, he observed that it rendered Egypt "completely open . . . totally accessible to European scrutiny"[7] in a way that Egypt could never hope to do to

France. Knowing precedes and necessitates dominating. It is "the construction of an object, for investigation and control."[8] Here lies the nexus of travel (literature) and imperialism.

But there are other, insurgent kinds of knowledge that can only be grasped by the subaltern, the dispossessed, the very people who inhabit Shamshatoo camp and others like it. Winterbottom's film shares this knowledge with those so far removed from it. It offers a way of seeing that is radically opposed to the typical "monarch of all I survey" mode of travel writing, a visuality of those who are surveyed. To put this vision on the screen requires the deconstruction of the travel genre as it is understood in the West. Winterbottom does this by designing a road movie in reverse: an epic of travel from the unknown into the known. How stable those two categories really are becomes obvious by the end of the film, when the center must endure interrogation by its margins.

Of course it makes sense, both statistically and politically, to position Afghans as the paragons of marginalization, migrancy, and vulnerability. As the largest refugee population on earth, they stand for all migrants everywhere. But they are also identified in the popular Western mind with radical Islam, the most vociferous foe to modernity. This makes them doubly Other, the reification of everything that lies outside the borders of the "civilized" metropolis. Afghans are the global "other half."

To chart their journey requires more than a simple act of revisionism. That would imply a basic faith in the system doing the representing, one that simply needs fine-tuning. *In This World* does not seek to balance the scales of cultural representation in this manner, to integrate the Other into the modern episteme. Rather, it fires a cinematic salvo aimed directly at the value of modernity itself.

Jamal and Enayat's perspective bears little resemblance to that of the standard world traveler. They do not journey to a place to "see" it. In fact, during their travels there is relatively little to see. They do not spend their time navigating the city, taking in the sights, going to museums, beaches, cafés. Instead they furtively inhabit paint-peeled, anonymous rooms, stripped of their home, their language, their identity. They do not view Turkey or Iran as destinations but as obstacles to be surmounted, barriers that must be overcome.

There is hardly a moment in the entire film when our eyes can rest on any single object or when a piece of landscape lies before us for contemplation. Instead the camera cuts frenetically from figure to figure in long-range shots, close-ups, jump cuts, and transitions that wrest us from one scene and thrust us into another, in a state of constant flux. The images inhabit a space both deeply unsettled and unsettling that permits no stability, where meaning itself migrates.

This restless vision manifests itself as soon as their journey commences. The sequence begins with birds careening through the sky. In an establishing shot, we see Peshawar, picturesque with mosque and the spiritual song of the muezzin, still and peaceful. In an abrupt cut, a car harshly and loudly moves across the field of vision, and Jamal and Enayat are revealed walking down the other side of the street from where the camera stands. A car pulls up to them, obscuring them from view. Inside the car, Enayat speaks to an invisible driver from the backseat before the camera shifts to a new point of view from Jamal in the front seat. The changing world beyond the windows provides, paradoxically, the only constant in the camera's incessant motion. Even the characters' conversation focuses on movement, as the driver asks Jamal about a family member who lives in London.

Establishing the shifting borders of physical space, the director next focuses on the instability of perception and point of view. The two suddenly appear in a teeming crowd, viewed frontally in a medium close-up. Then, just as suddenly, the camera pulls back to reveal even more people, so many of them that Enayat and Jamal become lost to view. Inside Enayat's father's store, they approach the counter, from behind which we view them. Swiveling around, the viewer's gaze embraces those behind and in front of the counter as Enayat introduces Jamal to his father and relatives. The next scene shows them all sitting at a table, viewed from multiple angles as silhouettes, bodies, hands, and close-ups, each line of dialogue corresponding to another reconfigured position.

A shot of the driver's eyes initiates the next stage of this meditation on the meaning of Peshawar, as he drives to the cattle market at night. Winterbottom employs night-vision photography in a grainy, digital black and white that, combined with constant intercutting, abstracts the images of men and cattle in an envelope of darkness. Lingering on the whitened eye of a cow, the camera switches to a daytime setting where the animal is being slaughtered for a meal to celebrate Enayat's departure. Only here, with the men involved in an age-old ritual, does the camera rest—if only briefly. A group of men surround the beast, wrestling it to the ground where they partially decapitate it, in halal fashion. The ensuing gore is audial rather than visual, with the gurgling death noises obscured by the same peaceful music that characterized the earlier scenes of the mosque and sky.

From this extended sequence emerges a radical critique of Western notions of developing-world essentialism. Rituals become demystified, prosaic. The exotic atmosphere of the Orient with its mosques and muezzins collapses with the appearance of a single automobile. Indeed, Enayat and Jamal are not alien to the modern world of technology but implicit in it. Rather than using these "machines in the garden" to simply disrupt a pure, primeval order, the film constantly intercuts frenetic modernity with the traditional life of the tribal.

To a refugee, this relationship is self-evident. Especially for Afghans, living in the twenty-first century implies a certain set of self-contradictions: an ongoing identity crisis. They know all too well that nothing is permanent and that their lives are as contingent as their fortunes or social meaning. One moment they have homes, nations, and families. The next these are bombed out of existence. It is no surprise, then, that their minds become the breeding ground for militant Islam and its apocalyptic, regressive spirituality. For the desperate, there are but two choices: conversion or flight.

Following the *zabihah* (ritual slaughtering), Jamal reveals just such a longing for a sacred absolute, for a place of stillness. Winterbottom takes us into this interior space, transitioning from Enayat's face to the still twitching legs of the butchered cow to Jamal standing by a coursing river, its waters the color of the mud banks surrounding it. For a fraction of an instant, the camera lingers on him, surveying the scene much like Caspar David Friedrich's figure in his painting *Wanderer above the Sea of Fog* (1817). As if to dispel the romanticism, Jamal's legs, seen in close-up now, plunge into the brown water. The scene then shifts to a more comprehensive view of the river, with earthen huts emblazoned with the acronym of the International Red Cross (IRC) presiding over a landscape that recedes into an unremitting perspective of barren desolation, interrupted only by a child wading across the river in the foreground.

In the European version of this encounter, the traveler has just climbed the mountain to become the monarch of all he surveys. He observes from a fixed position, and the image itself is frozen in time, archetypal. Jamal, on the other hand, cannot seem to keep the distance between him and the destructive force of nature. Instead he immerses himself in it, not simply through philosophical detachment but through direct, physical contact. In the final shot, Winterbottom situates this ostensibly natural space within the frame of the refugee camp, itself a creation of international organizations like the IRC. Here he (and by extension the viewer) must confront the misery of his human-made environment as well as the context of a global order that appears at once accessible to him through his study of English and use of cell phones and at the same time also impossibly, implacably distant. For Afghans, it is not simply a metaphysical exercise to confront the sublime. It is a matter of survival.

This transition from the *zabihah* to the river resembles a pillow shot in the manner of Yasujiro Ozu, a visual non sequitur detached from the previous action. But unlike Ozu's motionless camera, Winterbottom's pillow shots are, like the scenes they punctuate, never still. His camera is constantly on the move, ranging in and out of crowds that are themselves in flux. Jamal and Enayat both stand apart from these crowds and become lost in them. Winterbottom represents the men of Peshawar like a cubist, desperate to envision the human form from all possible angles at once. In doing so, he rewrites the "cosmopolitan script" of travel, challenging the idea of fixed categories and most especially the relationship between subject and object, viewer and viewed. The film does not constitute meaning through a steady progression from ignorance to wisdom, lack of vision to true sight, but instead through a fragmentation that sustains itself.[9] Reality is the brown river and the street, never the same, never abiding, with no destination or source that can be seen. Any attempts at classification, the scientific bedrock of imperial domination, seem utterly futile.

Despite such aestheticism, the film remains grounded in the material conditions of its subjects. This frustrates a cosmopolitan tendency to view the idea of migrancy as a revelatory epistemological breakthrough, a liberating insight into the contingency of reality. Exponents of this position often simply appropriate and intellectualize the experience of refugees and migrants to better philosophize upon such abstractions as cultural difference and modernity. As Terry Eagleton has observed, "One is allowed to talk about cultural difference, but not—or not much—about economic exploitation."[10] Winterbottom, on the other hand, talks about it a great deal. The goal of his film appears to be a movement past romanticism and intellectualization to a deeply felt human connection with the reasons for why these people must live in the conditions that they do.

The typical consumers of road movies live in an environment where travel is a privilege, an opportunity for the rich and powerful. No such luxuries exist for the film's Afghans. They cannot possess or even interpret the scenes unwinding before their eyes. They do not travel in the Western sense. They struggle, they suffer, they endure. For Jamal and Enayat, travel is a necessity, a matter of life and death that highlights their inferior, object position in global politics and economics.

Winterbottom critiques this inequity by deconstructing what Mary Louise Pratt has called the "balcony vantage point."[11] In her book *Imperial Eyes: Travel and Transculturation,* Pratt discusses the work of several travel writers, including Alberto Moravia and Paul Theroux, who transfer their panoptic visuality to "the balconies of hotels in big third-world cities."[12] Although they are not natives of the cities they are describing (they are, in fact, transient tourists), they still feel empowered to pronounce upon what they are seeing and its meaning in the most authoritative language. In the wake of decolonization, these writers tended to view the developing world with contempt, if only because it was slipping from their grasp. Nevertheless, a continuity exists between how they limn the city they are observing and how it was evoked by earlier, triumphalist travel writers, penning their works in the heyday of empire.

One can view the "balcony vantage point," then, as the modern promontory, not unlike the position of the figure in Friedrich's painting. Whoever occupies such a position becomes de facto omniscient and omnipotent. The world appears more or less as a chaotic mist from which the observer constitutes an ordered and visible object. The epistemological relevance lies not in what is being described. Rather it resides in the ability of the writer to place him- or herself in that position that validates the account. Because they are there, we are simply to trust in their powers to relate to us what that place is really like.

In This World calls this privileged observer status into question in a scene that immediately follows the two Afghans' arrival in Istanbul. Here it is an Afghan, Enayat, who inhabits the balcony in a city that literally bridges the gap between East and West. We see him from behind, framed by the door to the outside, looking down at the street. Before him stand a series of walls, windows, clotheslines, and buildings the color of dishwater. Assuming his viewpoint, the camera peers downward onto the brick-cobbled street corner. Two men stand talking as boys and a man with a wagon pass by. Then the gaze shifts to a pair of colorfully dressed, Western-looking girls strolling down the litter-strewn street, their bright clothes juxtaposed with the soggy, gray browns of the surrounding walls. We see a close-up of Enayat's face in profile, a dreary cityscape beside and behind him like a Renaissance painting's window to the world. But he does not focus on the dreariness of the neighborhood. Instead the camera descends to the street to watch what catches his eye: a boy playing soccer with his friends. In an abrupt jump cut, Enayat suddenly appears down there with them, playing along.

This sequence acts in diametric opposition to the "white man's lament" of modern travel writers. Rather than focusing on the squalor, Enayat (and we) dwell on the lives of the people there, not as depersonalized parts of a crowd but as individuals, wrapped up in their lives, in the slow unwinding of a day and its slipping into dusk. His gaze, at first clearly positioned in that promontory perch, is able to do what many of the writers Pratt discusses cannot (or will not) do: It descends into the street, at first as mere observer but then as participant. No separation exists any longer between Enayat and the people he watches. He becomes one of them, playing with them, talking to them. The dismal tones of the slum dwellings give way to sunset reds that suffuse the scene in peaceful, joyous colors. The final cut to the Blue Mosque, one of the most beautiful buildings in Istanbul, is the natural outcome of Enayat's observations. He doesn't even actually see the building but rather feels it through his own visual (and spiritual) experience. The mosque becomes the beauty, the solidarity, the resonance with community and history that are his now, predicated on a way of seeing that remains deeply inimical and inconceivable to the standard "balcony vantage point" mentality of modern, Western travelers. It is the most revelatory, insurgent moment in the film—a glimmer of light and hope before the film's descent into terror and suffering.

Afghanistan Discovers the West

At the beginning of Joseph Conrad's *Heart of Darkness,* his narrator Marlowe observes that London is "one of the dark places of the earth." This begs the question: Just what is Conrad referring to in his title? Is it the Congo or England?

The quest of Jamal and Enayat helps clarify the issue. After they begin their journey, their first stop is Quetta. There the two Afghans walk into a tailor's shop with a barefoot man operating an antique sewing machine, the image a shorthand for developing world color. But right behind him, on the wall, are pictures of George Bush, Tony Blair, Osama bin Laden, and the World Trade Center in flames. Unlike the United States, this impoverished part of the globe cannot afford to ignore world events. After all, these people are on the receiving end of most of them.

As the Afghans journey farther west, such foreboding signs become more prevalent, mirroring the passage of Marlowe down the Congo River. For Conrad's narrator, the environment grows increasingly threatening, the landscape more primeval and inscrutable. Even so, there is little difference between Outer and Inner Station. Both embody the chaotic, irrational, and savage impulses that infect both the native inhabitants and their colonizers. *In This World,* on the other hand, shows a different kind of darkness, the kind that hides itself behind the lies Marlowe tells to Kurtz's Intended. Although its scattered traces are omnipresent, it takes a determined, honest observer to put them together. The Swedish writer Sven Lindqvist writes of such savagery: "It is not knowledge we lack. What is missing is the courage to understand what we know and draw conclusions."[13]

With each step Jamal and Enayat take, the contrast between the life of Shamshatoo camp and the rest of the world becomes more marked. On the road to Iran, this manifests itself in the perplexing image of a bombed truck on the side of a road, similar to Marlowe's encounter with the Outer Station and its slaves and decaying machinery. In a reversal of Conrad's narrative, however, the farther the Afghans move from the periphery, the more this chaos and violence will become sublimated, mystified, as will their own poverty. By linking the destination point, London, with the point of origin, Shamshatoo camp, Winterbottom implicates the West in a predatory relationship to the rest of the world, the cause of Afghanistan's effect. The real savagery lies not in the jungle of course—as Marlowe himself well knew—but in the whitewashed sepulchres of the colonial metropolis. As the Afghans soon learn, this link can only be discerned by connecting the two dots of East and West.

This system of exploitation threatens the two travelers as soon as they enter Iran. The first Iranian they meet, Behrooz, is initially shown poring over gay pornography on the internet. He speaks in English, a language that from now on the two will use with increasing frequency. Proceeding to chat up Jamal, Behrooz betrays a barely suppressed sexual interest in the young boy. Subsequently he demands pay for housing the Afghans even though they have already paid the smugglers in Pakistan. When he asks the two to take their clothes off, one anticipates the worst. Instead Behrooz demands a violation of a different type: that they change their Afghan clothes for more modern Iranian attire. Just as a corrupt border guard has stripped Enayat of his Walkman (a parting gift from his uncle), so now will both of them be forced to surrender the things that bind them to their ancestral way of life. "You have to be like an Iranian," Behrooz tells them. Taking their clothes he says, "This is bloody fucking shit. We don't need it anymore."

The simple moral of the episode is that Afghans living in the West are condemned to be whatever the West is not—unless of course they consent to sacrificing their identity. The traditional clothes must go, and the language must be left behind, used only in the home. Even their religion becomes a source of embarrassment and scorn. The refugees' desire to cling to culture while yearning for the benefits of modernity almost seems an affront to all the benevolence being extended to them. Being modern means being modern on the West's terms: accepting a total package of assimilation and renunciation. This is why in Tehran the camera lingers on a traffic island, surrounded by a black-and-white border, encircled by speeding cars. In the middle of it stands a lone palm tree, stunted, surrounded by barren sward. It lingers tenaciously in the midst of this modern city like the revenant of a dimly remembered past. In mosques its shape once conjured up the vision of paradise. Now it grows in the midst of urban sprawl, almost choked out of sight. Transculturation may exist, but it never undermines the balance of real power. There is no question of who owns the controlling share here. That's what the vast arsenals of the West are for.

It may seem strange that Iran, of all places, should be the first outpost of the West for these young Afghans. *In This World,* in fact, provides no easy answers as to where exactly the West begins and the East ends. Iran, far from being the draconian theocratic state portrayed in the U.S. media, here appears as the epitome of sophistication. In a few shots of Iranian girls, we see their hijabs as well as their sunglasses, jeans, and denim jackets. One has her hair dyed blonde. Similarly, there is little to distinguish Turkey from Trieste. Both have their trucking depots, industrial wastelands, and heavily trafficked streets with honking cars jostling for position.

Only when Jamal begins hawking trinkets at Italian cafés do we get an indication of the real arbiter of modernity: money. The more the film moves westward, the richer the cities look: cleaner, more expansive, more divorced from the material conditions that enable them. Like Orientalism, modernity appears to be not necessarily a purely Western concept but a floating signifier. It only acquires meaning in its relation to a fixed other, an illusion that *In This World* demystifies. As a result, such terms as *hybridity* and *modern* cease to have any real meaning. They are synonymous effects of a root cause that the film illustrates so indelibly: the web of global military and economic power.

Jamal and Enayat discover for us the defining truth of this web: that developing and developed worlds are one; that both Shamshatoo and London and everything else between them are all "in this world." When they finally come face-to-face with this reality, it is a terrifying vision of darkness. Nearing the border of Turkey, Jamal and Enayat huddle in the back of a truck on a road in the middle of nowhere. Poised behind the windshield, the camera fixates on the looming vastness of a mountain range. The road, completely devoid of any sign of life or movement, curves toward the mountains, shrouded by an impinging storm. Darkness crawls across the landscape like the tendrils of a slow-moving predator. Now and then, bolts of lightning punctuate its absolute blackness. This is where Asia meets Europe, where the intimations of a great darkness are suddenly not simply inferred but seen.

Next they must cross that darkness. Departing from a friendly Kurdish village with a local boy as guide, they make a perilous night crossing of the mountain. The scene begins with yet another antiromantic image: Enayat standing outside the home of their hosts, the mountains before him vast, implacable. He is not elevated above them, gazing from the standard promontory. Rather he stands with the villagers on a muddy road, looking away from the mountains at something we cannot see—tentative, patient, fragile.

The journey over the mountain itself, done in digital video with night vision, has the graininess of news footage, a clandestine sliver of reality. The effect nearly dematerializes the three figures, identifiable from the snow-covered rocks only because they are moving in stumbling slow motion. Far from being above nature, contemplating it from a safe distance, the Afghans are plunged into it, made one with barely recognizable shapes among them. Their voices are lost in the howl of the wind. In the nearly absolute darkness, a far-off city appears intermittently, shimmering, impossibly remote. The moving camera cannot hold the distant lights in its frame. They trail across the stygian canvas like a Jackson Pollock painting. The night vision achieves a new kind of clarity, illuminating the boys in negative-image white versus the wall of black to which they stumble—the bridge between two worlds.

Warned by men leading their horses across the same path, the boys crouch in the snow as a border patrol draws near. Below them, the city road dematerializes itself completely. A policeman emerges from the car and fires his gun into the air. The figures disintegrate, with the film giving way to frantic sound and the random chiaroscuro of city lights and mountain nothingness. Between the frames, there is no continuity, just jerking, frantic, stumbling movements that mirror the passage of Enayat and Jamal over the mountain. At first Enayat walks during the descent, his feet sinking into the snow, but finally the ordeal brings him to his hands and knees as he makes his way toward the now invisible city. This is the position demanded by the West for those who would see it as it is. They do not sail into a harbor, guns blazing. They simply crawl into a darkness. Before we see them reach their goal, the mountain appears again, immobile, an abstract silhouette against a deeper night.

For the Afghans, this redoubtable image reifies the West as metaphysical and physical boundary. Earlier in the journey, the first English words Jamal teaches Enayat are *mountain* and *snow,* providing a harrowing vision of what it means to cross the border between worlds, between the powerful and the powerless. Unlike the Romantic travelers who seek out the abyss and assert themselves over it, positing their reason and their civilization against the irrationality and savagery lying there in wait, the Afghans discover that the heart of darkness is also the heart of civilization.

The true moment of revelation and discovery comes soon afterward, when Jamal and Enayat endure their final journey together. Here the abyss reveals itself as not contiguous with modernity but intrinsic to it, the enactment of a globalized nightmare. To make the passage from Turkey to the West proper, the city of Trieste, they must submit to being locked inside a trailer and loaded on a ship for a nearly two-day trip. Here at last there is nothing to do, nothing to see, nothing to say. All that can be done is to wait. Winterbottom's camera captures their horror vividly as the air starts to give out and terrors rise. They are helpless and completely in the dark (literally and metaphorically) about where they are going and how long it will take. Devoid of visual, historical referents, the scene becomes archetypal, transcending the contemporary moment and arriving at its historical terminus: the transatlantic slave ship. Like the millions of African slaves in the past, these Central Asian refugees now pay a price for their passage that is at best servitude, at worst death.

In Trieste the past continues to fuse with the present, and the naked ugliness of money and power reveals itself in plain view. Jamal walks the streets with an African man, both of them peddling trinkets to tourists. Trying his best to raise some funds for the last leg of the journey, Jamal is rebuffed by one posh establishment after another, ejected by a tuxedoed mâitre d' and a blonde woman, stand-ins for Western elegance and glamour. He has no place in their rarefied atmosphere. Finally, out of desperation, he snatches a tourist's purse and buys a ticket to France.

To enter England, Jamal and his new friend, Yusef, must surrender themselves to speed, the liberating force that enables Western travelers to find themselves in new romantic landscapes. But for Jamal and other migrants, speed is a destabilizing, terrifying force completely beyond his control. From one city to the other, Jamal and Enayat have experienced the dizzying, disturbing power of speed and its alienating dissonance with their tribal way of life. Now, in this last passage, Jamal must surrender to it, crawling beneath a truck and letting invisible machines convey him to a destination he cannot foresee. His desperation has forced him into a bewildering tunnel with no light at the end, just the infinite stream of bulbs ticking off a distance he himself cannot measure. The film abruptly cuts to a squalid English pizzeria, with Jamal washing dishes there. With all the ordeals he had to endure, even this dismal existence is an improvement on the place from where he came.

The Kindness of Strangers

In This World is a film about the meaning of a global order that causes children to risk their lives—to even die—for jobs most Westerners would not even dream of doing. The refugee camp serves as the crucible of modernity. Just as it benefits from the technology and information the West produces, so, too, does it provide the raw materials—human and otherwise—that enable those benefits. This exchange is not "free trade," a give-and-take between equals, but a carefully managed system of exploitation. Sooner or later, however, out of the raw material of the dispossessed and desperate, wars are inevitably waged against the modern world and all that it stands for—as if that world were somehow different from their own.

Of course, material benefits exist for some of those who come searching for a "better life." Jamal seeks the light at the end of the Channel Tunnel and finds it. To compare even the worst part of London to the best part of Shamshatoo camp is to understand what it really means to live in the developing world. For some postcolonial theorists like Iain Chambers, the city emblematizes a liberating mélange of the rootless, the contingent, the dialogic.[14] But *In This World* takes a more critical view of the metropolis and its incarnations from Iran to England, highlighted by a series of shots that situate Jamal in a receding perspective of industrial buildings or market stalls, alienating him through an endless and impersonal monotony.

Nevertheless, *In This World* seeks to criticize not the Western city itself but the ideology fueling it. Modern morality, the ethos of the globalizing order, reduces men to packages on the back of a truck, of no more intrinsic worth than a crate of fruit. Throughout the film, this cynical and amoral materialism is challenged by a spirituality and communality that transcends language, class, or tradition. The simple and pious Enayat embodies these qualities. In the desert, amid a swirling dust storm, he kneels to God while Jamal simply watches. In the teeming Iranian city, he prays again while cars and pedestrians pass by apathetically. For Jamal, the discovery of the mosque comes only when he has completed his journey. There, among strangers who have perhaps undergone a similar ordeal, he finds a peace and community that is otherwise denied to him. The mosque represents a piece of home that has taken hold in the West, almost miraculously, as the West has taken hold of faraway Shamshatoo camp with its cell phones, videos, and blue jeans.

Continuities abound in the film, both negative and positive. The difference in kind lies in their propensity for coercion. The world itself is as a constant struggle between centripetal and centrifugal forces—human relations that either enslave or uplift. In the Kurdish village, the Afghans encounter the first caring community outside their own. The mother of the family pets Jamal's head affectionately when he walks in her door, expressing her pity for him and invoking God's blessing. Later the little boy who will be their guide across the mountains buys Jamal a new pair of shoes. Here they can play soccer again, talk to children, and experience genuine empathy and kindness. When they depart, the young women see them off with a burning *espand,* waving the smoke at them for good fortune. These people, also without a state of their own, can understand the position and the plight of these two young Afghans. Winterbottom, in his turn, sees beyond the decrepit shacks in which they live and the muddy streets they walk to reveal their dignity and humanity. If there is an answer to the abyss that kills Enayat, it lies within the heart of this simple Kurdish woman and her family.

Children Looking into the Camera

In This World never reveals Afghanistan as a geographic and political territory. It doesn't have to. Afghanistan is not simply a place but a calamity, a situation, a diaspora. All of the films previously made about Afghanistan or Afghans focused, often very narrowly, on specific events within the country. All of them were predominated by a coercive way of seeing, no matter what the provenance of the film. But here Afghanistan emerges all the more forcefully through its connection with the rest of the world. It appears not simply as a series of marvels and exotica—of burqas and mullahs, machine guns and mosques—but as a collection of individual human beings who, in the midst of terrible suffering, long for dignity and freedom from fear and want. Far from being a closed-off primitive island, Afghanistan is implicated in a global savagery that in many ways dwarfs as well as enables the homegrown kind. The courage of the film lies in its ability to peer past the politics and ideology, the history and the religion, to meet these two Afghans on their own terms. It presents a new way of traveling and learning.

Winterbottom and screenwriter Tony Grisoni first made this journey themselves, scouting out locations. They rode on the back of trucks, underwent interrogations at checkpoints, met with refugees and migrants, and witnessed Afghans demonstrating against the U.S. bombing of their homeland. When shooting began, the two Afghan leads (real names Jamal and Enayatullah) played themselves. "The film," Winterbottom said, "is a fiction. They are acting the journey." But it is also true, he stated, that "it is a document of the journey we organized. . . . We weren't trying to get them to pretend to be anything other than what they were."[15] There was no script for the actors, who themselves were not professionals but ordinary Afghans living in Peshawar. Winterbottom and his crew simply described the situation and let the two behave within that framework in whatever way they chose. Thus the film is itself the product of the very hybridity that it seeks to represent. For this reason, *In This World* conveys something powerful, truthful, and real about Afghanistan.

A strange thing happens at the end of the film. Jamal has made his way to England. He then calls Enayat's father and tells him that his son is dead. A moment of despair, of hopeless defeat in the face of insurmountable power, appears to conclude Enayat and Jamal's story. And then suddenly the scene changes, returning to Pakistan, to the same camp that was the boys' point of departure. Here are all the little Sharbat Gulas that never made it to the cover of *National Geographic*. The children crowd around, curious, staring into the camera. Some of them glare; some shyly turn away. Knowing they are being filmed, the girls turn out in their best dresses, which glimmer in the sunlight. One little one stares from a doorway with a friend or sister. Her companion rubs the girl's shaved head, causing a smile. This is the last image we have of the camp. Winterbottom explained that the purpose of these shots was to show that Afghans were "just as interested in us as we are in them."[16] Not long after Winterbottom finished production, Jamal again made the same journey he had previously made on film, this time reenacting the journey in earnest. Like the character he portrayed, the Afghan boy from Peshawar made for London, where he sought asylum. Life mirrors art, which mirrors life.

Daring to view Afghanistan and its people in such a way takes profound courage and compassion. It necessitates a letting go of one's self and one's eyes and letting the Other direct you, revealing elements of him- and herself to you that otherwise would never be seen. To do so implies the terrifying but liberating belief that it is altogether necessary not simply to see but to be seen, not just to discover but to be discovered. *In This World* stands as a perfectly realized representation of Afghanistan for just this one very human sentiment.

7 The Poetry of Silence

Ellipsis

Films like *Kandahar* and *Osama* played important parts in creating a visual discourse that, whether inadvertently or not, legitimized the war in Afghanistan that began on October 7, 2001. Like its cinematic counterparts, the televised bombardment of Kabul and other cities provided a blitz of antinarrative, a spectacle in every sense of the word, replete with explosions,

Afghanistan Unveiled: Gul Afrooz crosses the border.

crowds cheering their American liberators, and, most important, one Afghan woman after another lifting her blue burqa.

Thus *Kandahar*'s obsession with the burqa finds its way to the cover of *Time*'s December 3, 2001, issue, one among many that furnished photographs of women "lifting the veil." *Time*'s version shows a woman named Saliha staring into the camera with a confident smile. The cover story title says it all: "About Face." The light shining on that face draws attention to her eyes, while darkness obscures the hijab she still wears. Saliha provides a mirror image to the Sharbat Gula of *National Geographic*. Here the Afghan woman, liberated and yet still submissive, dutifully avoids the confrontational, defiantly direct contact with our own eyes. Inside, the copy cannot compete with the persuasiveness of the photographs: a two-page spread of veiled women preceding another of a mother's face, now exposed to view, as she stares into the eyes of her daughter. The accompanying captions are either redundant or misleading.[1]

Cinematic spectacles are likewise very much "about face," providing a feast for the eyes while allowing viewers to bypass their critical faculties. One has only to think of the mindless summer movies whose sole purpose appears to be to delight gut and groin while avoiding not just great ideas but any ideas whatsoever. American director Howard Hawks summed up this worldview perfectly when he said, "I never made a statement. Our job is to make entertainment. I don't give a damn about taking sides."[2] Of course, Hawks's films, like anyone's, are rank with ideology. All art, and thus all cinema, is political, whether it addresses the world and its problems or flees from them. But the genius of spectacle lies in its ability to mystify this reality by exploiting the very nature and power of images.

We have a host of presuppositions about photographs: "The camera never lies," "a picture is worth a thousand words," and so on, which testify to the camera's ability to somehow capture the essence of the real. Photographs, not pencil sketches or oil paintings, are admissible evidence in murder trials. That these images, especially now, can be (and have been) altered in innumerable ways does not negate the power of the photographic and cinematic image to construct reality. Whether it be the cinema, entertainment television, the news media, or advertisements, all employ a relatively coherent language of visual persuasion that more often than not is used to sell us something. In the case of Afghanistan, this visual language promoted the multibillion-dollar U.S. intervention there in much the same way that advertisers sell the public on any other new product that they don't in fact need.

The cinematic spectacle is a direct corollary of the commercial. In many ways they are identical, very frequently employing the same professionals, including directors and actors. Advertising's appropriation of the photograph and of cinema has led to new kinds of discourse that seem to transcend logic, in which images supersede narrative, rendering it meaningless. Thus the diptych of veiled/unveiled Afghan woman becomes "something which simply happens, shows forth, but that can't be told."[3] How does one argue with the image of an Afghan woman unveiling? As Neil Postman noticed, this kind of commercial, persuasive visuality cannot be addressed by a logic that deals with written or spoken language. Rather it places these images beyond logic and into the world of aesthetics.[4] The question becomes not "Is it true/valid/cogent?" but "Do I like it (enough to buy it)?"

Few Americans in the fall of 2001 were concerned with any kind of warranty on the Afghan war they'd just purchased. Thus film critic Richard Schickel's review of *Kandahar* (propelled to international fame by the U.S. bombardment) enthused over the film's "gorgeous" and "lovely" imagery. For him, the ultimate burqa film was a "primitive and sophisticated . . . near documentary" that "achieves moments of something akin to aesthetic bliss."[5] Such gorgeous displays exist for their own sake, obviating any criticism. They are true because they are beautiful, because they please us, or because we want to buy them.

A Dissident Voice

The scarcity of knowledge regarding Afghanistan left a vacuum quickly filled by this persuasive language of consumable images. Whatever ethnographic and historical knowledge Americans did not acquire from *The Kite Runner,* the mainstream media furnished them through accounts characterized by an astonishing lack of critical inquiry. Certainly no one could mourn the Taliban's passing (if they had indeed passed on), but neither could the public, so embroiled in the antilogical spectacle of Afghanistan's "unveiling," find the means to ask what should happen next. None of the media provided information to contextualize, historicize, contradict, or complicate the visual "narrative" of Islamic fundamentalist terror and misogyny being defeated by enlightened Marines and feminists. The conflict was so defined by these tropes that, typical of spectacle, nothing existed outside the frame.

Once the war in Iraq commenced and Afghanistan receded from the headlines, a multitude of documentaries ensured continued domestic support for the Afghan war from the liberal intelligentsia, who had proved such stalwart supporters from the beginning. Of these films, *Afghanistan Unveiled* (which aired on PBS in 2004) was the most accomplished. Shot by three young Afghan women, the short film paints a harrowing picture of their country after the defeat of the Taliban. Yet after following these native informants into the Afghan heartland, the viewer can be reassured of the postinvasion progress. Despite the fact that all three girls wear the hijab, they still dare to trade barbs with crowds of men, dispute the Qur'an with them, and discuss their plans for a brighter future. Sometimes they inadvertently stumble on some embarrassing information, such as when a young widow mentions how U.S. bombs killed her husband. More typically, however, they keep the narrative upbeat, enthusing about the Taliban's fall as they venture once more into a brave, new world.

The documentary's optimistic rhetoric dwells exclusively on the new and improved status of women in the country. More important, it focuses on young Kabulis, educated urbanites whose security depends on the presence of foreign soldiers. These young women, of all those in Afghanistan, were therefore the ones who would most likely accept not only Western values but also intervention. Although there is much of interest in the film, the fact that it was funded by the U.S. State Department should be duly noted.

Naturally in the absence of any other information, one might conclude (invalidly) that these young women speak for all Afghan women and that like the rest of U.S. history (as exemplified by the pabulum of our high school textbooks) the Afghan war involved a march of progress from hardship to success, from ignorance to wisdom, from war to victory. Certainly media coverage, as well as films on Afghanistan, all seemed to echo this hopeful but ultimately uncritical view.

All except one: *Seh Noqta* (*Ellipsis* or, literally, *Three Dots*), released the same year as *Afghanistan Unveiled*. *Ellipsis* is the debut effort of Roya Sadat, the first female director in Afghan cinematic history. A native of Herat, she was born in 1981, during the height of the Russian war. Surviving the conflicts of that period and the later depredations of the Taliban, Sadat taught herself filmmaking by reading a book by Hollywood screenwriting guru Syd Fields, translated into Farsi. After the success of *Osama,* she received two thousand dollars and assistance from Siddiq Barmak (who hired her as a scriptwriter for two short films) as well as Japanese television.[6] Despite such generosity, she was still forced to film *Ellipsis* in low-grade digital video during a shoot that lasted less than two weeks. The finished product, although at times crude in material and technique, nevertheless provides a much-needed palliative to discourse on Afghanistan in the West. It is not surprising, therefore, that the film remains largely unknown.

The narrative centers on Gul Afrooz, a young widow who is so desperately poor that she must become a drug courier for the local warlord in order to gain medical treatment for her sick child. After failing in every way to circumvent the warlord's machinations, she eventually crosses the border into Iran, where police quickly apprehend and incarcerate her—for life. The bleak storyline superficially resembles many other tales of Afghan abjection. But unlike so many of them, *Ellipsis* offers an antispectacle that thrusts the viewer into the world of historical contingency to finally face the challenge of continued Afghan suffering.

To begin an analysis of *Ellipsis,* it makes sense to ascertain what it is not, compared to other films like *Kandahar* and *Osama.* For one thing, it's not a "burqa film." The *chadari* makes only one brief and bitterly ironic appearance when a child bride is married off to a leering, middle-aged stooge of the local warlord. Instead of the U.S. military, her new husband "lifts the veil" this time, revealing tears of grief, not joy. Here, in the dusty wilderness far removed from Kabul and President Hamid Karzai's besieged government, gender oppression continues, enabled by the American government's support of warlords who continue the misogyny where the Taliban left off.

In a sense, *Ellipsis* is the sequel to *Osama.* The latter picture clamored for international intervention, depicting a nation gone mad, in desperate need of a savior. Sadat's film shows the even more horrible moment after the apocalypse. And in that aftermath, when the world should be transformed and the great evil shaken to its very foundations, we find that instead nothing has changed. Women and men continue to live miserable lives of deprivation and heartbreak. Against a barren monotone of dust, Gul Afrooz and the other Afghans assert themselves with a desperation that punctuates, defiantly, the unremitting emptiness of the wasteland they inhabit.

Sadat refuses to subject this bleak environment to the aestheticization of spectacle. Using every neorealist trick in the book, she consistently undermines the essentializing expectations of an Orientalizing gaze. In one early scene, night has come to Gul Afrooz's village. For most of the day, she has been employed baking and delivering bread to the local warlord's compound. One initially incomprehensible act, locking the bread inside her home where her children cannot reach it, only becomes sensible later in the film as the children share a stale piece of naan. When her son splits the morsel left to them, it makes a loud and dismal cracking sound. The realization that these people are starving necessarily spoils the previous sense of the picturesque achieved while watching their mother bake bread at a nearly prehistoric-looking oven or transporting the huge sheaves on her head to the warlord. These Afghans do not simply form part of the mise-en-scène. Beyond our vision, inside them, something horrible is happening.

At the end of the day, Gul Afrooz returns home to finally feed her ravenous children. In the interior, the only illumination comes from a tiny lantern and a small open-air furnace. There Gul Afrooz bakes the bread for her family, slapping the dough on a tarnished and battered metal plate, flames licking her fingers, wizened beyond her age. There is no time for banter, no time for anything but work. Her children are waiting outside in the night to be fed. The dim but lambent light of the fire resembles the mystic, solemn quality of a Georges de La Tour painting. She watches the flame quietly, the silence disrupted only by the sound of her hand slapping the dough. For Afghans like her, the fireside does not offer a site of warmth or comfort but simply the means to (barely) live for another day.

The woman named Gul Afrooz (the film uses her real name) clearly *knows* the ritual. One can see it in the way her hands expertly slap the dough, avoiding the open flames. Her eyes, reflecting the glimmering oven, are distant, exhausted. There is no joy, but there are no tears of self-pity either. Watching her watch the fire, one feels the weight of many nights such as this that have passed and many more that shall come, struggling one last moment that her children might live. In *Ellipsis* one cannot witness such grinding poverty without constantly being redirected to the contexts that underlie it: the warlord's luxury, drought, drug addiction, war.

Too often Western viewers are able to detach from the suffering they see. The possibility of this detachment has historically compromised realism as an artistic method. While admirably striving to show the dignity of common people as well as the seriousness of their economic oppression, the beauty of nineteenth-century realist art often diluted its call to action. The most obvious illustration would be Jean-François Millet's *The Gleaners,* which depicts three French peasant women picking up the remains of the harvest. In the painting, the peasants' backs bend in harmony, frozen in a composition that, while showing the poverty of the women, also manages to make it beautiful. The gleaners and their desperation become something lovely, something to be passively watched and enjoyed. It would take later realist artists and photographers like Jacob Riis and Lewis Hine to more accurately document the misery of economic oppression with starker, unromantic eyes.

Ellipsis follows in their footsteps. In one such instance, Gul Afrooz goes into the desert surrounding her village, using a long knife to cut thorny scrub brush from the rocky ground. But this woman does not simply stoop above the earth, a frozen spectacle to be enjoyed. Rather, a series of jump cuts show her hacking away at brush, standing up, throwing more bushes on a pile, nursing a pricked finger. This is a gleaner who moves, who toils, whose back aches and whose fingers sting with pain. The young widow bows to her work with no visible ground line to frame her. Instead, the desert appears to stretch behind her infinitely, the only demarcations of space being a mother and child idly watching her in the distance.

The barren landscape provides a fitting metaphor for what Afghanistan has become. Nothing transpires here except unremitting work in the face of death, actions in a void, emptiness within emptiness. In terms of visual pleasure, there is nothing of interest here, just the dust-covered monotone of dirt and village dwellings. It looks like a ghost town, yet *Ellipsis* reminds us that people actually inhabit this terrifyingly lonely place. They are not actors, and they pay little heed to the intrusion of a film crew in their midst. As the narrative progresses, the villagers' lives go on unimpeded in the periphery. Now and then, they interrupt the story's action as the camera stops to focus on them for a fleeting moment. An errant child kicks the dust. A woman with bare feet burned and cracked almost beyond recognition tears water from a well, rimmed by a rubber tire. Such a place reduces everything and everyone to the barest essence, to whatever is necessary for survival. Even the mosque has no walls, only a grandiose mihrab, shining absurdly white against the dusty brown background.

Other filmmakers have artificially created sets that bear this minimalist stamp. Carl Dreyer, the director of *La Passion de Jeanne d'Arc* (1928), stripped his interiors to their barest, whitewashed essence and isolated faces from bodies in extreme close-up in order to probe into the soul of his characters. Similarly, Sadat has stated that her goal was to "express people in a way they cannot express themselves."[7] Thus she employs a number of arresting close-ups of Gul Afrooz, almost Dreyer-like in their stark and elegant power. Such shots tend to invite voice-over narration, allowing us to get into the character's inner world while providing a breathing space in the narrative. But here, the voice-over, paradoxically, can be heard only in its utter silence, as wordless intertitles punctuating the visual. There are no words, after all, to contain the enormity of what this widow (and by extension her nation) has seen and experienced. Instead we simply have only her image to contemplate, most powerfully in one scene in which Gul Afrooz stares through a tiny window devoid of glass. The dark interior frames her face, while we are submerged within, watching her as she glances inside, hoping to see something. Maybe it's simply food. Or maybe it's another set of eyes—our own—that can return her gaze and step outside to welcome her.

In its pure expressiveness, this iconic presentation of the young mother obviates the need for mediation, connecting the spectator directly with a truth that it at once reflects as well as embodies. To see Gul Afrooz cradling her dying son in her arms toward the film's conclusion is to witness a living, breathing Pietà. Shortly thereafter, the mother and child ride into the desert on a donkey, accompanied by an older man, both drug runner and guide. It looks for all the world like a Christmas card, an Afghan "Flight into

Egypt." Except here the mother and child, rather than fleeing from death and imprisonment, are propelled toward it, into Iran. In *Ellipsis* the Magi (who were Persian Zoroastrian priests) are modern-day Iranian police who bring no gifts. Instead they throw the mother in prison and bear away her screaming child.

Of course this Christian story also belongs to Islam. The Qur'an itself describes the nativity of Jesus in a sura entitled "Mary" (Q. 19:16–34). Iconically, however, *Ellipsis* portrays a new kind of Passion, similar to that of Joan in Dreyer's film, where the familiar story of suffering appears without its concurrent redemption. Whether Sadat intended to employ imagery familiar to a Christian audience, she succeeded in establishing a link between two worlds and faiths, a spiritual expressionism rooted firmly in the material world. Like those of a Byzantine icon, the eyes of Gul Afrooz confound any attempts to view her or her story as simply art. Instead they draw the viewer into a desperate and distant world bound by and within our own.

Watching Afghan Women

In March 2007, as the war in Iraq continued to claim Iraqi and American lives alike, the newly elected Democratic majority in the U.S. Congress issued its proposal for troop withdrawal. Their stated aim was to "redirect more of our resources to the war against al Qaeda and the Taliban in Afghanistan, fighting the right war in the right place against the people who attacked us," although none of the Taliban nor any Afghans for that matter had anything to do with attacking the United States.[8] *The Nation*, a bastion of liberal opinion, early on averred that the Afghan war was the "first just war since World War II."[9] Conservative pundits were quick to observe the left's curious propensity for protesting the Iraq occupation while championing a similar occupation of Afghanistan.[10]

Such unflinching support ignores the fact that U.S. and other troops in Afghanistan committed crimes similar to those in Iraq, including killing civilian road crews in Nuristan, bombing wedding parties, and supervising the live burials of hundreds of prisoners of war.[11] With the onset of hostilities, American depleted uranium rounds almost immediately began impacting Afghans' health and safety.[12] Elsewhere the mismanagement and outright fraud perpetrated by foreign contractors have been matched only by Afghans' growing despair over the corruption of their own government.[13] The combined picture suggests the nation as a whole fared little better than it did during the Taliban era.

Consequently, large demonstrations occurred throughout Afghanistan with increasing frequency, reflecting the Afghans' concern for their safety as well as their anger at the arrogance and indifference of the soldiers ostensibly deployed there for their welfare. Many joined insurgent groups—not all of which are Taliban-oriented—seeking nothing more than to eject yet another round of foreign invaders who have killed or maimed their families.[14] Others hoped the Americans would stay if only to forestall another civil war that they have enabled, indeed incubated, ever since 1989.

To build political support for the invasion, policy makers initiated a long-standing propaganda campaign to unite right-wing militarism with the sentiments of American progressives. Their efforts were effective in pitching the war in Afghanistan not as a struggle for strategic positioning in Central Asia, with its vast energy resources and proximity to all of America's potential rivals (China, Russia, Iran, India), but as a war of liberation, most especially a liberation of Afghan women.

The media followed their lead, enlisting some of the most eminent feminist writers as celebrity endorsers of American imperialism. These included Margaret Atwood, who stated in a *New York Times Magazine* essay that *The Handmaid's Tale* (notorious for its depiction of a patriarchal police state) was in part inspired by prewar Afghanistan, which she limns by focusing on its most primitive and stereotypical features: *buzkashi,* "'Arabian Nights' dwellings," and, of course, the *chadari* (which she mistakenly refers to as the "chador"). Showing little more than a tourist's knowledge of Afghanistan, Atwood pontificates on the nature of her purple *chadari* (bought as a novelty) by saying it turns her "into negative space, a blank in the visual field, a sort of antimatter." By ignoring the past thirty years of history, she equates the meaning of the burqa today to its meaning in the 1970s, essentializing Afghanistan as a permanently benighted and misogynistic place in time-honored Orientalist fashion.[15]

Other feminist writers and organizations eagerly climbed on the anti-Taliban bandwagon, especially after the efforts of the Feminist Majority and its celebrity endorsers succeeded in making it a public issue even before 9/11. The organization would later take credit for liberating Afghan women after the invasion, angering Afghan members of the Revolutionary Association of Afghan Women (RAWA), who, unlike their American counterparts, had actually been working in the country for years, risking their lives to further the same goal.[16] Within months of the U.S. invasion, Afghan women became a media cottage industry. Through films like *Kandahar* and books like *My Forbidden Face* to Feminist Majority campaigns to end Afghan "gender apartheid," the Afghan woman (and the developing world Muslim woman she represents) has been developed into a "Blue Burqa" brand, referring to the slew of books and films that have used nearly identical images of faceless women in blue *chadaris*.[17]

In seeking to draw attention to the plight of Afghan women, Western media have done their share of "epistemic violence" by objectifying them as victims needing to be rescued.[18] As with most Western representations of the Islamic world, the "Blue Burqa" exists outside any historical context, simplifying the nature of patriarchy in Afghanistan by ignoring the ways in which gender, race, religion, and class are shaped not only by conflicting views within their society but also by the globalizing forces of the West. These accounts portray Western secular feminism as the model of female liberation that all Afghan women need to emulate, whether they want to or not. On the other hand, Islam frequently appears as a monolithic entity assumed to be inimical to the interests of Afghan women.[19] Such rhetoric reveals a profound ignorance of Afghan mores or the potential of Islam to generate its own social critiques. Afghan women activists themselves, on the other hand, understand that "arguments based on principles of universal human rights or on what international conventions say don't persuade many Afghans to support reforms. . . . Only religious arguments hold sway."[20]

The narrative of *Ellipsis* uses its own kind of visual rhetoric to also suggest that the ongoing agency of Afghan women (and men) "is not exhausted by their victimization in patriarchal and misogynist contexts."[21] When compared with *Osama*'s vision of cloistered women, imprisoned in their own homes, Gul Afrooz does indeed seem liberated. She has the freedom to move, to allow her hair to escape from beneath her chador, to walk unaccompanied by a man, to work outside the home. Similarly, other women in the village work alongside her, sewing, caring for their children, making flour. If anything characterizes this Afghan woman, it is not passivity but rigorous labor, whether it be fetching water from a well or stream, delivering bread to the warlord, feeding her children, cutting down scrub brush, begging for food from friends, tending the oven fire, or, ultimately, trekking to Iran loaded with opium. She does not simply stay at home, under parda. She cannot afford to do that, for her sake or her children's.

Despite this validation of female agency, Sadat does not shirk from portraying the many ways in which predatory males destroy women's lives. The Afghanistan of *Ellipsis* remains a place where men can do with women what they wish, a place where money buys the mullah's conscience and children are sold like slaves to leering middle-aged husbands. If women are the ones who do all the work, then most men in *Ellipsis* seem to do little more than gratify their own sensual desires. When Gul Afrooz attempts to resist their control, one of the khan's thugs reminds her, "You don't know whose dog you are and where you eat from." Immediately after this scene, the film cuts to the desert where five girls sing a folk song about marriage. The destabilizing movement of the camera, the close-ups, and the empty backgrounds all position the girls in a liminal setting where past meets future, childhood anxiety encounters the wisdom of age, and men (and women) are forced to question the repressive worldviews they uphold:

> Girls pick flowers but don't smell them.
> Stay in fathers' homes! Don't get husbands!
> Fathers give us wheat bread
> But husbands sting us like scorpions.
> Oh, father I'm a good girl!
> Don't marry me off to an old man
> As I am young, with black hair.
> Don't marry me off to an old man
> Or I will be banished from my family.
> I will go mad in far-off, black mountains.
>
> You married me off far-away.
> I was not content but you did it by force.
> I didn't agree but it was my fate.
> You used me as firewood in this furnace.

This scene makes it clear that tradition is never simply the provenance of men. Women have their say as well. They craft folk songs like this one, laments that by their very existence testify to their powerful presence within the traditional culture. Their criticism of marital customs and kinship taboos goes hand in hand with those practices themselves. Afghan women have opinions and desires that even children can articulate. They are not simply voiceless victims.

Along with depicting the harsh realities of child marriage and misogyny, *Ellipsis* shows that women themselves experience divided loyalties and that, regarding the oppressive conditions of patriarchy, "Women are produced by these relations as well as implicated in their formation."[22] The mother of Shir (one of Gul Afrooz's suitors) embodies this dividedness against herself. She appears in several scenes as both counselor and arbiter to her brutish son, scheming to get him the woman he so desires. As her pudgy fingers work incessantly at rolling cotton thread, she resembles a mythical fate weaver and cultural authority. Far from a veiled victim, Shir's mother ruthlessly enforces hierarchy and protects privilege, in every way like a female counterpart of the warlord. It is she who colludes with the khan and her son to once again compel Gul Afrooz into an unwanted marriage, one that will force her (because of custom) to abandon her own children. Through this kind of collaboration, Shir's mother becomes a comprador colonized from within, and a reminder that patriarchy is a cooperative enterprise.

These sorts of insights rarely see the light of day in mainstream discourse on the Islamic world, especially regarding Afghanistan. The film's vision of Afghan gender relations in fact drastically differs from that of the West, which (whether inadvertently or not) seeks to pit the sexes against each other there. This strategy has always been effective in driving a wedge through an otherwise united people. The French employed it in Algeria, the British in India. Identifying women as the exploited and their own husbands, brothers, and fathers as the exploiters allows the imperial power of the moment to divide and rule more effectively.

Ellipsis deconstructs this process in the film's most important scene, a flashback to Gul Afrooz's all-too-brief moment of happiness. Here she works not alone but with her betrothed, the young and handsome Firooz, as they build the wall of a house they shall someday inhabit together. Joy transfigures her usually careworn face. Gone is the black chador, the pallor of defeat in her face, the emptiness in her eyes. Here, in the past, she wears a bright green scarf, her hair freely showing beneath. She decorates her eyes with kohl and wears red lipstick, a deep red to match her vermilion folk dress. The richness of color mirrors the warmth between them. After dumping some mud on the wall, Gul Afrooz stands back to watch Firooz smooth it into shape. For the first time in the film, she is not at work. Her hands rest on the shovel's handle, her eyes lost in contemplation of her future husband. Returning to work, she suddenly, almost miraculously, smiles.

In one brief scene that lasts a total of three minutes, *Ellipsis* has done something extraordinary. It has shown us Afghan women happy with Afghan men. Unlike typical Western accounts of her country, which luridly dwell on child marriages or polygamy, Sadat portrays a youthful but mature couple, engaged by mutual consent and attraction. Firooz bears no resemblance to the typical turban-clad primitive of popular culture. He is attractive, clean-shaven, and wears a Western shirt to match Gul Afrooz's folk dress. The two truly marry the modern and traditional, bound together not just by the wall they construct (a future shaped by their own hands) but also by the reed flute Gul Afrooz hands her lover.

This musical instrument evokes the *Masnavi* of Jalaluddin Rumi, the thirteenth-century Afghan Sufi whose works are the best-selling poetry in twenty-first-century America.[23] The first section of Rumi's masterpiece of mystic verse is "The Song of the Reed," and its opening lines are famous throughout the Persian-speaking world: "Listen to this reed as it makes complaint, telling a tale of separation."[24] For Gul Afrooz, the separation soon comes when some strongmen abduct Firooz and her father. Watching his betrothed forcibly married to one of the khan's thugs, Firooz goes insane. He takes to wandering about the village, mindlessly playing the flute, a mute witness to the continued suffering of the woman he still loves.

The flashback alludes to the story of Majnun and Layla, two star-crossed lovers of Central Asian folklore. Many poets have adapted the tale, including the greatest names in Persian literature—Nizami, Jami (from Sadat's hometown of Herat), and Rumi himself. The story appears in the *Masnavi*, used there as a Sufi metaphor for a soul (Majnun) who extinguishes himself in contemplation of the divine (Layla). But Sadat uses the same story for a quite different purpose, albeit through the interpretative framework of what Fatemeh Keshavarz has called Rumi's "poetics of silence":

> In the poetic universe that Rumi builds . . . human beings realize and acknowledge the imperfection of their verbal medium of expression. Abstinence from self-expression through language will, it is hoped, cure us of the illusion that we possess a powerful, autonomous and exclusively human expressive tool. We will come to realize that our sense of freedom and independence is a self-delusion, for we are completely dependent for our inner experiences on the universe and the divine forces that created it.[25]

If Rumi's poetics of silence reveal the inherent constructivism of human knowledge, then Sadat uses that insight and the story of Majnun and Layla itself both to criticize patriarchy in her culture and to deconstruct the West's negative view of Afghan gender relations. In the silence of this scene, the rhetoric of Orientalism stands contradicted by the mythical lovers and their passion for each other, a political and cultural critique stemming not from Western humanism but from the most profound work of Muslim spirituality after the Qur'an. *Ellipsis* testifies to the ability of Afghans to furnish their own critiques of oppression from deep within their own spiritual and cultural traditions.

The Other Ground Zero

Like Marina Golbahari in *Osama*, Gul Afrooz had had no dramatic training when Roya Sadat discovered her. In the absence of a shooting script, she was free to improvise and subsequently invested a great deal of her own personality into the role. Unfortunately Gul Afrooz's decision to act in *Ellipsis* was met with extreme resistance by her husband, who would not allow her to participate in the project. Her response to him and other family members was at once horrifying and heroic: "If they prevent me, I will kill myself."[26] Evidently her husband took the threat seriously enough to cease his objections, instead demanding that he be present during her every scene and stipulating that his wife have no extended dialogues with men.

Like her lead, Roya Sadat also took risks making the film in the dangerous rural areas surrounding Herat. To minimize potential threats both to performers and to technicians, she shot the film clandestinely in only ten days. Despite this precaution, local tribal officials drove her and her crew from the village at gunpoint halfway through the production. "They said we were strangers and would have a negative influence on their women," Sadat later stated. "The clans had never seen a film team on which men and women work together."[27]

Such patriarchal values were by no means uncommon in that region of the country. In fact, once the Northern Alliance was given control of Afghanistan, they did little to change the repressive policies of the Taliban, with which they sympathized. These were, after all, the same fundamentalist warriors (also known as "freedom fighters" during the Ronald Reagan era) whose zealotry the United States had used to topple the Afghan communist regime. One such mujahedeen commander and former U.S. ally, Gulbuddin Hekmatyar, had begun his career in the early 1970s by throwing acid at the faces of unveiled women and later orchestrated the assassination of Meena, leader of the Revolutionary Association of Afghan Women.

On the opposite side of the political spectrum, Ismail Khan, who governed Herat from 1992 to 2004, instituted a number of draconian policies after the U.S. invasion that led one UN official to label Herat "the worst province for women in Afghanistan."[28] While being lauded in the Western press for such accomplishments as installing "traffic lights that drivers actually obey,"[29] the U.S.-backed warlord also banned coeducation and proclaimed that "it's better that [women] would be in their houses than going outside."[30] Women were forced to wear the *chadari* (a decree enforced by religious police), and those who appeared in public with men who were not their family members could be arrested and forced to submit to gynecologic exams to see if they had recently had intercourse. Ismail Khan's repressive policies resulted in two to three suicide attempts a week among young women. In one particularly horrific case, a fourteen-year-old Herati girl attempted suicide by immolation after she had been given in marriage to a sixty-year-old man with grown children.[31] President Karzai removed the governor from power in 2004, only to appoint him to the cabinet position of energy minister.

U.S. bombardment notwithstanding, Sadat obviously did not begin her project in an open atmosphere of liberation. "We are busy dealing with reality," she has said of her film, "which is unfortunately composed of misery, poverty and injustice."[32] This is the awful truth of *Ellipsis:* that nothing has changed. Women are still oppressed; the power of the gun trumps the power of law; and health care, education, and basic safety are still dim dreams. The only difference appears to be that Afghan women are now at the mercy of fundamentalists of a different stripe, backed not only by their own firepower but by that of a "deeply masculinized foreign institution, the U.S. military."[33] The media, meanwhile, continue to effuse over Afghan women's need for political clout, proffering political assurances that they are "on their way" to achieving it. But something is missing in this obsessive focus on empowerment, namely, a critique of the very concept of power itself.

In Afghanistan, as elsewhere, power means being at the top of a social and economic order that entails pain for the many and pleasure for the few. The film's widow, like so many unseen millions, has no mobility. She cannot simply up and leave, go to the city and get a job. There are no jobs. There aren't even many cities to speak of. They've been bombed out of existence. Materially, the khan holds complete sway. His compound is both factory and company store, an outpost of progress. Only there can Gul Afrooz acquire the medicine she needs to save her child from dying of pneumonia. But the khan does not simply give that medicine away. Instead he demands her complete and abject submission to him in exchange for her child's life. The baby is a thing, his life a commodity to exchange for another, in this case a bag of dope. Gone are the tribal loyalties, religious pieties, and nationalist sentiments that once formed the backbone of Afghan society. Now the amoral selfishness of the marketplace reigns supreme.

To finally identify and interrogate the system of oppression that holds her fast, Gul Afrooz must leave her village and cross into Iran. Between the two places lies an almost cosmic chasm. On arriving at the other side, she encounters the face of the enemy: a police car, blaring its red lights at the smugglers. The Afghans stand transfixed in its beams as a disembodied voice shouts one word at them: "Stop!"

The car seems to erupt out of the night. Its sudden appearance wrests us out of the timeless village of the Afghans and into the modern world, with its borders and security, its legal systems and prisons. In fact, these things more or less *are* the modern world, or at least all that people like Gul Afrooz can know of it. Such knowledge, however, comes with a steep price: imprisonment and the annihilation of her family. She has finally crossed the border to the other side of 9/11, where each village becomes a Ground Zero. Economic and military aggression wreak havoc daily. Living in their awful wake, Gul Afrooz sees the distinctions between East and West, private and public, political and personal vanish in a terrible epiphany, revealing the symbiosis between local patriarchal exploitation and a global economic enslavement that strips the young mother of everything that she loves. The film ends here, leaving us to fill the empty space between our own private and political ellipses. If we listen to those quiet, unfinished thoughts and intentional omissions, we might finally hear the still, small voice in the silence, telling us that to understand Afghanistan is to understand the world.

8 A Way to Feel Good Again

The Kite Runner

Khaled Hosseini's 2003 novel *The Kite Runner* was a sleeper of a book. Published only two years after the U.S. invasion of Afghanistan, it attracted a smattering of attention in the critical press when issued in hardcover. But in between its debut and its trade paperback publication, a plethora of Afghanistan tales fertilized the market, from the release of *Osama* to the onslaught of Afghanistan documentaries, historical novels, and burqa-clad women's memoirs. With the way paved, *The Kite Runner* achieved critical mass at an astonishing speed, spread by word of mouth through the reading circles of America. Hosseini's story soon appeared on the *New York Times* best-seller list in 2005 and stayed there for years to come.

Afghanistan in the Cinema: Hassan (Ahmad Khan Mahmoodzada) and Amir (Zekeria Ebrahimi) before the war

Almost overnight the book was adopted by universities, reprinted in several different editions (even an illustrated one), became the subject of numerous high school study guides, and inevitably inspired a Hollywood feature film. The book's success was so great that it allowed Hosseini, an Afghan American physician living in San Jose, California, to give up his medical practice for an even more lucrative career as a full-time author. His next work, *A Thousand Splendid Suns,* was published in 2007 to warm critical response and even warmer sales. It's not an exaggeration to say that *The Kite Runner* has become not only the single most important source of information on Afghanistan for American readers but also the most widely read American story ever written about the modern Islamic world.

The Kite Runner's appeal has a great deal to do with its thoroughly gripping plot, a tale of sin and fall, guilt and redemption. The two main characters are Amir and Hassan, two boys living in Afghanistan's capital in 1978. Amir belongs to the educated elite, his father (Baba) a Westernized and affluent Pashtun Afghan with enough clout to have Ahmad Zahir play at his son's birthday. Hassan, on the other hand, is their servant's son, a Hazara and thus the victim of both racial and religious prejudice (the majority of Hazaras are Shias as opposed to the mostly Sunni Pashtuns). Amir and Hassan nevertheless ignore these differences and join together in a variety of boyhood pastimes, from reading Ferdowsi's book of Persian legends, the *Shahnameh,* to flying kites in spectacular competitions. After the two friends win the citywide kite-fighting contest, a vicious Pashtun boy named Assef corners Hassan and rapes him. Amir, who witnesses the terrible crime from a distance, does nothing to stop it.

Tormented by the memory of his cowardice and guilt, he eventually drives Hassan and his father from his home, only to lose that home himself when the Russians invade. Baba and the child flee Afghanistan, settling in Fremont, California (the largest community of Afghans in the United States). There Amir becomes an American, marries Soraya, the beautiful daughter of an Afghan general in exile, and comes into his own as a storyteller, eventually achieving success as a writer of fiction. His father, on the other hand, cannot adapt to Western ways and soon succumbs to cancer. As the immigrant narrative reaches its conclusion, Baba's friend summons Amir back to Afghanistan to save Sohrab, the son of his old and much-maligned friend Hassan. Stealing into Taliban country in disguise, Amir finds the child in the clutches of Assef, still engaging in psychopathic violence but this time as an Islamic fundamentalist. Rescuing the boy and returning to the United States, Amir, Soraya, and Sohrab become a new family in a land of peace and opportunity.

Like its literary source, the Hollywood version of *The Kite Runner* was also a cultural milestone. As director Marc Forster put it, the purpose of the film was to "humanize that part of the world . . . [to] give a face and voice to a country that's been in the news for three decades, and create an emotional connection beyond culture or race."[1] For Americans, the film provided the first-ever cinematic view of urban Afghanistan before the Soviet invasion. John Frankenheimer's Afghans in *The Horsemen* were rustic *chapandaz*, archetypal warriors of the Hindu Kush. Forster's, on the other hand, are city dwellers quite comfortable with the trappings of American culture, from Ford Mustangs to 1970s plaid sports jackets. They listen to the radio, watch Steve McQueen movies, and live in sumptuous homes with marble floors, framed pictures on the walls, and heavily stacked library shelves. Most important, they don't appear to obsess about Islam. Baba, for example, drinks alcohol unapologetically, declaring that he "pisses on the beards" of the mullahs. These moderate, sophisticated Afghans are a world away from those of *Kandahar* or *Osama*.

Although shot primarily in the Xinjiang region of China (on the Afghan border), *The Kite Runner* nevertheless goes out of its way to present as authentic a picture of prewar Afghanistan as possible. Thus there are crowd scenes that portray, along with women in burqas, Westernized and unveiled women decked in the latest 1970s fashions. At Amir's birthday party celebration, they dance in public without any shame to the music of Ahmad Zahir, the most popular Afghan singer of the twentieth century (who is even represented by an actor who bears a passing resemblance to him). By inserting these images, the film reveals an Afghanistan in dialogue (and not even necessarily in conflict) with the world of modernity. Here for the first time, the Western viewer can watch Afghans who are literate, complex, cosmopolitan, and relatively tolerant. Even though a vast abyss exists between that optimistic past and the dismal present, this vision still holds a promise of what might be once again.

Nevertheless, *The Kite Runner* has been criticized by some of the very Afghan diaspora whose vicissitudes it seeks to chronicle. At a meeting of the Society of Afghan Professionals in Fremont, Hosseini himself encountered some hostility stemming from his treatment of ethnic tensions between Pashtuns and Hazaras.[2] The anger was not so surprising. After all, Hosseini was airing the dirty laundry of Afghanistan in public at a time when it was already getting more than its share of negative press. But what galled some older-generation Afghans even more perhaps was Hosseini's debunking of prewar nostalgia. To discuss racism against Hazaras, one must admit that all was not well in the paradise lost. Confronting this reality is essential not just from the viewpoint of history but also because in many ways these ethnic tensions have only become more exacerbated in recent decades. The racial violence between

Sunni Pashtuns and Shia Hazaras in the 1990s was, according to *The Kite Runner*'s author, "worse than anything the country endured under the Taliban."[3] Subsequently, Persian-speaking Tajiks and Hazaras used the overthrow of the Taliban to settle scores with the Pashtuns of Kabul and elsewhere. Meanwhile, Pashtun insurgents perpetrated new atrocities on ethnic minorities in Hazarajat, while Hazaras themselves murdered Kuchi nomads.

Of course Afghanistan's seemingly endless war is not simply a tale of race. A great deal of the conflict has been religiously based, pitting Shias versus Sunnis, and within Sunnism the Wahhabis against the more moderate Hanafi school. At the same time, many foreign countries like the United States, Pakistan, Iran, and Saudi Arabia continue playing the New Great Game, backing one faction against another.

The Kite Runner, however, glosses over these tensions to present a more simplified picture of Afghanistan as an arena of civil rights struggle that closely resembles America's own convulsions of the 1960s and 1970s. Although Marc Forster has said that he hopes to give Afghanistan a face for movie audiences, what he actually provides are two faces, a split image of Amir before and after that alters the meaning of Afghanistan in the 1970s (and by extension today). From a potentially empowering, subversive array of images, something far more compromised emerges. Border crossing may still be possible, even desirable, but as the film's villain Assef says, "Nothing is free."

Predatory Identities

Immigrant narratives have been a mainstay of American film ever since Charlie Chaplin's *The Immigrant* of 1917. In the era of globalization, they have grown in number as well as importance, becoming crucial staging grounds for the rearticulation of American identity. Various recent films have focused on a number of immigrant ethnicities including Greeks (*My Big Fat Greek Wedding*), Indians (*Mississippi Masala, The Namesake*), Vietnamese (*Heaven and Earth, Catfish in Black Bean Sauce*), Chinese (*The Joy Luck Club, Combination Platter, The Wedding Banquet*), Mexicans (*Lone Star, Bread and Roses, Spanglish*), and Iranians (*House of Sand and Fog*).

The struggle for self-definition in the New World cuts both ways. Just as the immigrants must grapple with a preestablished national narrative, so, too, must the nation itself revise the American story in order to accommodate these new strangers. Some writers view this process as one of national renewal. Thus the linguistic, racial, and religious differences of these new immigrants enable them to "sense personal and national contradictions."[4] Although this may be true on a limited level, to say that such a process "force[s] an interrogation of American identity and accepted national norms"[5] may be giving such narratives too much subversive potential.

Instead, these tales of immigration often participate in a kind of nationalistic narrative of reform, confronting retrogressive and reactionary elements in society that contradict the vision of America as a refuge of tolerance and equality, open to all. In this regard, they resemble the mainstream tales of racial tolerance promoted in the civil rights era and ensconced in public school curricula. Such narratives seldom rock the boat in a radical way, unless one considers it radical to say that America is not by definition a white and Judeo-Christian nation. Instead they absorb the impact of change or unrest in order to reconstitute an embattled status quo, through acts that often amount to little more than tokenism. While there may be multicultural modifications to American identity, certain basic assumptions persist no matter which immigrant group does the interrogating, even a group as recalcitrant and mysterious as the Afghans.

Like other immigrants before him, Amir's coming to America involves not just travel but also transformation and personal growth. Only when he makes the transition to California can he be portrayed as a man rather than a child. This metamorphosis occurs in a dissolve from the tanker in which Amir and Baba ride through the desolate Afghan night to a BART train, gliding smoothly over a suburban paradise basking in California sunshine. His presence in Fremont enables things that were hitherto impossible, like taking charge of the family from his redoubtable father, educating himself, having an intimate relationship with a woman (the only woman of any consequence in the entire film), and achieving economic success through his writing. Most important, by virtue of his American identity, Amir gains the ability to undo the sins of his past. No longer willing to be a passive looker-on, he confronts not only his own racism but also that of others, changing the world for the better as a result. As indicated by the transitional dissolve, Amir has crossed the threshold from benighted Eastern world to the glorious day of the West.

Such visual binaries (night/day, Afghanistan/America, concealment/exposure, imprisonment/freedom) attest to the ubiquitous presence of doubling in *The Kite Runner,* from the central scenes of kite flying in both Old and New Worlds, to the doubling of the main characters themselves, who are not only friends but also half brothers. Amir represents a distinct type: independent, educated, secular, wealthy, and dressed in the latest Western fashions. Hassan is the polar opposite: pious, loyal, illiterate, and always appearing in traditional clothes. They crown themselves the "sultans of Kabul," but their rubble-strewn kingdom is a graveyard and their relationship never elides the taint of class. Only in kite flying can they, like the kite itself, achieve a transcendence that is as exhilarating as it is ephemeral.

But Amir has many other selves. He and his father form one such pair. In Afghanistan Baba (which simply means "Dad") reigns supreme at the top of the social ladder as well as the family hierarchy. For the son, he represents (much like Tursen did for Uraz in *The Horsemen*) an almost unattainable goal of masculine power. Baba, in his turn, views Amir as a coward, a person who cannot take action. The earlier confrontations between Amir and Assef, the racist and rapist Taliban-to-be, serve to validate this judgment. Luckily for Amir, the journey to America effectively reverses the roles between father and son, rendering Baba weak and powerless while Amir becomes the leader of the family.

If it is true that, as Frederic Jameson has written, "the story of the private individual destiny is always an allegory of the embattled situation of the public third-world culture and society,"[6] then Amir's multiple personalities are indicative of not just himself but his homeland as well. They offer before-and-after images of what happens to Afghanistan when it comes in contact with the rehabilitating and empowering potential of American identity. The doubling of Amir and Assef illustrates this point. Although they belong to the upper class, wear Western clothes, and attend the same parties, their identification takes on a more sinister and sadistic tone when Amir's passive complicity enables Assef to rape Hassan, his best friend and half brother. This mirroring only comes to an end during the climactic fight in Taliban-era Kabul. In one corner stands Assef, the bearded, psychopathic Muslim fundamentalist. In the other is the gentle Amir who, stripped of the false beard he'd been wearing as a disguise, represents the forces of tolerance and rationality. The beating he subsequently receives casts him in the role of defenseless victim, redeemed only when an Afghan boy (Hassan's son) uses violence to save him.

At stake in this brutal showdown is the nature of *afghaniyat,* the Afghan sense of national identity, with the two fighters representing antipodal definitions. One exhibits a catalog of Orientalist stereotypes—lascivious, sadistic, fanatical, veiled behind his sunglasses. The other represents an ideal of the assimilated Other: passive, secular, moderate, and vulnerable. Along with these traits, Amir possesses the higher moral values that come with his newfound citizenship. The three figures in the blank, whitewashed room embody an Afghan mind at war with itself: Sohrab the tender ego besieged by a vicious id that can only be checked by a Westernized superego. Happily the latter wins out, and Sohrab does what is expected of him, taking arms against the fanatic within and submitting himself to the civilizing mission.

Sohrab and his father are the only truly blameless Afghans in the film—pure victims, loyal to a fault as well as humbly pious. Obviously ignorant, they nevertheless betray a thirst for knowledge while always managing to maintain a healthy respect for their social betters. When Amir seeks to expunge his own guilt over what happened to Hassan by provoking a fight with him, he smears the boy's face with a pomegranate. Hassan continues the disfigurement himself in an act of abject humiliation and self-abnegation. How different this is from the fierce, defiant gaze of Sharbat Gula, who, despite her poverty, never surrenders herself.

The dichotomy between those two images resembles the difference between reading *To Kill a Mockingbird* and *The Autobiography of Malcolm X*. These iconic texts of the civil rights era represent two very different solutions to race relations in the United States.[7] Harper Lee's novel depicts African Americans as hapless victims, with racist and nonracist whites the only ones capable of action. Malcolm X's story, on the other hand, portrays a proud and powerful opponent to white hegemony. More radically, it offers Islam as a universalizing ideology in competition with the Christianized values of America. Not surprisingly, Lee's book remains on high school reading lists across America, while Malcolm X appears far less frequently. The contrasting definitions of *afghaniyat* in *The Kite Runner* follow this pattern closely as they do the discourse of racial minorities in America in general, providing textbook descriptions of what it means to be a "good Indian" and a bad one.

Reading *Wuthering Heights* in Little Kabul

Although good Indians seldom seemed to benefit a great deal from white domination, *The Kite Runner* indicates that far greater rewards are in store for those Afghans who assimilate—rewards like the view from Amir's apartment, where he moves after his marriage. This is not only the first interior location in the film but also where Amir receives the author copies of his first published novel, the sign that he has "arrived." Unlike the rather shabby quarters he occupied with his father, Amir's new residence displays a commanding "balcony vantage point" of the Bay Area of San Francisco. As discussed in chapter 6, such a position has traditionally been the prerogative of imperial power, a sure token of Amir's new national identity. The kite-flying scenes employ a similar vista, revealing both Kabul and the Bay Area to the camera's transcendent eye. Visually detached from the hands that guide it on the ground, the kite becomes a free and hybrid agent, occupying a liminal space between earth and sky. Such transcendence embodies, paradoxically, domination as well as freedom. Far from being just a colorful toy, the kite functions as a competitive weapon that destroys all the others, taking the sky for its own. The question of who most deserves to wield this power remains itself up in the air until the film's conclusion, when Amir as an adult not only replicates his great triumph of the past but also atones for the moral cowardice that had marked his life as an Afghan child.

While gently requiring the surrender of inner weaknesses associated with the old country, America also allows Amir to retain many elements of his heritage, like the Dari language and Afghan cuisine. In this way, he becomes simply another "ethnic" while still espousing the basic values of American society. The end result can only be a positive one, as Baba's friend Rahim Khan later says to Amir, "America's infused you with her optimism." This peculiar brand of sanguinity naturally incurs from the bountiful material conditions in his new home.

One can hardly question the statement that America provides opportunities for safety and health, not to mention education and affluence, which are inconceivable in Afghanistan today. The environment of greater openness and tolerance that the film's Afghans experience in the United States is certainly not mere fantasy. The fact remains that they have entered a place where honor killings and burqas, parda and female illiteracy are anathema. In this virtual utopia, the American majority (religious or racial) never seems to hinder Amir in any way in his climb to the top. He graduates with them, lives among them, makes money when they buy his books. Yet the two cultures do not seem to mix in any substantial way. The only time he interacts with non-Afghans is in a dingy bar, where he and his father drink a toast with some white pool players as they curse the Russians, their common enemy. Apparently Amir has every opportunity to join the mainstream—but only if he pays for their drinks and espouses the proper politics.

Meanwhile he must learn English. While alluding to such Persian literary giants as Ferdowsi and Rumi, *The Kite Runner* takes numerous opportunities to indicate the high status and universal utility of English literature as well as Western values. Amir uses his mastery of this literature to reap financial rewards that are beyond the reach of his father. In one scene showing the two men in their apartment, Baba pores painstakingly over a newspaper while Amir demonstrates his facility by typing at lightning speed. For him, English offers a passport to social and economic success, as proved by Baba's exile to a dirty gas station while his son attends book signings at tidy strip malls. But the language serves an even more important purpose: creating a common ground between Amir and the love of his life, Soraya.

They first meet at the San Jose flea market, where many respectable Afghans (men and women alike) are vendors, including Baba and General

Taheri, Soraya's father. In the more open American environment, Taheri feels free to leave her alone at the stand to wait on strangers (something that would have been inconceivable for a general's daughter in Afghanistan). Amir seizes the opportunity to introduce himself, commenting on her choice of reading material: Emily Brontë's *Wuthering Heights*. A tale of passion, vengeance, and intergenerational cruelty, this canonical novel alludes to the primacy of romantic love in the West versus Afghan tradition. For the two immigrants, this sexual liberation promises the hope of a new emotional shelter beyond history to replace the homeland that was lost.[8]

The film visualizes the moment when the Afghan Americans finally forsake homeland and tradition to create a particularly Western nuclear unit. During their first family-sanctioned meeting, Amir and Soraya emerge from her Fremont ranch home, with her mother chaperoning them at a safe distance. Soon, however, the two outpace her and the Old World morality she represents. The house itself fades out of focus as the two individuals fill the frame. In this new state of detachment from the old code of family honor and personal shame, the young woman can finally confess her great sin to Amir: that years before she had run off with an older Afghan man and lived with him as lover, not wife. This crime (and certainly its public admission) would have made her effectively unmarriageable in Afghanistan. The film shows no indication of the tremendous risk Soraya takes in making such a confession or of the degree of humiliation she would suffer. Nor does it address (as Hosseini's book does) the amount of repugnance Amir feels despite his enlightened sensibilities. To do so would be to complicate a moment of effortless border crossing, one of the chief benefits of Amir's fusion with a new nation of unrestricted movement and effortless transformation. And so Amir sloughs it off, nonplussed for only a moment before professing his continued desire to marry her. Unlike in *Wuthering Heights*, their coming to America averts romantic tragedy, supplying the Hollywood ending—free from regret—that everyone deserves.

America the Beautiful

For many postcolonial theorists, the hybridity of people like Amir heralds an emancipatory new vision of identity. "Such a journey," Iain Chambers glowingly writes, "is open and incomplete, it involves a continual fabulation, an invention, a construction, in which there is no fixed identity or final destination."[9] Edward Said has also written of the advantages of living in exile, a condition that allows one to "cross borders, break barriers of thought and experiences."[10] Yet in spite of fellow theorist Homi Bhabha's similar identification of a productive "third space," the same one-way traffic from periphery to center continues. Indeed, Bhabha's hybridity "depends upon a presumption of the existence of its opposite for its force," and consequently "those who oppose the dominant power on its own terms or in its own language are necessarily caught up in its logic and thus perpetuate it."[11] Rasheed Araeen has questioned the intellectually liberating potential of border crossing, declaring it "a fallacy to presume that migration in itself creates displacement, loss and exile." In fact, exile and migration can often provoke a very different set of reactions, including extreme aversion to the past and the culture that was left behind as well as a fierce loyalty to the adopted country.[12]

The term *hybridity* itself is often imbued with a kind of absolute quality of indeterminateness that by its very nature challenges the fixedness of national borders and cultures. By essentializing it in this fashion, one ignores the fact that this concept can be and has been used for very different purposes, such as in reinforcing the very center it presumably challenges. Rather than imagining it as a single quality, one might envision a hybridity "spectrum" that includes, along with the destabilizing kind Bhabha and others privilege, an assimilationist hybridity that reinforces national boundaries rather than dissolves them.[13]

Like many other immigrant narratives, *The Kite Runner* privileges assimilation into a general national identity. The danger of Amir's difference becomes subsumed in the "tradition" and "heritage" of multiculturalism, which constructs cultures "as essentially equivalent and therefore interchangeable in their various parts, leading inevitably to an emphasis on assimilation to the dominant."[14] *Afghaniyat* is thus reduced to a peppering of Dari, the eating of *bulani* and *aushak,* and kite flying on weekends. If Muslim worship persists in the United States, the film only shows it during weddings and funerals. Thus the empire does write back, but not in the way that postcolonial theorists have cast it. Rather, power reinscribes its narrative and ways of seeing on the new immigrant.

While still in the United States, Amir's transformation goes unnoticed. But on his return to Afghanistan, one can easily discern the change. This is the before-and-after moment of the film, when Amir confronts not only his double, the Talib Assef, but also the memory of his Afghan childhood, tinged with shame and failure. Like him, not a single other Afghan escapes being morally compromised, except for the hapless Hassan, who is hauled off and shot for his loyalty to a faithless friend. Amir's Afghan identity has become, like Afghanistan itself, a fallen state.

As the emigrant traverses his homeland, this dark side of Afghanistan grows more ineluctable. Whereas the land of his youth was a place teeming with people and especially children, the camera reveals nothing now but desert, juxtaposed by snowcapped mountains, rife with rubble and meandering livestock. The country has been transformed into the archetypal landscape of imperialist discourse: a sublime emptiness. The only human inhabitant of the desolation is a burqa-clad woman who squats beside a demolished tank. "What happened to the trees?" Amir asks his driver. "The Russians chopped them down," the man replies. As their journey continues, they drive by a man with his prosthetic leg for sale. Down the street, a body swings on an improvised gallows. The street where they park reeks of diesel instead of the long-ago aroma of lamb kabobs. There is no electricity, Amir learns, so people are using generators nonstop. The next moment, the scowling Taliban drive by in their pickup trucks, while Amir says, "I feel like a tourist in my own country."

In fact, this is the same Afghan chamber of horrors visited by many tourists and native informants before him, from Rambo to Nafas. When Amir witnesses a woman being stoned in Ghazi stadium, she appears in a long shot, distant and abstract. Her perfunctory death does little to move Amir or the viewer because she is not so much a human as a set piece of Afghan gothic. Later, Sohrab dances before the pedophiliac Assef in a sequence that looks for all the world like the cinematic adaptation of Jean-Léon Gérôme's *Snake Charmer* painting. By evoking these mainstream images of Islamic world benightedness, the film palliates the earlier image of a civilized, moderate Afghanistan and returns the audience to the familiar violence and erotic excess of Orientalist imagery.

Such an epistemological regression bolsters Amir's American identity by casting him as the lead in a Wild Eastern replay of the captivity narrative. There's just one difference: In the twenty-first century, the borders of civilization have gone global, and everyone on the planet has the possibility of becoming an American held hostage by the duly designated savages. Thus the hero redeems Sohrab from the perversities of the Taliban, allowing him to take his place as ward of a greater and more virtuous power. Civilization has once again triumphed over savagery.

Naturally, Amir never questions the nationalist assumptions of the narrative in which he plays a part. Nor does the film portray an America that in actuality is every bit as divided against itself and fallen from grace as Afghanistan. Rather, it shows the United States as it wishes to be seen: as a haven of tolerance and harmony, a place where the kind of racism seen in 1970s Kabul has long since been extirpated. Only after Amir enacts the American myth of Indian fighting can he return (wiser and battle-hardened) to Little Kabul and tell off his racist father-in-law, completing the final act in the grand epic of American exceptionalism.

One can make the argument that *The Kite Runner,* although employing a nationalist rhetoric, nevertheless draws much-needed attention to some very real evils in the world. After all, racism against the Hazaras, Taliban fanaticism, and the victimization of orphan children are still realities in Afghanistan. But the point at issue here is not the facticity of Afghan abjection but the way certain well-honed narratives make sense of this information. The stock imagery of the Wild Eastern suggests some alternatives to the current state of the country while ignoring others, but most of all it demonstrates little faith in the notion that Afghans might solve their own problems if left alone.

El Cid Is Playing

This book began with an examination of the ways in which Hollywood used the international setting of Afghanistan throughout the 1970s and 1980s to address the domestic "problem" of the Vietnam syndrome, reflecting the hypernationalistic quality of an American culture that seeks to shape the world in its own image in order to better absorb it.[15] The tradition of American exceptionalism provides the impetus for this cultural project by imagining the United States as a "privileged site for the integration of racial and ethnic difference . . . an experiment in democracy," the like of which the world has never seen.[16] And because, by its very nature the United States is assimilative (like the most successful empires of old), it can cast itself as "the universal nation" whose purpose is to "enlighten the world."[17]

In his study of Cold War America, *The End of Victory Culture,* Tom Engelhardt demonstrates how an ideology of political and spiritual liberation became fused, from the very beginning of European colonialism in North America, with a policy of extermination. This synthesis gave birth to the most fundamental of American narratives: the war story or "victory culture" that rhetorically justifies imperialism as a "settling and ordering of a wilderness of human horrors into a celebratory tale of progress through devastation."[18] Against "e pluribus unum" stands a host of monolithic enemies, always scheming to end the democratic experiment. What makes their extirpation palatable is the promise of eventual reconciliation between people of different races, languages, and creeds.

If one takes the conquest of the wilderness to be the U.S. equivalent of a cosmogony, then to question this vision of war as liberating and redemptive ultimately threatens the spiritual core of American nationalism. To overcome the trauma of the political defeat in Vietnam as well as economic and cultural pressures at home, 1980s patriotic mythmakers began rehabilitating mindless killing machines like John Rambo to renew hostilities against developing world insurgents. The Gulf War soon provided those in power with an opportunity to "lick Vietnam Syndrome for good" (as the elder George Bush put it) by rehabilitating just war theory. Dusting off the old imperialist tropes, the cinema followed in lockstep with the news media and the Pentagon, envisioning a new world order in which the entire planet provided a new frontier in which to conduct a now endless civilizing mission that was America's birthright. More than any other conflict since World War II, Afghanistan offers the American war story (like *The Kite Runner*'s Amir) a "way to be good again," and Americans a chance to feel good again about the use of excessive force. Just how excessive was made clear in the fall of 2001:

> During the first four weeks of the war, half a million tons of bombs were dropped on Afghanistan, 20 kilos for every man, woman, and child. During eight and a half weeks of U.S. bombing, a documented 3,763 civilians were killed.[19]

To justify such violence, the media transformed the Taliban from U.S.-supported guerillas (at least throughout the Bill Clinton era) and retrofitted them with all the trappings of America's most archetypal villains, the Nazis. Hence the coining of the term *Islamofascism* and the obsession with "gender apartheid." With an entire nation held captive by fanatics, America had no choice but to continue the bombing and troop surges as well as to enlist Afghans themselves in the fight against the elusive al-Qaeda and the protean Taliban. *The Kite Runner* similarly serves to "Afghanize" the war against terror. Far from a simple tale of immigration and redemption, the film uses multiculturalism in much the same way that it was used in the combat movies of previous eras: to direct anger over internal racial and economic inequities to a demonized and externalized Other.[20] This rainbow coalition of the willing demonstrates American exceptionalism while at the same time offering war against fundamentalist Islam as a universalizing alternative to those whom the global market has failed to liberate.

Not everyone was sanguine about the new war. Noam Chomsky labeled the Afghan invasion "a major war crime."[21] Others chronicled the continued suffering of Afghans "enduring freedom" at the hands of the U.S. military, from books like Ann Jones's *Kabul in Winter,* to a host of documentary films like *Kabul Transit* and *The Boy Who Plays on the Buddhas of Bamiyan.* In the mainstream political circles of America, however, such sentiments were few and far between. Rather, as the U.S. war story collapsed in Iraq under the weight of Abu Ghraib and other My Lai–like atrocities, authorities touted Afghanistan as a way to keep feeling good about war.

As usual, the cinema played and continues to play a crucial role in this process, both at home and abroad. Early in *The Kite Runner,* Baba mentions that "*El Cid* is playing" at the local Kabul cinema. One of the great costume dramas of the 1960s, *El Cid* chronicles the life of Rodrigo (played by Charlton Heston), a patriotic knight at war to liberate Spain from its evil Muslim occupiers. Even before his arrival in America, Amir has been encouraged to identify with the white, European, and Christian hero and his liberating mission. Meanwhile, *El Cid* disparages the Afghans' own religion and cultural heritage, viewing Muslim Spain not as the "ornament of the world," as a contemporary Christian described it, but as an alien and oppressive regime needing to be annihilated. In such a way, American frontier mythology colonizes global identity, transforming the "invader into the invaded and [creating] the foundation for any act of retribution that might follow."[22] Orientalist epics like *El Cid* serve a useful ideological purpose, teaching Afghans about who they are, how they should behave, and the ultimate consequences of resisting America's "march of progress." As the Borg, *Star Trek*'s infamous aliens, put it, "Resistance is futile, prepare to be assimilated."

The Kite Runner inadvertently expresses this connection between U.S. cultural exports and military domination in another scene in which Amir overhears his father call him a "boy who won't stand up for himself." The film then cuts to a movie theater where Hassan and Amir watch Charles Bronson in *The Magnificent Seven,* the cinematic quintessence of Kennedy-era interventionism.[23] In this classic Western, a group of hapless Mexican peasants enlists the aid of hypermacho Americans Yul Brynner, Steve McQueen, and Charles Bronson to protect them from their fellow countrymen, a gang of evil bandits under the leadership of Eli Wallach (wearing a not-too-subtle red shirt). It was a dress rehearsal for Vietnam, an example of how natives like Amir can learn to "stand up for themselves," primarily by allowing U.S. soldiers into their country.

Affluent, anticommunist, and possessing a wealth of powerful connections, Baba alone among the film's Afghans has the self-confidence and authority to solve his nation's problems without foreign interference. A truly heroic character, he stands up to regressive forces in his own society, while championing the honor of his people against the invading Russians, even if it means his own death. Unfortunately, his communal ties in Kabul are far more important to him than the competitive individualism so privileged by the global economy, as when he writes a check to found an orphanage. In a still-tribal society where "material things . . . are morally inconsequential" and "personal integrity" within one's clan determines social status, Baba truly exists only within his community.[24] Amir's father thus exemplifies the kind of homespun "crony capitalism" and traditional tribalism that are anathema to transnational corporate power. There is no way to translate him into the world of American capitalism. Baba winds up toiling at a grungy gas station, a broken shell of a man.

But things are different for his son. Quick to grasp the ideology of the marketplace, Amir survives the move to Fremont because neither community nor borders mean anything to him. During one of his talks with Soraya at the flea market, he observes her taking a five-dollar bill from a customer. "Not much of a haggler, are you?" he says approvingly. Such haggling is part of the bazaar culture, after all, an Afghan way of doing business that stresses communal bonding. These old ways must be eschewed to favor materialism and competitive individualism over the Islam and tribalism that characterized Afghan society. That Soraya, like Amir, has assimilated these values of American capitalism only makes her more attractive to him.

The film's second-generation Afghan Americans willfully immerse themselves in a brave, new worldview of economic apocalypticism. Under the San Jose flea (or free) market tent, everyone is equal, or as the general declares, "Everyone here is a storyteller," capable of writing their own narrative. True, the Afghan young ones have lost their old home. But happily their adopted country's rise to power heralds the inevitable "end of history" that will banish starvation and war and create "greater opportunity for all people to realize their potential and aspirations."[25] Cultural tensions ineluctably diminish as people of all religions and ethnicities declare their loyalty to the free market. Through rational self-interest, capitalism has (in the words of the Organisation for Economic Co-operation and Development) "accelerated the material progress of the human race at a pace difficult to comprehend."[26]

The local-based, honor-bound society Baba represents never promised such limitless opportunities. This is why *The Kite Runner* locates *afghaniyat* not in Kabul but in the San Jose flea market, or to put it more simply, in the market itself. Ultimately Amir does not stay in Afghanistan to administer an orphanage for Hazara children. Nor does he set up a school that teaches tolerance or participate in the government there. If he were to do that—if he were to stay there—he might be able to make a positive change in Afghan society, though certainly at enormous personal risk to himself. The film ultimately discourages such a path to change, however, by asserting (through Amir) that Afghans can only escape the conflagration by assuming their place in the Western-dominated transnational scheme of things. The logic naturally resembles that of Mohsen Makhmalbaf's essay on *Kandahar,* the only difference being that America, unlike Iran, is able and willing to intervene on an international scale, much as it does nationally, to help the free market along in keeping with the best principles of neoliberalism. Although that market is supposedly free, it is a freedom presided over by an imperial power that accounts for nearly half of the entire globe's military spending.[27]

Alas, there are other ideologies, like Islamic fundamentalism, that stand opposed to this imbalance of power while providing their own, very different visions of a borderless world. Unlike the old era of colonialism, the issue at stake in the twenty-first century is not who draws the borders but who dissolves them. Naturally, if it's a choice between the Taliban and America, *The Kite Runner* opts for the latter (and who wouldn't?). This Manichaean perspective easily configures military intervention as a "way to be good again," and not simply a crass ploy to absorb Afghanistan into the sphere of U.S. power. With Assef representing sexual depravity, misogyny, racism, and psychopathy, Amir's Americanized worldview becomes absolute good by default. But although Amir and Soraya embrace the imperial logic of rational self-interest and military hegemony, they would do well to remember a proverb from their old home: No flowers without thorns.

From Kabul to Karbala

Any analysis of *The Kite Runner*, while weighing the politics underlying the narrative, must also take into account the reasons for the film's popularity, and even more so its literary source. For many American readers and moviegoers, the story's simple and compelling tale of redemption resonates with great power. It taps a hidden reservoir of guilt and shame, stemming from childhood wrongs unrighted. Readers love Amir's story because he, like all of us, has numerous flaws, fails time and again, and yet ultimately does the right thing. He can do what we want to believe is possible: reach back into the past and undo the damage he (or we) inflicted there. At the same time, Amir's story soothes our conscience over Afghanistan and our war there, allowing us to express sympathy, gain a little knowledge of their history and traditions, and reaffirm the civilizing mission that he champions.

In spite of the sheer storytelling involved, the political undercurrents of the film (and even more so the book) cannot be denied. As proof positive that Hollywood, Washington, DC, and even Wall Street sprang from the same DNA, *The Kite Runner*'s screenwriter David Benioff happens to be the son of Stephen Friedman, at various times the chairman of both Goldman Sachs and George W. Bush's Foreign Intelligence Advisory Board.[28] If this potential convergence of ideologies problematizes the film's narrative, author Khaled Hosseini can still provide the proper Afghan credentials of authenticity. Hosseini's authorship, however, does not impress some scholars like Fatemeh Keshavarz, who has been quick to judge both the popularity and the politics of *The Kite Runner*. In her *Jasmine and Stars: Reading More than Lolita in Tehran*, she writes off Hosseini (along with Azar Nafisi and others) as a "New Orientalist."[29] What makes New Orientalism new is its use of native informants with liberal sensitivities to sustain the same stereotypes. Although this rings true to a certain extent, such a reading oversimplifies the novel's internal political and religious schisms. Unfortunately, the cinematic version does its best to minimize this complexity and, by doing so, deprives the story of Amir of any destabilizing potential it might possess.

More often than not, the screenplay tends to homogenize Amir politically, ethnically, and socially, censoring Hosseini's narrative when necessary. Gone are the constant references to Afghan food, proverbs, and a great deal of history. At the same time, Baba and Amir's politics go unmentioned, including their support (which mirrored that of practically every Afghan exile in the States) for Ronald Reagan, who helped the mujahedeen down Russian aircraft by supplying Stinger missiles. Naturally, such rampant Republican boosterism would alienate the target liberal audience. Therefore it was excised, as was the entire climax of Hosseini's book, in a glaring and politically revealing omission.

The elision comes toward the end of the film, after Amir flees with Sohrab to Pakistan. Once there, the boy suddenly disappears from their hotel room. Distraught, Amir wanders around aimlessly, eventually winding up in a mosque where he silently and awkwardly prays. When he returns, Sohrab is waiting there for him, ready to depart with his uncle for a better home and future. While remarkable for showing Amir at prayer, this profession of Muslim faith does not change him in any way, nor does it have much relevance to his relationship with Sohrab or Hassan.

This complete bowdlerization of the novel leaves out Amir's attempts to legally adopt Sohrab and thus get him into the United States. When he finds it extremely difficult to do so and lets slip to Soraya that he may have to leave the boy there, Sohrab overhears the conversation and attempts suicide by slitting his wrists in the bathroom. The absence of this scene in the screenplay further cements the film's role as a suppressant to conflict and complexity regarding Afghanistan and Afghan Americans. Its vision of "America the Beautiful" precludes any mention of the tremendous difficulties people face when immigrating here, of the sacrifices that must be made, of the lives that are often shattered. But even more dishonestly, the film suppresses the most radical element in Hosseini's narrative, the real transformation of Amir that in many ways supersedes the birth of his American identity: the moment when Amir experiences a religious conversion. With Sohrab near death in the hospital, Amir instinctively turns to the only one who can help him:

> There is no God but Allah and Muhammad is His messenger. I see now that Baba was wrong, there is a God, there always had been. . . . I bow to the west and kiss the ground and promise I will do *zakat*, I will do *namaz*, I will fast

during Ramadan. . . . I will think of Him every day from this day on if He only grants me this one wish: My hands are stained with Hassan's blood; I pray God doesn't let them get stained with the blood of this boy too.[30]

This is the turning point in Amir's life and the climax of *The Kite Runner*. Unfortunately for the filmmakers, it also vastly complicates Amir's absorption into the American collective. With this conversion, Amir pledges his allegiance to another kind of universal truth, in a different language and with a different way of seeing than those of his new home. Amir's conversion does not simply provide a counternarrative that rehegemonizes the center. The universality of Islam exists independently of that center, while engaging with American exceptionalism in a state of unresolved tension. The omission of the Shahada in the shooting script indicates that the literary character of Amir may not be so different from Sharbat Gula, that the Afghan within him remains defiant, even strengthened by his encounter with the West.

The film carefully refashions and dilutes this potent force of difference. Although there are references to Afghan culture (the mythic father-and-son conflict of Rostam and Sohrab, the character's namesake), these are left unexplained in a visual rhetorical space that privileges readily recognizable American cultural exports like Ford Mustangs and *The Magnificent Seven*. By doing so, the film mystifies the narrative heart of *The Kite Runner*, the most sacred story of its author's faith: Shia Islam.

In the year 680 on the tenth day of the month of Muharram (the first month of the Muslim calendar), the Prophet Muhammad's grandson Hussein set out with a small band of followers to restore Islam to its spiritual roots by removing the Umayyads from power. Deserted by many of his comrades along the way, Hussein struggled on until he was attacked at Karbala. Rather than flee, he and his remaining followers fought to the death and perished, with only one boy left alive.

This act of betrayal, of sacrifice and devotion to the truth, is the foundation of Shiism. Memorializing the event every year during Yawm Al-'Ashura, Shias engage in ritualized expressions of grief, in some countries even striking themselves with sharp blades, bleeding in mystic union with Hussein. Elsewhere, miniature shrines (*taziyas*) are built, resembling that of the Imam, who still lies in Karbala, Iraq, in one of Islam's most sacred monuments. Although long established as an expression of personal piety and community solidarity in the face of persecution, Ashura has become in the modern era "a commemoration inspiring active engagement in bringing about social, political and religious change."[31] In modern Iran, Ali Shariati invoked the "Karbala paradigm" to cast the Islamic revolution against the shah in the sacred language of Shiism.[32] Through Shariati's writings, Hussein became for many Shias a "key figure of revolutionary struggle" and a paragon of "political action, martyrdom and sacrifice."[33]

The seventh-century Muslim betrayal of Hussein provides the historical antecedent for Amir's betrayal of Hassan. Just as Amir has Hassan's blood on his hands (symbolically wounding Hassan with the pomegranate), so, too, do Shias experience Hussein's blood on their own hands, a reminder of the ways in which humans fail to follow God's will. But this identification leads to redemption by enabling others to imitate Hussein's selfless example. Amir, by risking his life to save Sohrab, very clearly follows in Hussein's footsteps.

If one can read the novel's take on Hussein as potentially depoliticizing, the fact remains that the Karbala paradigm, the spiritual signature of Shia Islam's "clashing civilization," lies at the spiritual and political heart of one of America's most beloved narratives in recent memory. Shiism also works through Hosseini's novel to challenge the American war story's appropriation of narrative, especially of the themes of sacrifice and redemption. Many films like *The Kite Runner* and others I have discussed serve to obfuscate these furtive meanings, hypernationalizing the Islamic world in America's image. In spite of their efforts, thankfully, the hybrid voices embedded in the narrative cannot be so easily repressed, enduring as persistent challenges to a victory culture under siege once again. To emerge from this particularly dangerous mindset requires immersion in something other than one's own cultural absolutism. Rather, it involves dialogue and compromise, a dismantling of ideological borders instead of their feverish reassertion. Staring into those haunted eyes of Sharbat Gula and so many other Afghans of film and fact, one might finally learn that if that dialogue is not freely offered, it will sooner or later be demanded.

Conclusion

Ending Charlie Wilson's War

Clearly Afghanistan has become a hot property, politically and culturally, the place more than any other where the resurgent victory culture of the United States stakes its future. Many Americans feel they have come to know it intimately, thanks to native informants like Nelofer Pazira and Khaled Hosseini. Afghanistan has served as a backdrop for action in liberal political films like *Lions for Lambs* and right-wing superhero twaddle like *Iron Man*, as well as for critically acclaimed documentaries like *The Beauty Academy of Kabul* and *Taxi to the Dark Side* (which won an Academy Award). Elsewhere, Bollywood has chimed in with *Kabul Express* (banned in Afghanistan for its perceived racism toward the Hazaras), and various other directors from France, Iran, and Afghanistan itself (most notably Atiq Rahimi and his *Earth and Ashes*) continue to make films about the country that for various reasons remain almost impossible to view in the United States. Along with these films, there is also a significant body of work that chronicles the experiences of the Afghan diaspora, from America's *Fire Dancer* to France's *Nelofer in the Rain* and Iranian films like *Baran* and *Djomeh*.

The crucial question I have addressed in this book has been: What is the nature of the knowledge these films impart? By drawing attention to the many popular and influential films that portray Afghanistan from positions of extreme cultural, political, and religious bias, I am suggesting that our perception of Afghanistan and its people is often warped to fit the needs of aggression and profit, not democracy and liberation.

There are arguments from within the academy, inevitably, about our ability to truly "know" the native. Gayatri Spivak, for example, calls the subaltern an "inaccessible blankness circumscribed by an interpretable text."[1] Such a critical focus on textuality and theory often fails to notice more mundane topics like human rights reports, war casualties, land-mine fatalities, and the news media that make these bitter realities so "inaccessible." The subsequent flight into abstraction leaves the field open for those who support the war in Afghanistan and elsewhere. For these ideologues of aggression, the divide between an academic criticism that dwells on theory and a mainstream readership that craves facts and practical applications leaves a void in which they can make their continued pitches for a just war that continues ad infinitum, no matter which party happens to be in the White House.

Cultural production and consumption in the United States, as I have shown, are responsible for shaping our views of Afghanistan as well as our policies there. Clearly, American audiences are interested in Afghanistan and seek a human connection with its people. Scholarship should make it easier for them to decode the various "faces" of Afghanistan they are shown. Pointing out Orientalist bias (or any other) is a good first step. But we must go further into *remedies* for that bias. Often, idealistic souls surmise that to simply allow Afghans to speak for themselves will balance the rhetorical scales. But as this book has shown, it takes more than one or two auteurs to speak for an entire nation or religion. Neither can Eastern voices be expected to pose necessarily objective counterarguments for an ill-conceived New Great Game. As Mohsen Makhmalbaf's film shows, Orientalism is simply the Western dialect of a hybridized and globalized imperialist lingua franca, an Esperanto of exploitation and oppression.

My purpose in this book has been to demonstrate that concerned people of any nationality can take control of the process of representation and use it to challenge military, economic, and cultural power. To that end, the cinema can be used to initiate a dialogue between very different peoples—to find common ground, to negotiate difference, and to empower a complexity and cosmopolitanism that may be the only antidotes to fundamentalisms of all stripes. Once that dialogue begins, it should become clear to all involved that there is no such thing as the Other, only others.

Yearning to know the real Afghanistan—to put a face on an abstraction— prevents us from knowing real Afghans. Absurd pronouncements about the "Afghan mind-set" tell us nothing about actual Afghan minds, especially when they come from people who've never *spoken* to Afghans. The "real" Afghanistan cannot be reduced to a few films and points of view. Rather, it may be grasped, albeit tenuously, only by listening to a plethora of different voices, all of which need to be heard as the nation directs itself toward an uncertain future. While the real Afghanistan might not exist, real Afghans do. The kind of truth we acquire from listening to them is not absolute but, rather, cumulative, an epistemological process that, like science, builds upon itself slowly, relentlessly, and inescapably. It can be used, also like science, to build or destroy real lives in the real world. If warmongers can turn *Kandahar* into war propaganda, then certainly those who actually care about Afghans must use film and film criticism to aid Afghans in their quest for peace and self-determination.

The issue of representation is literally one of life or death. Huge segments of the population view films like *The Kite Runner* and *Osama,* basing their opinions on national policy, the nature of the Islamic world, and the righteousness of their own cause, on what they see in the darkened cinema, in their classrooms, and in their homes. To view films on Afghanistan and examine them critically, then, is not some empty academic exercise. As Pablo Picasso put it regarding his painting *Guernica,* art is not simply something with which to decorate the walls but a means to make war on the enemy. Films have played a crucial part in framing the Afghan conflict and rallied public opinion in support of the "war against terror." At the same time, Afghanistan as represented in these films has come to stand for the West's Islamic Other (as well as Iran's)—everything that must be opposed because it opposes, feared because it is not afraid. While *The Man Who Would Be King, The Kite Runner,* and *Kandahar* effectively veil Afghanistan, *Osama, Ellipsis,* and *In This World* reveal the Sharbat Gula stare of the Afghan people, the ability to look back at us, judge us, and repudiate what we contend are universal, liberating values to which all must submit.

While it is probably a good thing to be wary of crusades to right wrongs in other peoples' cultures, the fear of "reverse ethnocentrism" does not absolve educated people in the West from their responsibility to use knowledge (not military invasions) to empower others and to be empowered by those others. In a recent book, a frustrated Terry Eagleton posed the question: "Is the point to understand the cannibals rather than to change them?"—an either-or fallacy characteristic of not only neoconservatives but also Marxists.[2] Not even entering Eagleton's thought process (or that of many others, of every political persuasion) is the idea that maybe "the point" is not how we can change *them* but how they can change *us.* To look at Afghanistan in film, one must be prepared for Afghanistan to look back, with both anger and the hope of reconciliation, in an exchange based not on domination but on reciprocity. It is up to each of us to decide whether this is a crisis to be avoided or an opportunity to be seized.

Notes

Introduction: Haunted Eyes

1. Newman, "A Life Revealed."
2. Ibid.
3. Alloula, *The Colonial Harem*, 7.
4. Spurr, *The Rhetoric of Empire*, 22.
5. Newman, "A Life Revealed."
6. Gabrieli, "Apology for Orientalism," 83.
7. Said, *Orientalism*, 3.

Chapter 1: Getting in Touch with Our Inner Savage

1. Boyle, "Grab the Goat and Ride, Omar!"
2. Pratley, *The Films of Frankenheimer*, 112.
3. Since the Afghans Frankenheimer encountered would not allow him to photograph their female family members, he had members of his crew don the burqa; Pratley, *The Films of Frankenheimer*, 118. For an interview with Leigh Taylor-Young about *The Horsemen*, see Taylor-Young, "The Horsemen."
4. Clark, "Introduction," 2.
5. Champlin, *John Frankenheimer*, 123.
6. Thomas Gray in a letter to Richard West, November 16, 1739. From Woods, *English Poetry and Prose of the Romantic Movement*, 70.
7. Rousseau, *The Confessions of Jean-Jacques Rousseau*, 167.
8. Slotkin, *Gunfighter Nation*, 14.
9. Prats, *Invisible Natives*, 2.
10. Corkin, *Cowboys as Cold Warriors*, 213, 220–21.
11. Ebert, "The Horsemen."
12. Regarding Habib, Frankenheimer enthused, "This guy's a real monster. He's killed people!"; Boyle, "Grab the Goat and Ride, Omar!"

13. Champlin, *John Frankenheimer,* 123.

14. Pratley, *The Films of Frankenheimer,* 119.

15. In the real society of the Afghan steppes, the *chapandaz* are indeed the elite, their horses so valuable that only the wealthy landowners can afford to stable and breed them; Michaud and Michaud, *Horsemen of Afghanistan,* notes 26, 27. As such, they combine the qualities of cowboys and ranchers, both settled and free. Uraz exemplifies their ethos of rugged individualism, living and nearly dying by his society's primitive code.

16. Zereh, the lone woman in the film and thus representative of Afghan women as a whole, is fiercely independent and more importantly *unveiled.* She is, in short, the antithesis of the silent, chador-shrouded women of the post-9/11 media. The veiled women in the film, shown walking the streets of Kabul, certainly indicate that it was neither radical Islam nor the Taliban that introduced veiling to Afghanistan. And Zereh's character demonstrates that Sharbat Gula's defiance has long been the counterpoint to the veiled victim of popular imagination. What this tells us is that not only are Afghan women constructed by the cinema but also that the cinema's representation of Afghanistan is itself shaped by political forces that view the country much as Western discourse views nature. In such a cultural way of seeing, Afghanistan (or Afghan women) can, like nature itself, be portrayed as whatever the political forces seeking to control it demand, as noble savage in primeval paradise or imperiled woman in Islamic hell. Afghanistan—as it represents the non-Western other—serves a very "practical function in colonial discourse, which is always that of designating difference and of assigning hierarchical or ethical value to the distinctions that inhere in the structures of power"; Spurr, *The Rhetoric of Empire,* 169.

17. As quoted in Chomsky, *Media Control,* 33.

18. Canby, "Screen: Honor and 'The Horsemen.'"

19. Bacevich, *The New American Militarism,* 70.

20. McAlister, *Epic Encounters,* 187–92.

21. Bacevich has noted that "the Israeli way of war has placed a premium on early offensive action" as well as "mandated a forward-leaning military posture with an eye toward eliminating threats before they could fully develop." Such military actions, he states, "defy easy moral justification"; Bacevich, *The New American Militarism,* 133. George W. Bush administration neoconservatives, who had made careers out of preventing Americans from "seeing both sides," would later enthusiastically apply these same questionable policies of preemption in completely different contexts, first in Afghanistan and then in Iraq, with predictably tragic results.

22. Champlin, *John Frankenheimer,* 123.

23. Frankenheimer and the reactionary America interpolated by his film do not take kindly to the Sharbat Gula stare. Like *The Horsemen*'s Zereh, *Black Sunday*'s Dahlia offers another nightmare vision: the seductive and lethal Palestinian terrorist. Eroticized (she appears naked) and demonized (she racks up quite a body count), Dahlia "veils" her true self by mimicking Western dress—even going so far as to impersonate a nun! The implicit message is that we should not trust even those Muslims who seem the most innocent. Dahlia's aggressive (read: assertive) femininity meshes in the Orientalist imagination with the fear of an increasingly defiant Palestinian people and Muslim world in general through the 1970s; see Semmerling, *"Evil" Arabs in American Popular Film,* 93–123.

Chapter 2: Butch and Sundance in Afghanistan

1. Fowler, "'Replete With Danger,'" 168.

2. Reeves, "Read Kipling to Understand Afghanistan or Iraq."

3. Macintyre, *The Man Who Would Be King*, 4–5.

4. Sailer, "What to Do about Afghanistan?" Sailer is a former correspondent for UPI, a conservative press service owned by the Unification Church. It is no surprise that he would be attracted to Huston's film, which depicts the dangers of miscegenation. In Sailer's articles for publications such as the *National Review*, he fulminates against "unattractive" and "unfeminine" African American women. He also is a firm opponent of interracial marriage: "By the end of the century, Hispanics may be three times as numerous as blacks. We'll enjoy equally large groups of black and Hispanic jailbirds. Quite a legacy to leave our great-grandchildren"; Sailer, "America and the Left Half of the Bell Curve."

5. Engelhardt, *The End of Victory Culture*, 274–75.

6. Voeltz, "John Huston, Sean Connery, Michael Caine, and the Epiphany of The Man Who Would Be King," 42, 49.

7. Zinn, "Machiavellian Realism and U.S. Foreign Policy," *Howard Zinn on War*, 125.

8. Ryan and Kellner, *Camera Politica*, 239–40.

9. Pratley, *The Cinema of John Huston*, 191.

10. Beckerman, "On Adapting 'The Most Audacious Thing in Fiction,'" 186.

11. Kozloff, "Taking Us Along on The Man Who Would Be King," 190.

12. Ibid, 191.

13. Brill, *John Huston's Filmmaking*, 47–48.

14. Lindqvist, *Exterminate All the Brutes*, 51.

15. Bachmann, "Watching Huston," 22.

16. Kozloff, "Taking Us Along on The Man Who Would Be King," 190.

17. Conrad, *Heart of Darkness*, 4.

18. Pratley, *The Cinema of John Huston*, 192.

19. Dwyer, *Beyond Casablanca*, 384.

20. Voeltz, "John Huston, Sean Connery, Michael Caine, and the Epiphany of The Man Who Would Be King," 42.

21. Kipling, "The Young British Soldier," in *The Works of Rudyard Kipling*, 418.

22. Moore-Gilbert, "A Sense of Insecurity," in *Kipling and "Orientalism,"* details the effect of the mutiny and constant warfare with Afghans and others on Anglo-Indian society and literature.

23. Ibid., 37.

24. Oppel, "Marines Respect Taliban's Abilities." Oppel quotes another Marine who expressed not only admiration but also surprise that Afghan guerillas did "the same thing we do" and used military tactics to not only "hit and run" but "maneuver." U.S. strategists learned this lesson in Vietnam but presumably have forgotten it in the ensuing years, thanks in part to a pervasive Orientalism that stereotypes Muslims as hopelessly backwards and inept. In the month this article was written, July 2009, they learned differently as American casualties reached their highest point since the October 2001 invasion.

25. Card, "Uncle Orson's List of the Best Films Ever Made."

26. Kipling, *The Works of Rudyard Kipling*, 45.

Chapter 3: The New Great Game

1. Russian General Staff, *The Soviet-Afghan War,* 9.

2. Coll, *Ghost Wars,* 58–59.

3. Ibid., 99.

4. Valenti, "Hollywood and Washington."

5. As quoted in the video documentary "An American Hero's Journey" included in the 1998 VHS release of the film.

6. After *buzkashi,* soccer is the Afghan national pastime. The country joined the FIFA in 1948, with the national team playing in Ghazi National Olympic Stadium in Kabul (with a capacity of 55,000 spectators) into the mid-1980s.

7. Waller, "Rambo: Getting to Win This Time," 122–25.

8. Parenti, *Make Believe Media,* 49.

9. Power, "Kabul's Grass Is Green at Last."

10. Kakar, *Afghanistan,* 213–51.

11. Sikorski, "Why Rambo's Not Right."

12. Studlar and Desser, "Never Having to Say You're Sorry," 102.

13. Coll, *Ghost Wars,* 173.

14. Stevens, "Getting the Picture."

15. For an example of how this worked in World War II combat films, see Slotkin, "Unit Pride."

16. Canby, "*The Beast.*"

17. Haines, "'They Were Called and They Went,'" 108.

18. A term that descriptively encompasses all the revisionist Westerns that used the nineteenth century as an allegory for America's war in Asia; from Cook, *Lost Illusions,* 174–75.

19. Emadi, *Culture and Customs of Afghanistan,* 136.

20. Gannon, *I Is for Infidel,* 18.

21. Lobe, "Human Dignity, Crazy Mike, and Indian Country."

22. Pincus, "Spending Bill Suggests Long Stay in Afghanistan."

23. Synovitz, "Afghanistan."

24. Crawford et al., "The Real 'Surge' of 2007."

25. Heller, "Worst Movie of the Year."

26. McGuigan, "War, Peace and Mike Nichols."

27. "Unlawful Killings Continue at Heavy Rate in Afghanistan, UN Rights Expert Says."

28. McGuigan, "War, Peace and Mike Nichols."

29. Appadurai, *Fear of Small Numbers,* 121.

30. Johnson, "Imperialist Propaganda."

31. Ibid.

32. Ibid.

33. McGuigan, "War, Peace and Mike Nichols."

34. Voeltz, "Rambo, Kipling, and Shirley Temple," 48–50.

Chapter 4: Land without Images

1. Goodson, *Afghanistan's Endless War*, 148–49.

2. Unemployment in Kabul in 2000 was estimated at 70 percent; "Afghanistan," *Washington Post Country Guides*. After the American invasion, 40 percent of the entire country was unemployed from at least 2005 to 2008; Central Intelligence Agency, *CIA Factbook*.

3. A Reuters February 24, 2005, report stated that two hundred children had died of cold-related illnesses that winter; Brunnstrom, "Up to 200 Kids Said Dead of Cold in Afghan Province." In 1999, there were one hundred fifty cases of polio in Afghanistan, one of the last ten countries on Earth to be afflicted by this preventable disease; "Unicef in Afghanistan."

4. Hertenstein, "Here Comes the Sun."

5. Saeed-Vafa, "Location (Physical Space) and Cultural Identity in Iranian Films," 204–5.

6. Ibid., 206–7.

7. A perfect example of this is the *New York Times Magazine*'s January 12, 1997, article on Afghanistan; Loyd, "A Market in Human Remains." It is not so much a story as it is an epitaph. Like a Puritan gravestone, macabre and dismal, the headline proclaims "A Market in Human Remains," while surmounting a photograph of a human skull. "Under the strict new Taliban regime," it states in terse memento mori prose, "desperate Afghani children raid graveyards. Bones bring money. Families survive." This is a postcard from hell, otherwise known as Kabul. Photographs show children atop mounds of human and animal bones, the text describing in gruesome detail how twelve-year-old boys scavenge for tibiae and craniums among the eroded grave soil of Afghanistan's capital city. They sell the bones of their ancestors to merchants, who then convert the remains into useful things like "cooking oil, soap, chicken feed, sometimes even buttons." For his efforts, one young grave robber can net as much as twelve dollars a month. "You see what we have come to," a teacher tells the journalist. "A generation with no education, that has only known war. This is what it comes to . . . human remains sold as animal bones. Look at our miserable lives." Possibly somewhere, somehow there were Afghans who were not forced to rob graves and that not all Afghans had descended into the depravity of violating their ancestors and their dignity. Such a suggestion does not dispute the reality of the events in the article but does challenge the picture of Afghanistan as essentially depraved, barbaric, and benighted. If this is the only picture we receive, the only transmission from another world, then one might be tempted (as people so often are) to inductively reason that that picture represents not *a* reality but *the* reality.

8. Smith, "Poe's Arabesque," 43.

9. Ibid.

10. Ibid., 45.

11. Farahmand, "Perspectives on Recent (International Acclaim for) Iranian Cinema," 87.

12. Ibid., 103.

13. According to Farahmand, this explains the popularity of Abbas Kiarostami's films, which focus on aesthetics and universalizing "everyday life" issues, as opposed to critiques

of Iran's religious life and politics in a more cosmopolitan setting. The same critique was leveled against the first breakout film from Indian cinema, Satyajit Ray's *Pather Panchali* (1956), which, like many Iranian films, dwelled on the trials and tribulations of rustics living in a largely premodern environment. This seems to lend credence to Farahmand's argument that the West will watch films from the East as long as they are exoticized and essentialized to taste. Nevertheless, there are many films emerging from Iran that directly confront contemporary social issues. Most notable among these is Jafar Panahi and Kiarostami's *Crimson Gold* (2004), a brutally naturalistic Iranian noir set in Tehran that highlights the country's class conflicts.

14. Tapper, "Introduction," *The New Iranian Cinema*, 20–22.

15. Farahmand, "Perspectives on Recent (International Acclaim for) Iranian Cinema," 103.

16. Maiwandi, "Osama Empowers Afghans."

17. An example is Zolnoor, "An Exclusive Interview with Mohsen Makhmalbaf and Niloofar Pazira."

18. Grady, "Kandahar Bound."

19. Roland Barthes as quoted in Spurr, *The Rhetoric of Empire*, 48.

20. Bisley, "Paths of Glory." Fisk's high opinion of the film may have something to do with his friendship with the film's star, Nelofer Pazira.

21. Makhmalbaf, "Director's Interview: Kandahar."

22. Thomas, "Introduction," *Reading Images*, 7.

23. Alloula, *The Colonial Harem*, 28.

24. Ibid., 129, note 11.

25. Césaire, "Discourse on Colonialism," 176.

26. Nugent, "A Killer in 'Kandahar?'"

27. Mohanty, "Under Western Eyes," 213.

28. Egan, *The Films of Makhmalbaf*, 186.

29. Said, *Orientalism*, 183.

30. Williams, "Kim and Orientalism," 482.

31. Lawrence, *Seven Pillars of Wisdom*.

32. Melman, *Women's Orients*, 60.

33. Alloula, *The Colonial Harem*, 74.

34. Ibid.

35. Daly, "The 'Paarda' Expression of Hejaab among Afghan Women in a Non-Muslim Community," 157.

36. Ibid.

37. Fanon, *A Dying Colonialism*, 36.

38. Yeğenoğlu, *Colonial Fantasies*, 48.

39. Ibid., 28.

40. Shirazi, *The Veil Unveiled*, 39–61.

41. Yeğenoğlu, *Colonial Fantasies*, 57.

42. Alloula, *The Colonial Harem*, 13.

43. A point made not just by hawkish commentators but also by liberal voices like Gary Trudeau in his "Doonesbury" comic strip in the fall of 2001.

44. Fanon, *A Dying Colonialism*, 37–38.

45. Kramer, "The Camera and the Burqa."

46. Physicians for Human Rights, "Women's Health and Human Rights in Afghanistan."

47. Kramer, "The Camera and the Burqa."

48. Mosley, "Mohsen Makhmalbaf's *Kandahar*," 180. Mosley compares the Taliban to "European fascist regimes of the 1930s" (183) and calls the U.S. soldiers in Afghanistan "peacekeepers" whose purpose is to "help start the long, slow process of relieving and reconstructing a country" (198). The descriptions mirror George W. Bush administration rhetoric perfectly, which says a great deal about their validity.

49. Kramer, "The Camera and the Burqa."

50. Dabashi, "Dead Certainties," 129.

51. Egan, *The Films of Makhmalbaf*, 81.

52. Dabashi, "Dead Certainties," 134.

53. Dabashi, *Close Up*, 188–89.

54. Varzi, "Picturing Change," 931–34.

55. Dabashi, "Dead Certainties," 137.

56. The source for these quotes is Makhmalbaf, "The Buddha Was Not Demolished in Afghanistan; He Collapsed Out of Shame."

57. Shirazi, *The Veil Unveiled*, 89–90.

58. Sardar and Davies, *American Terminator*, 24.

59. Egan, *The Films of Makhmalbaf*, 186.

Chapter 5: Afghan Gothic

1. A phrase from Abdel-Malek, "Orientalism in Crisis," 50.

2. Shaheen, *Reel Bad Arabs*. Shaheen's "best list" of twelve films includes: *Three Kings*, *The 13th Warrior*, *Lion of the Desert*, and Kevin Reynolds's (*The Beast*) *Robin Hood: Prince of Thieves*. In an interview for the Media Education Foundation's 2007 *Reel Bad Arabs* documentary, Shaheen also recommends *Kingdom of Heaven*, *Hideous Kinky*, *Syriana*, and *Paradise Now*.

3. Eisele, "The Wild East," 68.

4. Ibid., 72.

5. Ibid., 79.

6. Radio address by Laura Bush, November 11, 2001.

7. But not *the* first, despite many an erroneous write-up. That distinction goes to *The Speculator*, a film by Sayed Farud Haybat, which was shot in 2002 for Afghan television.

8. Adams, "Making History."

9. Kennedy, "From Guerilla to Director."

10. Woodward, *In Ruins*, 23–31.

11. Ibid., 203.

12. Sigmund Freud on Wilhelm Jensen's 1903 novel *Gradiva*, as quoted in Woodward, *In Ruins*, 55.

13. Smiley, "Women's Crusade."

14. As quoted on CNN's Web site, February 4, 2005; "General: 'It's Fun to Shoot Some People.'"

15. Abu-Lughod, "Do Muslim Women Really Need Saving?" 789.

16. To illustrate the extreme forms this argument takes: In the June 27, 2005, issue of *The Nation,* Deborah Scroggins lionized Ayaan Hirsi Ali, a Somali-born Dutch politician who has called the Prophet Muhammad a pedophile and demands that her government and other European nations save Muslim women from Muslim men. With sentiments like these, *The Nation* and *The National Review* can finally be on the same page. There's a sequel to the story. After lying about her immigration status as well as many details of her past, Ayaan Hirsi Ali resigned from parliament and moved to the United States, where she landed a job as propagandist for the right-wing American Enterprise Institute.

17. Spurr, *The Rhetoric of Empire,* 110.

18. Spivak, "Imperialism and Sexual Difference," 225.

19. Mulvey, "Visual Pleasure and Narrative Cinema," 58–69.

20. Coward, "The Look," 34.

21. Mernissi, *Scheherazade Goes West,* 19.

22. Ibid., 51.

23. Merskin, "Reviving Lolita?" 119–29. Fatema Mernissi similarly criticizes the transformation of children into sexual objects, asserting that the Western media insist "that in order to be beautiful, a woman must look fourteen years old"; Mernissi, *Scheherazade Goes West,* 213.

24. Ryan and Kellner, *Camera Politica,* 12.

25. Carbonell, "The Exotic Space of Cultural Translation," 81.

26. Said, "Orientalism Reconsidered," 347.

27. Said, *Orientalism,* 63.

28. Cardullo, "An Afghan Is a Woman."

29. Macnab, "A Woman's Place."

30. "An Interview with Samira Makhmalbaf for the Movie '5 in the Afternoon' in the Cannes Film Festival 2003."

31. Ryan and Kellner, *Camera Politica,* 14.

32. Siddiq Barmak quoted in Adams, "Making History."

33. Meek, "Through the Dark Black Smoke of War."

34. Ibid.

35. Adams, "Making History."

36. Meek, "Through the Dark Black Smoke of War."

37. Ibid.

38. Rashid, *Taliban,* 27–28.

39. Fisk, *The Great War for Civilisation,* 27.

40. Edwards, *Before Taliban,* 171–73.

41. Ahmad, "Kabul's Beggar Children Working the Streets."

42. Meek, "Through the Dark Black Smoke of War."

Chapter 6: The West Unveiled

1. Goodson, *Afghanistan's Endless War,* 149.

2. "Refugees from Afghanistan."

3. Maass, "How a Camp Becomes a City."

4. Fermer, "War, Incorporated."

5. "Testimony from Afghan Refugees."

6. Feinstein, "Michael Winterbottom."

7. Said, *Orientalism*, 83.

8. Gayatri Spivak as quoted in Young, *Postcolonialism*, 8.

9. Modernity as defined by Chambers, *Migrancy, Culture, Identity.*

10. As quoted in Moore-Gilbert, *Postcolonial Theory*, 148.

11. Pratt, *Imperial Eyes*, 222.

12. Ibid., 216.

13. Lindqvist, *Exterminate All the Brutes*, 172.

14. Chambers, *Migrancy, Culture, Identity*, 92–114.

15. From an interview on the film's DVD release.

16. Ibid.

Chapter 7: The Poetry of Silence

1. For example, in the photograph of a man whipping a crowd of children, both boys and girls, the caption says, "Crowd Control: A man whips a group of women and children. The Taliban often beat women with steel cables as punishment for petty crimes." What is not mentioned is that the man with the whip is wearing a *pakul* cap. The significance here is that the Taliban wore turbans while these particular hats were worn by the Northern Alliance, the group supported by the U.S. government. Naturally it would not do to blame our allies for conduct similar to the Taliban, so the caption's slant ignores this particular detail.

2. As quoted in Sardar and Davies, *American Terminator*, 90.

3. Polan, "Above All Else to Make You See," 130.

4. Postman, "The Public Mind."

5. Schickel, "A Gorgeous Journey Through Hell."

6. Dasgupta, "'John Is as Good Looking as Any Afghani Man.'"

7. Cordoni, "Roya Sadat."

8. Cowan, "Democrats Seek 2008 Troop Withdrawal."

9. *The Nation*, as quoted in Kolhatkar and Ingalls, *Bleeding Afghanistan*, 170.

10. Goldberg, "The Body Democratic."

11. On the deaths in Nuristan: Batty, "U.S. Air Strikes Kill Civilian Roadworkers in Afghanistan." On the wedding party bombing, which killed as many as two hundred fifty people: "Civilian Catastrophe as U.S. Bombs Afghan Wedding." And on the U.S. involvement in the live burial of Taliban prisoners of war: "U.S. Implicated in Taliban Massacre."

12. Durakovic, "The Quantitative Analysis of Uranium Isotopes in the Urine of the Civilian Population of Eastern Afghanistan after Operation Enduring Freedom."

13. Nawa, "Afghanistan, Inc."

14. Jones, "Commentary: Afghanistan's Local Insurgency." Jones, who works for the conservative RAND Corporation, states that the majority of Afghan insurgents are "primarily young men from rural villages who are paid to set up roadside bombs, launch rockets and mortars at NATO and Afghan forces, or pick up a gun for a few days. Most

are not ideologically committed to jihad. Rather, they are motivated because they are unemployed, disenchanted with the lack of change since 2001, or angry because a local villager was killed or wounded by Afghan, U.S. or NATO forces."

15. Atwood, "When Afghanistan Was at Peace."

16. Farrell and McDermott, "Claiming Afghan Women," 35.

17. Kolhatkar and Ingalls, *Bleeding Afghanistan,* 106.

18. Ayotte and Husain, "Securing Afghan Women," 112–33.

19. A notable exception is Armstrong, *Veiled Threat.*

20. Carroll, "Inside Islam, a Woman's Roar."

21. Ayotte and Husain, "Securing Afghan Women,"126.

22. Mohanty, *Feminism without Borders,* 26.

23. Tompkins, "Rumi Rules!"

24. Arberry, *Tales from the Masnavi,* 21.

25. Keshavarz, *Reading Mystical Lyric,* 61.

26. The interview with Gul Afrooz is part of a behind-the-scenes program produced by Roya Sadat for the DVD version of the film.

27. Farsaie, "Afghan Cinema."

28. "'We Want to Live As Humans.'"

29. "Profile: Ismail Khan."

30. Kolhatkar and Ingalls, *Bleeding Afghanistan,* 114.

31. Ibid.

32. Farsaie, "Afghan Cinema."

33. Enloe, *The Curious Feminist,* 283.

Chapter 8: A Way to Feel Good Again

1. Tourtellotte, "'Kite Runner' Makers Hope to Bridge World Cultures."

2. Newman, "'Kite Runner' Rises against a Hard Wind."

3. Ibid.

4. Muller, *New Strangers in Paradise,* 10.

5. Ibid., 15.

6. Jameson, "World Literature in an Age of Multinational Capitalism," 140.

7. For a critical comparison of liberal and radical views of civil rights and their place in high school curricula, see Lindstrom, "Following the Flame."

8. A thought suggested by Berger, *And Our Faces, My Heart, Brief as Photos,* 66.

9. Chambers, *Migrancy, Culture, Identity,* 25.

10. As quoted in Chambers, *Migrancy, Culture, Identity,* 2.

11. Moore-Gilbert, *Postcolonial Theory,* 129.

12. Araeen, "A New Beginning," 11.

13. Nederveen Pieterse, *Globalization and Culture,* 73–74.

14. Moore-Gilbert, *Postcolonial Theory,* 125.

15. Rowe, "Culture, U.S. Imperialism, and Globalization," 576.

16. Davies, "'Diversity. America. Leadership. Good over Evil,'" 399.

17. Ibid., 401.

18. Engelhardt, *The End of Victory Culture,* 42.

19. Caldicott, *The New Nuclear Danger,* xiii.
20. Gulf War films intensified this process; McAlister, *Epic Encounters,* 235–65.
21. Chomsky, *What We Say Goes,* 86.
22. Engelhardt, *The End of Victory Culture,* 23.
23. Corkin, *Cowboys as Cold Warriors,* 164–204.
24. Edwards, *Before Taliban,* 70, 172.
25. As quoted in Spring, *Education and the Rise of the Global Economy,* 161–62.
26. Ibid.
27. "U.S. Military Spending vs. the World."
28. Longsdorf, "Scripting with Sensitivity."
29. Keshavarz, *Jasmine and Stars,* 3.
30. Hosseini, *The Kite Runner,* 346.
31. Deeb, "Living Ashura in Lebanon," 137.
32. For an in-depth discussion of this process, see Fischer, *Iran.*
33. Egan, *The Films of Makhmalbaf,* 53.

Conclusion: Ending Charlie Wilson's War

1. Gayatri Spivak in "Three Women's Texts and a Critique of Imperialism" as quoted in Moore-Gilbert, *Postcolonial Theory,* 88.
2. Eagleton, *After Theory,* 150.

Bibliography

Abdel-Malek, Anouar. "Orientalism in Crisis." In *Orientalism: A Reader,* edited by A. L. Macfie, 47–56. New York: New York University Press, 2000.

Abu-Lughod, Lila. "Do Muslim Women Really Need Saving? Anthropological Reflections on Cultural Relativism and Its Others." *American Anthropologist* 104, no. 3 (September 2002): 783–90.

Adams, Sam. "Making History: With *Osama,* Siddiq Barmak Tries to Rebuild Afghanistan's Past." *Philadelphia Citypaper,* February 26–March 3, 2004, http://citypaper.net/articles/2000–02–26/movies2.shtml, accessed April 11, 2006.

"Afghanistan." *Columbia Encyclopedia.* 6th ed. 2001–5. Bartleby.com, http://www.bartleby.com/65/af/Afghanis.html, accessed April 11, 2006.

"Afghanistan." *Washington Post Country Guides,* http://www.washingtonpost.com/wp-srv/world/countries/afghanistan.html, accessed August 16, 2009.

"Afghanistan: ILO to Tackle Unemployment." *IRIN,* UN Office for the Coordination of Humanitarian Affairs. December 6, 2004, http://www.irinnews.org/report.asp?ReportID=44532&SelectRegion=Central_Asia&SelectCountry=AFGHANISTAN, accessed April 14, 2006.

Ahmad, Sardar. "Kabul's Beggar Children Working the Streets." *RAWA News,* June 9, 2007, http://www.rawa.org/temp/runews/2007/06/09/kabul-s-beggar-children-working-the-streets.html, accessed August 13, 2009.

Alloula, Malek. *The Colonial Harem.* Minneapolis: University of Minnesota Press, 1986.

Appadurai, Arjun. *Fear of Small Numbers: An Essay on the Geography of Anger.* Durham, N.C.: Duke University Press, 2006.

Araeen, Rasheed. "A New Beginning: Beyond Postcolonial Cultural Theory and Identity Politics." *Third Text,* no. 50 (2000): 3–20.

Arberry, A. J. *Tales from the Masnavi.* London: RoutledgeCurzon, 2002.

Armstrong, Sally. *Veiled Threat: The Hidden Power of Afghan Women.* New York: Viking Penguin, 2002.

Atwood, Margaret. "A Novelist Remembers When Afghanistan Was at Peace." *New York Times Magazine,* October 28, 2001, http://www.nytimes.com/2001/10/28/magazine/28LIVES.html, accessed August 18, 2009.

Ayotte, Kevin J., and Mary E. Husain. "Securing Afghan Women: Neocolonialism, Epistemic Violence, and the Rhetoric of the Veil." *NWSA Journal,* 17, no. 3 (Fall 2005): 112–33.

Bacevich, Andrew J. *The New American Militarism: How Americans Are Seduced by War.* New York: Oxford University Press, 2005.

Bachmann, Gideon. "Watching Huston," *Film Comment,* January–February 1976, 22.

Batty, David. "U.S. Air Strikes Kill Civilian Roadworkers in Afghanistan." *Guardian,* November 28, 2007, http://www.guardian.co.uk/world/2007/nov/28/afghanistan.davidbatty, accessed August 18, 2009.

Beckerman, Jim. "On Adapting 'The Most Audacious Thing in Fiction.'" In *The English Novel and the Movies,* edited by Michael Klein and Gillian Parker, 180–86. New York: Ungar, 1981.

Berger, John. *And Our Faces, My Heart, Brief as Photos.* New York: Pantheon, 1984.

Bisley, Alexander. "Paths of Glory: Robert Fisk on Film." *The Lumière Reader,* April 2, 2006, http://www.lumiere.net.nz/reader/item/432, accessed August 16, 2009.

Boyle, Robert H. "Grab the Goat and Ride, Omar!" *Sports Illustrated,* May 17, 1971, http://vault.sportsillustrated.cnn.com/vault/article/magazine/MAG1084870/index.htm, accessed August 17, 2009.

Brill, Lesley. *John Huston's Filmmaking.* Cambridge: Cambridge University Press, 1997.

Brunnstrom, David. "Up to 200 Kids Said Dead of Cold in Afghan Province." *Reliefweb,* February 24, 2005, http://www.reliefweb.int/rw/RWB.NSF/db900SID/DDAD-69WUA3?OpenDocument, accessed April 14, 2006.

Caldicott, Helen. *The New Nuclear Danger: George W. Bush's Military-Industrial Complex.* New York: New Press, 2002.

Canby, Vincent. "Screen: Honor and 'The Horsemen': Afghan Tale Opens at Local Theaters Lead Roles Shared by Sharif and Palance." *New York Times,* July 22, 1971.

———. "*The Beast:* Sort of Like *Red Dawn,* Except in Afghanistan, and Real Mujahedeen Kick the Commies Around." *New York Times,* September 16, 1988, http://movies2.nytimes.com/mem/movies/review.html?title1=&title2=BEAST%2C+THE+%28MOVIE%29&reviewer=Vincent+Canby&v_id=4458&pdate=19880916, accessed May 22, 2007.

Carbonell, Ovidio. "The Exotic Space of Cultural Translation." In *Translation, Power, Subversion,* edited by Roman Alvarez and M. Carmen Africa, 79–98. Bristol, Penn.: Multilingual Matters, 1996.

Card, Orson Scott. "Uncle Orson's List of the Best Films Ever Made." N.d., http://www.hatrack.com/osc/reviews/alltimefilmlist/index.shtml, accessed August 17, 2009.

Cardullo, Bert. "An Afghan Is a Woman." *Hudson Review* 58, no. 2 (Summer 2005), http://www.hudsonreview.com/cardulloSu05.pdf, accessed August 18, 2009.

Carroll, Jill. "Inside Islam, a Woman's Roar." *Christian Science Monitor,* March 5, 2008, http://www.csmonitor.com/2008/0305/p13s03-lign.html, accessed August 17, 2009.

Central Intelligence Agency. *CIA Factbook: Afghanistan,* July 30, 2009, https://www.cia

.gov/library/publications/the-world-factbook/geos/af.html, accessed August 17, 2009.

Césaire, Aimé. "Discourse on Colonialism." In *Colonial Discourse and Post-colonial Theory, a Reader,* edited by Patrick Williams and Laura Chrisman, 172–80. New York: Columbia University Press, 1994.

Chambers, Iain. *Migrancy, Culture, Identity.* London: Routledge, 1994.

Champlin, Charles. *John Frankenheimer: A Conversation with Charles Champlin.* Burbank, Calif.: Riverwood, 1995.

Chomsky, Noam. *Media Control: The Spectacular Achievements of Propaganda.* New York: Seven Stories Press, 2002.

———. *What We Say Goes: Conversations on U.S. Power in a Changing World.* New York: Metropolitan Books, 2007.

"Civilian Catastrophe as U.S. Bombs Afghan Wedding." *Guardian,* July 1, 2002, http://www.guardian.co.uk/world/2002/jul/01/afghanistan, accessed August 16, 2009.

Clark, Steven H. "Introduction." In *Travel Writing and Empire: Postcolonial Theory in Transit,* edited by Steven H. Clark, 1–28. London: Zed, 1999.

Coll, Steve. *Ghost Wars: The Secret History of the CIA, Afghanistan, and bin Laden, from the Soviet Invasion to September 10, 2001.* New York: Penguin, 2004.

Conrad, Joseph. *Heart of Darkness.* Mineola, N.Y.: Dover, 1990.

Cook, David A. *Lost Illusions: American Cinema in the Shadow of Watergate and Vietnam, 1970–1979.* Berkeley: University of California Press, 2002.

Cordoni, Michael. "Roya Sadat: A Woman in Afghanistan." September 9, 2004, http://cordoniproductions.com/Roya.html, accessed August 17, 2009.

Corkin, Stanley. *Cowboys as Cold Warriors: The Western and U.S. History.* Philadelphia: Temple University Press, 2004.

Cowan, Richard. "Democrats Seek 2008 Troop Withdrawal." *Reuters,* March 8, 2007, http://www.alertnet.org/thenews/newsdesk/N08455398.htm, accessed August 17, 2009.

Coward, Rosalind. "The Look." In *Reading Images,* edited by Julia Thomas, 33–39. New York: Palgrave, 2001.

Crawford, Neta C., Catherine Lutz, Robert Jay Lifton, Judith L. Herman, and Howard Zinn. "The Real 'Surge' of 2007: Non-Combatant Death in Iraq and Afghanistan." *Carnegie Council for Ethics in International Affairs,* January 22, 2008, http://www.cceia.org/resources/articles_papers_reports/0003.html, accessed August 17, 2009.

Curphey, Shauna. "Women in Afghanistan Fear New Taliban-like Rule." *Women's eNews,* May 15, 2003, http://www.womensenews.org/article.cfm/dyn/aid/1328, accessed August 16, 2009.

Dabashi, Hamid. *Close Up: Iranian Cinema, Past, Present and Future.* London: Verso, 2001.

———. "Dead Certainties: The Early Makhmalbaf." In *The New Iranian Cinema: Politics, Representation and Identity,* edited by Richard Tapper, 117–53. London: I. B. Tauris, 2002.

Daly, M. Catherine. "The 'Paarda' Expression of Hejaab among Afghan Women in a Non-Muslim Community." In *Religion, Dress and the Body,* edited by Linda B. Arthur, 147–61. Oxford: Berg, 1999.

Dasgupta, Priyanka. "'John Is as Good Looking as Any Afghani Man.'" *The Times of India,* December 13, 2006, http://timesofindia.indiatimes.com/NEWS/City_Supplements/Ahmedabad_Times/John_is_as_good_looking_as_any_Afghani_man/articleshow/807840.cms, accessed August 16, 2009.

Davies, Jude. "'Diversity. America. Leadership. Good over Evil.' Hollywood Multiculturalism and American Imperialism in Independence Day and Three Kings." *Patterns of Prejudice* 39, no. 4 (2005): 397–415.

Deeb, Lara. "Living Ashura in Lebanon: Mourning Transformed to Sacrifice." *Comparative Studies of South Asia, Africa and the Middle East* 25, no. 1 (2005): 122–37.

Durakovic, Asaf. "The Quantitative Analysis of Uranium Isotopes in the Urine of the Civilian Population of Eastern Afghanistan after Operation Enduring Freedom." *Military Medicine* 170, no. 4 (April 2005): 277–84.

Dwyer, Kevin. *Beyond Casablanca: M. A. Tazi and the Adventure of Moroccan Cinema.* Bloomington: Indiana University Press, 2004.

Eagleton, Terry. *After Theory.* New York: Basic Books, 2003.

Ebert, Roger. "The Horsemen." *Chicago Sun-Times,* August 6, 1971, http://rogerebert.suntimes.com/apps/pbcs.dll/article?AID=/19710806/REVIEWS/108060301/1023, accessed May 19, 2006.

Edwards, David B. *Before Taliban: Genealogies of the Afghan Jihad.* Berkeley: University of California Press, 2002.

Egan, Eric. *The Films of Makhmalbaf: Cinema, Politics and Culture in Iran.* Washington, DC: Mage, 2005.

Eisele, John C. "The Wild East: Deconstructing the Language of Genre in the Hollywood Eastern." *Cinema Journal* 41, no. 4 (Summer 2002): 68–94.

El Guindi, Fadwa. *Veil: Modesty, Privacy and Resistance.* Oxford: Berg, 1999.

Emadi, Hafizulla. *Culture and Customs of Afghanistan.* Westport, Conn.: Greenwood, 2005.

Engelhardt, Tom. *The End of Victory Culture: Cold War America and the Disillusioning of a Generation,* rev. ed. Amherst: University of Massachusetts Press, 2007.

Enloe, Cynthia. *The Curious Feminist: Searching for Women in a New Age of Empire.* Berkeley: University of California Press, 2004.

Fanon, Franz. *A Dying Colonialism.* New York: Grove, 1965.

Farahmand, Azadeh. "Perspectives on Recent (International Acclaim for) Iranian Cinema." In *The New Iranian Cinema: Politics, Representation and Identity,* edited by Richard Tapper, 86–108. London: I. B. Tauris, 2002.

Farrell, Amy, and Patrice McDermott. "Claiming Afghan Women: The Challenge of Human Rights Discourse for Transnational Feminism." In *Just Advocacy? Women's Human Rights, Transnational Feminisms, and the Politics of Representation,* edited by Wendy S. Hesford and Wendy Kozol, 33–55. New Brunswick, N.J.: Rutgers University Press, 2005.

Farsaie, Fahime. "Afghan Cinema: 'We Were Lacking Just About Everything.'" *Qantara. de: Dialogue with the Islamic World,* May 20, 2005, http://www.qantara.de/webcom/show_article.php/_c-310/_nr-187/_p-1/i.html?PHPSESSID=fccc07141f86230736adf82 7c5d0a423, accessed August 18, 2009.

Feinstein, Howard. "From Wanted Man to Golden Globe Winner; Siddiq Barmak Dis-

cusses 'Osama.'" *Indiewire,* February 3, 2004, http://www.indiewire.com/article/from
_wanted_man_to_golden_globe_winner_siddiq_barmak_discusses_osama/, accessed
August 18. 2009.

———. "Michael Winterbottom Talks about his Tragic Road Movie, *In This World." indieWIRE,* September 18, 2003, http://www.indiewire.com/article/michael_winterbottom
_talks_about_his_tragic_road_movie_in_this_world/, accessed August 15, 2009.

Fermer, Mike. "War, Incorporated." *Counterpunch.org,* July 17, 2002, http://www
.counterpunch.org/ferner0717.html, accessed August 18, 2009.

Fischer, Michael. *Iran: From Religious Dispute to Revolution.* Cambridge: Harvard University Press, 1980.

Fisk, Robert. *The Great War for Civilisation: The Conquest of the Middle East.* New York:
Knopf, 2005.

Fowler, Corinne. "'Replete with Danger': The Legacy of British Travel Narratives to News
Media Coverage of Afghanistan." *Studies in Travel Writing* 11 (2007): 155–75.

Gabrieli, Francesco. "Apology for Orientalism." In *Orientalism: A Reader,* edited by A. L.
Macfie, 79–85. New York: New York University Press, 2000.

Gannon, Kathy. *I Is for Infidel: From Holy War to Holy Terror: 18 Years Inside Afghanistan.*
New York: Public Affairs, 2005.

Gardesh, Hafizullah. "Old Faces for Karzai's New Cabinet?" *e-Ariana,* December 14, 2004,
http://www.e-ariana.com/ariana/eariana.nsf/allDocsArticles/A5ED14C6FF7564A8872
56F65007E4C60?OpenDocument, accessed August 18, 2009.

"General: 'It's Fun to Shoot Some People.'" *CNN,* February 4, 2005, http://www.cnn
.com/2005/US/02/03/general.shoot/index.html, accessed April 6, 2006.

Goldberg, Jonah. "The Body Democratic: Fight Today or Occupy Forever." *National Review
Online,* January 26, 2007, http://article.nationalreview.com/?q=ODIxNWQoZjE1Mzdl
OWRjYTIoZjNiNTY1OTZiZDJmMjY=, accessed August 18, 2009.

Goodson, Larry P. *Afghanistan's Endless War: State Failure, Regional Politics, and the Rise
of the Taliban.* Seattle: University of Washington Press, 2001.

Grady, Pam. "Kandahar Bound: Afghan Expatriate Nelofer Pazira Talks about the New
Film That Puts a Face on Her Country's Tragedy." *Reel.com,* n.d., http://www.reel.com/
reel.asp?node=features/interviews/pazira, accessed April 1, 2006.

Haines, Harry W. "'They Were Called and They Went': The Political Rehabilitation of the
Vietnam Veteran. In *From Hanoi to Hollywood: The Vietnam War in American Film,*
edited by Linda Dittmar and Gene Michaud, 81–97. New Brunswick, N.J.: Rutgers
University Press, 1990.

Heller, Stanley. "Worst Movie of the Year: Brzezinski and Charlie Wilson's War." *Coun-
terpunch,* December 26, 2007, http://www.counterpunch.org/heller12262007.html, accessed August 18, 2009.

Hertenstein, Mike. "Here Comes the Sun." *Imaginarium Online,* 2002, http://www
.cornerstonemag.com/imaginarium/movies/kandahar.htm, accessed April 11, 2006.

Hosseini, Khaled. *The Kite Runner.* New York: Riverhead, 2003.

"Interview with Samira Makhmalbaf for the Movie '5 in the Afternoon' in the Cannes
Film Festival 2003, An." *Makhmalbaf Film House,* April 2003, http://www.makhmalbaf
.com/articles.php?a=379, accessed August 13, 2009.

Jameson, Frederic. "World Literature in an Age of Multinational Capitalism." In *The Cur-*

rent in Criticism: Essays on the Present and Future of Literary Theory, edited by Clayton Koelb and Virgil Locke, 139–58. West Lafayette, Ind.: Purdue University Press, 1987.

Johnson, Chalmers. "Imperialist Propaganda: Second Thoughts on Charlie Wilson's War." TomDispatch.com, January 6, 2008, http://www.tomdispatch.com/post/174877, accessed August 18, 2009.

Jones, Seth G. "Commentary: Afghanistan's Local Insurgency." *International Herald Tribune,* January 31, 2007, http://www.rand.org/commentary/013107IHT.html, accessed August 18, 2009.

Kakar, M. Hassan. *Afghanistan: The Soviet Invasion and the Afghan Response, 1979–1982.* Berkeley: University of California Press, 1995.

Kennedy, Randy. "From Guerilla to Director; Siddiq Barmak's Road to 'Osama.'" *New York Times,* February 11, 2004, http://query.nytimes.com/gst/fullpage.html?res=9F06 E2D6143AF932A25751C0A9629C8B63, accessed August 18, 2009.

Keshavarz, Fatemeh. *Jasmine and Stars: Reading More than Lolita in Tehran.* Chapel Hill: University of North Carolina Press, 2007.

———. *Reading Mystical Lyric: The Case of Jalal al-Din Rumi.* Columbia: University of South Carolina Press, 2005.

Kipling, Rudyard. *The Works of Rudyard Kipling.* Ware, England: Wordsworth Editions, 1994.

Kolhatkar, Sonali, and James Ingalls. *Bleeding Afghanistan: Washington, Warlords, and the Propaganda of Silence.* New York: Seven Stories, 2006.

Kozloff, Sarah. "Taking Us Along on The Man Who Would Be King." In *Perspectives on John Huston,* edited by Stephen Cooper, 184–96. New York: G. K. Hall, 1994.

Kramer, Martin. "The Camera and the Burqa." *Middle East Quarterly* 9, no. 2 (Spring 2002), http://www.meforum.org/pf.php?id=177, accessed April 11, 2006.

Lawrence. T. E. "Chapter 93." In *Seven Pillars of Wisdom. eBooks@adelaide,* 2006, http://etext.library.adelaide.edu.au/l/lawrence/te/seven/chapter93.html, accessed April 11, 2006.

Lewis, Jon. "An Officer and a Gentleman: Male Bonding and Self Abuse." *Jump Cut,* no. 28 (April 1983): 13–14.

Lindqvist, Sven. *Exterminate All the Brutes.* New York: New Press, 1996.

Lindstrom, Jennifer. "Following the Flame: Choosing Literature That Empowers." *Rethinking Schools,* Summer 2007, http://www.rethinkingschools.org/archive/21_04/foll214 .shtml, accessed August 18, 2009.

Lobe, Jim. "Human Dignity, Crazy Mike, and Indian Country." *Antiwar.com,* September 25, 2004, http://www.antiwar.com/lobe/?articleid=3650, accessed August 18, 2009.

Longsdorf, Amy. "Scripting with Sensitivity." *Morning Call,* December 9, 2007, E1–E2.

Loyd, Anthony. "A Market in Human Remains." *New York Times Magazine,* January 12, 1997, 30–32.

Lutz, Catherine A., and Jane L. Collins. *Reading National Geographic.* Chicago: University of Chicago Press, 1993.

Maass, Peter. "How a Camp Becomes a City." *New York Times Magazine,* November 18, 2001, http://www.petermaass.com/core.cfm?p=1&mag=71&magtype=1, accessed August 18, 2009.

Macfie, A. L., ed. *Orientalism: A Reader.* New York: New York University Press, 2000.

Macintyre, Ben. *The Man Who Would Be King: The First American in Afghanistan.* New York: Farrar, Straus and Giroux, 2004.

Macnab, Geoffrey. "A Woman's Place." *The Guardian,* May 19, 2003, http://www.guardian .co.uk/film/2003/may/19/cannes2003.cannesfilmfestival, accessed August 13, 2009.

Maiwandi, Nadia Ali. "Osama Empowers Afghans." *Lemar-Aftaab* 3, no. 2 (April 2004), http://www.afghanmagazine.com/2004_04/film/osama_review.shtml, accessed April 11, 2006.

Makhmalbaf, Mohsen. "Director's Interview: Kandahar." *Makhmalbaf Film House,* n.d., http://www.makhmalbaf.com/articles.php?a=296, accessed April 11, 2006.

———. "The Buddha Was Not Demolished in Afghanistan; He Collapsed Out of Shame." *Makhmalbaf Film House,* March 2001, http://www.makhmalbaf.com/doc/060123175313English.doc, accessed April 1, 2006.

McAlister, Melani. *Epic Encounters: Culture, Media, and U.S. Interests in the Middle East, 1945–2000.* Berkeley: University of California Press, 2001.

McGuigan, Cathleen. "War, Peace and Mike Nichols." *Newsweek,* December 17, 2007, http://www.newsweek.com/id/74398/output/print, accessed August 18, 2009.

Meek, James. "Through the Dark Black Smoke of War: Osama, the Tale of a Young Girl's Struggle to Survive in Taliban-Ruled Afghanistan, Has Been Wowing Cinema Audiences around the World. James Meek Visits Cast and Crew in Kabul." *Guardian,* January 16, 2004, http://www.guardian.co.uk/arts/fridayreview/story/0,12102,1123636,00.html, accessed April 11, 2006.

Melman, Billie. *Women's Orients: English Women and the Middle East, 1718–1918, Sexuality, Religion and Work.* Ann Arbor: University of Michigan Press, 1995.

Mernissi, Fatema. *Scheherazade Goes West: Different Cultures, Different Harems.* New York: Washington Square Press, 2001.

Merskin, Debra. "Reviving Lolita? A Media Literacy Examination of Sexual Portrayals of Girls in Fashion Advertising." *American Behavioral Scientist* 48, no. 1 (2004): 119–29.

Michaud, Roland, and Sabrina Michaud. *Horsemen of Afghanistan.* London: Thames and Hudson, 1988.

Mohanty, Chandra. *Feminism without Borders: Decolonizing Theory, Practicing Solidarity.* Durham, N.C.: Duke University Press, 2004.

———. "Under Western Eyes: Feminist Scholarship and Colonial Discourses." In *Colonial Discourse and Post-colonial Theory: A Reader,* edited by Patrick Williams and Laura Chrisman, 196–220. New York: Columbia University Press, 1994.

Moore-Gilbert, Bart. *Kipling and "Orientalism."* New York: St. Martin's, 1986.

———. *Postcolonial Theory: Contexts, Practices, Politics.* New York: Verso, 1997.

Mosley, Philip. "Mohsen Makhmalbaf's *Kandahar:* Lifting a Veil on Afghanistan." In *Film and Television after 9/11,* edited by Wheeler Winston Dixon, 178–200. Carbondale: Southern Illinois University Press, 2004.

Muller, Gilbert H. *New Strangers in Paradise: The Immigrant Experience and Contemporary American Fiction.* Lexington: University Press of Kentucky, 1999.

Mulvey, Laura. "Visual Pleasure and Narrative Cinema." In *Feminist Film Theory: A Reader,* edited by Sue Thornham, 58–69. New York: New York University Press, 1999.

Nawa, Fariba. "Afghanistan, Inc.: A CorpWatch Investigative Report." *CorpWatch,* October 6, 2006, http://corpwatch.org/article.php?id=13518, accessed August 18, 2009.

Nederveen Pieterse, Jan. *Globalization and Culture: Global Mélange.* Lanham, Md.: Rowman and Littlefield, 2004.

Newman, Bruce. "'Kite Runner' Rises against a Hard Wind." *San-Jose Mercury News,* December 9, 2007, 4C.

Newman, Cathy. "Special Report: A Life Revealed." *National Geographic* 201, no. 4 (2003).

Nugent, Benjamin. "A Killer in 'Kandahar?'" *Time,* December 19, 2001, http://www.time.com/time/sampler/article/0,8599,189182,00.html, accessed August 18, 2009.

Oppel, Richard A. "Marines Respect Taliban's Abilities." *San Jose Mercury News,* July 25, 2009, A10.

Parenti, Michael. *Make Believe Media: The Politics of Entertainment.* Belmont, Calif.: Wadsworth Group, 1992.

Physicians for Human Rights. "Women's Health and Human Rights in Afghanistan: A Population-Based Assessment." *Physicians for Human Rights,* January 1, 2001, http://physiciansforhumanrights.org/library/news-2001-01-01.html, accessed August 18, 2009.

Pincus, Walter. "Spending Bill Suggests Long Stay in Afghanistan." *Washington Post,* July 14, 2008, A11.

Polan, Dana B. "'Above All Else to Make You See': Cinema and the Ideology of Spectacle." *boundary 2* 11, no. 1–2 (Autumn 1982): 129–44.

Postman, Neil. "The Public Mind: Consuming Images—Interview with Bill Moyers." PBS, 1989.

Power, Matthew. "Kabul's Grass Is Green at Last." *Slate,* July 21, 2004, http://www.slate.com/id/2104119/entry/2104123, accessed August 18, 2009.

Pratley, Gerald. *The Cinema of John Huston.* New York: A. S. Barnes, 1977.

———. *The Films of Frankenheimer: Forty Years in Film.* Bethlehem, Penn.: Lehigh University Press, 1998.

Prats, Armando José. *Invisible Natives: Myth and Identity in the American Western.* Ithaca, N.Y.: Cornell University Press, 2002.

Pratt, Mary Louise. *Imperial Eyes: Travel and Transculturation.* London: Routledge, 1992.

"Profile: Ismail Khan." *BBC News,* September 13, 2004, http://news.bbc.co.uk/1/hi/world/south_asia/2535261.stm, accessed August 18, 2009.

Rashid, Ahmed. *Taliban: Militant Islam, Oil and Fundamentalism in Central Asia.* New Haven, Conn.: Yale University Press, 2000.

Reeves, Richard. "Read Kipling to Understand Afghanistan or Iraq." *uExpress.com,* December 18, 2003, http://www.uexpress.com/richardreeves/?uc_full_date=20031218, accessed August 18, 2009.

"Refugees from Afghanistan: The World's Largest Single Refugee Group." *Amnesty International,* November 1, 1999, http://web.amnesty.org/library/Index/engASA110161999?OpenDocument&of=COUNTRIES%5CIRAN, accessed December 4, 2006.

Rosaldo, Renato. *Culture and Truth: The Remaking of Social Analysis.* Boston: Beacon Press, 1989.

Rousseau, Jean-Jacques. *The Confessions of Jean-Jacques Rousseau.* Translated by J. M. Cohen. London: Penguin, 1953.

Rowe, John Carlos. "Culture, U.S. Imperialism, and Globalization." *American Literary History* 16, no. 4 (2004): 575–95.

Russian General Staff. *The Soviet-Afghan War: How a Superpower Fought and Lost.* Translated and edited by Lester W. Grau and Michael A. Gress. Lawrence: University Press of Kansas, 2002.

Ryan, Michael, and Douglas Kellner. *Camera Politica: The Politics and Ideology of Contemporary Hollywood Film.* Bloomington: Indiana University Press, 1988.

Saeed-Vafa, Mehrnaz. "Location (Physical Space) and Cultural Identity in Iranian Films." In *The New Iranian Cinema: Politics, Representation and Identity,* edited by Richard Tapper. London: I. B. Tauris, 2002, 200–214.

Said, Edward. *Covering Islam,* rev. ed. New York: Vintage, 1997.

———. *Orientalism.* New York: Vintage, 1978.

———. "Orientalism Reconsidered." In *Orientalism: A Reader,* edited by A. L. Macfie, 345–61. New York: New York University Press, 2000.

Sailer, Steve. "America and the Left Half of the Bell Curve: Part 4: Helping the Left Half of the Bell Curve—the Not So Hot Ideas." *VDARE.com,* August 27, 2000, http://www.vdare.com/sailer/bell_curve_4.htm, accessed August 18, 2009.

———. "What to Do about Afghanistan?" *UPI,* September 26, 2001, http://www.isteve.com/Man_Who_Would_Be_King.htm, accessed August 18, 2009.

Sardar, Ziauddin, and Merryl Wyn Davies. *American Terminator: Myths, Movies and Global Power.* New York: Disinformation, 2004.

Saunders, John. *The Western Genre: From Lordsburg to Big Whiskey.* London: Wallflower, 2001.

Schickel, Richard. "A Gorgeous Journey through Hell." *Time,* December 3, 2001, 47.

Schowalter, J. E. "Some Meanings of Being a Horsewoman." *Psychoanalytic Study of the Child* 38 (1983): 501–17.

Semmerling, Tim Jon. *"Evil" Arabs in American Popular Film: Orientalist Fear.* Austin: University of Texas Press, 2006.

Shaheen, Jack. *Reel Bad Arabs: How Hollywood Vilifies a People.* Northampton, Mass.: Interlink, 2001.

Shirazi, Faegheh. *The Veil Unveiled: The Hijab in Modern Culture.* Gainsville: University Press of Florida, 2001.

Sikorski, Radel. "Why Rambo's Not Right." *National Review,* November 7, 1988, http://findarticles.com/p/articles/mi_m1282/is_n22_v40/ai_6790794, accessed August 18, 2009.

Slotkin, Richard. *Gunfighter Nation: The Myth of the Frontier in Twentieth Century America.* New York: Atheneum, 1992.

———. "Unit Pride: Ethnic Platoons and the Myths of American Nationality." *American Literary History,* 13, no. 3 (Fall 2001): 469–98.

Smiley, Jane. "Women's Crusade," *New York Times Magazine,* December 2, 2001, http://www.nytimes.com/2001/12/02/magazine/the-way-we-live-now-12-02-01-gaze-women-s-crusade.html, accessed August 18, 2009.

Smith, Patricia C. "Poe's Arabesque." *Poe Studies* 7, no. 2 (December 1974): 42–45.

Spivak, Gayatri. "Imperialism and Sexual Difference," *Oxford Literary Review* 8, no. 1–2 (1986): 226–40.

Spring, Joel. *Education and the Rise of the Global Economy.* Mahwah, N.J.: Lawrence Erlbaum, 1998.

Spurr, David. *The Rhetoric of Empire: Colonial Discourse in Journalism, Travel Writing, and Imperial Administration.* Durham, N.C.: Duke University Press, 1993.

Stevens, Richard. "Getting the Picture: Kevin Reynolds Becomes a Northwest Transplant to Make a Life—and a Movie—of His Own." *Seattle Times,* October 2, 2002, http://seattletimes.nwsource.com/pacificnw/2002/0210/cover.html, accessed August 18, 2009.

Studlar, Gaylyn, and David Desser. "Never Having to Say You're Sorry: Rambo's Rewriting of the Vietnam War." In *From Hanoi to Hollywood: The Vietnam War in American Film,* edited by Linda Dittmar and Gene Michaud, 101–12. New Brunswick, N.J.: Rutgers University Press, 1990.

Synovitz, Ron. "Afghanistan: Resurgent Taliban Slows Aid Projects, Reconstruction." *Radio Free Europe,* November 30, 2007, http://www.rferl.org/content/Article/1079214.html, accessed August 17, 2009.

Tapper, Richard, ed. *The New Iranian Cinema: Politics, Representation and Identity.* London: I. B. Tauris, 2002.

Taylor-Young, Leigh. "The Horsemen." *Leigh Taylor-Young* Web site, n.d., http://www.lty.com/70s/horsementext1.htm, accessed June 15, 2006.

"Testimony from Afghan Refugees: Hostility towards Afghans in Pakistan." *Human Rights Watch,* February 25, 2002, http://www.hrw.org/press/2002/02/afghan-testimony.htm, accessed August 18, 2009.

Thomas, Julia, ed. *Reading Images.* New York: Palgrave, 2001.

Tompkins, Ptolemy. "Rumi Rules!" *Time,* September 30, 2002, http://www.time.com/time/magazine/article/0,9171,501021007–356133,00.html, accessed August 18, 2009.

Tourtellotte, Bob. "'Kite Runner' Makers Hope to Bridge World Cultures." *Reuters,* December 18, 2007, http://www.reuters.com/article/filmNews/idUSN1743693420071219, accessed August 18, 2009.

"Unicef in Afghanistan: Year's First Nationwide Polio Immunizations to Continue Fight against Debilitating Diseases." *Unicef,* April 13, 2003, http://www.unicef.org/newsline/2003/03nn25afghanistan.htm, accessed April 11, 2006.

"Unlawful Killings Continue at Heavy Rate in Afghanistan, UN Rights Expert Says." *UN News Centre,* May 15, 2008, http://www.un.org/apps/news/story.asp?NewsID=26682&Cr=afghan&Cr1, accessed August 17, 2009.

"U.S. Implicated in Taliban Massacre." *Project Censored,* 2004, http://www.projectcensored.org/top-stories/articles/11-us-implicated-in-taliban-massacre/, accessed August 18, 2009.

"U.S. Military Spending vs. the World." *Center for Arms Control and Non-Proliferation,* February 22, 2008, http://www.armscontrolcenter.org/policy/securityspending/articles/fy09_dod_request_global/index.html, accessed August 18, 2009.

Valenti, Jack. "Hollywood and Washington: Sprung from the same DNA." Speech before the Los Angeles World Affairs Council on October 1, 1998, http://www.lawac.org/speech/pre%20sept%2004%20speeches/valenti.html, accessed August 18, 2009.

Varzi, Roxanne. "Picturing Change: Mohsen Makhmalbaf's *Kandahar.*" *American Anthropologist* 8, no. 2 (September 2002): 931–34.

Voeltz, Richard A. "John Huston, Sean Connery, Michael Caine, and the Epiphany of The Man Who Would Be King." *McNeese Review* (2002): 40–50.

———. "Rambo, Kipling, and Shirley Temple: From Hollywood to Afghanistan with Love." *Mid-Atlantic Almanack* 13 (2004): 47–59.

Waller, Gregory A. "Rambo: Getting to Win This Time." In *From Hanoi to Hollywood: The Vietnam War in American Film,* edited by Linda Dittmar and Gene Michaud, 113–28. New Brunswick, N.J.: Rutgers University Press, 1990.

"'We Want to Live As Humans': Repression of Women and Girls in Western Afghanistan." *Human Rights Watch* 14, no. 11 (December 2002), http://www.hrw.org/legacy/reports/2002/afghnwmn1202/Afghnwmn1202.pdf, accessed August 18, 2009.

Williams, Patrick. "Kim and Orientalism." In *Colonial Discourse and Post-colonial Theory: A Reader,* edited by Patrick Williams and Laura Chrisman, 480–97. New York: Columbia University Press, 1994.

Williams, Patrick, and Laura Chrisman, eds. *Colonial Discourse and Post-colonial Theory: A Reader.* New York: Columbia University Press, 1994.

Woods, George Benjamin, ed. *English Poetry and Prose of the Romantic Movement.* Chicago: Scott, Foresman, 1916.

Woodward, Christopher. *In Ruins.* New York: Pantheon, 2001.

Yeğenoğlu, Meyda. *Colonial Fantasies: Towards a Feminist Reading of Orientalism.* Cambridge: Cambridge University Press, 1998.

Young, Robert J. C. *Postcolonialism: A Very Short Introduction.* Oxford: Oxford University Press, 2003.

Zinn, Howard. "Machiavellian Realism and U.S. Foreign Policy." Chapter 19 in *Howard Zinn on War.* New York: Seven Stories, 2001.

Zolnoor, Behzad. "An Exclusive Interview with Mohsen Makhmalbaf and Niloofar Pazira." *Iran Press Service,* October 24, 2001, http://www.iran-press-service.com/articles_2001/oct_2001/makhmalbaf_pazira_interview_241001.htm, accessed April 11, 2006.

Index

MARK GRAHAM is the award-winning author
of *How Islam Created the Modern World* and other
works. He lives in Allentown, Pennsylvania.

The University of Illinois Press
is a founding member of the
Association of American University Presses.

———————————————————

Composed in 10.5/13 Adobe Minion Pro
by Jim Proefrock
at the University of Illinois Press
Manufactured by Thomson-Shore, Inc.

University of Illinois Press
1325 South Oak Street
Champaign, IL 61820-6903
www.press.uillinois.edu